Undigested P

The Holocaust in Lit

CW01662406

On the Boundary of Two Worlds: Identity, Freedom, and Moral Imagination in the Baltics
31

Founding and Executive Editor

Leonidas Donskis, Member of the European Parliament, and previously Professor and Dean of Vytautas Magnus University School of Political Science and Diplomacy in Kaunas, Lithuania.

Editorial and Advisory Board

Timo Airaksinen, University of Helsinki, Finland
Egidijus Aleksandravicius, Lithuanian Emigration Institute, Vytautas Magnus University, Kaunas, Lithuania
Stefano Bianchini, University of Bologna, Forlì Campus, Italy
Endre Bojtar, Institute of Literary Studies, Budapest, Hungary
Ineta Dabasinskiene, Vytautas Magnus University, Lithuania
Robert Ginsberg, Pennsylvania State University, USA
John Hiden, University of Glasgow, UK
Martyn Housden, University of Bradford, UK
Mikko Lagerspetz, Åbo Academy, Finland
Andreas Lawaty, Nordost-Institute, Lüneburg, Germany
Olli Loukola, University of Helsinki, Finland
Valdis Muktupavels, University of Latvia, Riga, Latvia
Hannu Niemi, University of Helsinki, Finland
Yves Plasseraud, Paris, France
Rein Raud, Rector of Tallinn University, Estonia
Alfred Erich Senn, University of Wisconsin-Madison, USA, and Vytautas Magnus University, Kaunas, Lithuania
André Skogström-Filler, University Paris VIII-Saint-Denis, France
David Smith, University of Glasgow, UK
Saulius Suziedelis, Millersville University, USA
Joachim Tauber, Nordost-Institut, Lüneburg, Germany
Tomas Venclova, Yale University, USA

Undigested Past

The Holocaust in Lithuania

Robert van Voren

Rodopi

Amsterdam - New York, NY 2011

The cover photo is of the statue of the “water carrier”, made by the Lithuanian sculptor Romas Kvintas and planned to be placed in a central location in the Old Town of Vilnius in remembrance of the Jewish past of the city as soon as the necessary funds are raised.

The paper on which this book is printed meets the requirements of “ISO 9706:1994, Information and documentation - Paper for documents - Requirements for permanence”.

ISBN: 978-90-420-3371-9
E-Book ISBN: 978-94-012-0070-7
© Editions Rodopi B.V., Amsterdam - New York, NY 2011
Printed in the Netherlands

Contents

Foreword

We are living in an era of monetary inflation but also of another kind of inflation – the devaluation of concepts and values. Sworn oaths are being debased before our very eyes. It used to be that by breaking an oath, a person lost the right to participate in society and to be a spokesman for truth and values. He would be stripped of everything except his personal and private life and would be unable to speak on behalf of his group, his people or his society. Promises have also suffered a devaluation.

Once upon a time, if you went back on your word you were divested of even the tiniest measure of trust. Concepts are also being devalued; they are no longer reserved for the explicit task of describing precise instances of human experience. Everything is becoming uniformly important and unimportant. One's very existence places one at the center of the world.

In my experience, the pinnacle of concept inflation was reached ten years ago when I came across articles in the American press describing the "holocaust" of turkeys in the run-up to the Thanksgiving holiday. This was probably not a simple case of a word being used unthinkingly or irresponsibly. Disrespect for concepts and language only temporarily masks disrespect for others; and this disrespect eventually bubbles to the surface.

In recent decades, the concept of genocide has undergone a perilous devaluation. Here, I would like to stress that the devaluation of this concept has not been underpinned by a concern for humanity as whole or for the condition of contemporary humaneness; just the opposite – it is a symptom of the history of the revaluation of the self as the world's navel and, concurrently, of an insensitivity towards humanity. Moreover, the immoderate use of this word threatens to stifle dialogue.

Since martyrdom-seeking politics have become, in our world, overwhelmed with total indifference and an efficient tool of attention seeking, if not a passport to the heaven of recognition, the Holocaust is perceived as a successful pattern of the politics of memory. Cynically speaking, it is treated as a success story in our world of comparative martyrology.

Therefore, the pie is expected to be sliced and shared equally among all victimized actors of history – Jews, Palestinian Arabs, African Americans, Native Americans, Latin Americans, Muslims, and Eastern Europeans alike. This is to say that a convincing martyrology or a plausible account of suffering becomes a password through the gates of power and recognition. We have to become a celebrity or a victim in our fluid modern times to get more attention and, therefore, to be granted visibility, which is the same as social and political existence nowadays, as Zygmunt Bauman would have it. The more convincing victims we are, the more attention and publicity we get. The more we try to think the unthinkable and to speak the unspeakable, the more likely we become to qualify for a niche in a power structure, whether local or global.

The struggle against meaninglessness, against insensitivity, against a failure to react and to extend recognition gives rise to such compensatory forms of struggle as a wildly spreading belief in conspiracy theories (which at least confirm your hunch that someone is trying to rub you out – in other words, there is somebody that does give a hoot about you) as well as an inflation of weighty words. Important terms referring to terrifying human experiences, such as *Holocaust*, *genocide*, *crimes against humanity*, *apartheid*, are being used ever more freely and ever more irresponsibly when talking about God knows what. They are adapted like old furniture to a more modern interior design: A once-vibrant form of life and culture is turned into a lifeless decoration. In this case, another's suffering and annihilation of humanity becomes, at best, a way of turning attention to oneself and one's own way of talking (or one's own "truth").

The hysterical conflation of semantic fields and the re-semantization of terms, undertaken for the purpose of calling attention to oneself or of fortifying one's faith or political doctrine (which essentially neither interests nor excites anyone until you announce that you know it will atone for the world's sins or at least show the true face of evil), have their roots here, too. As a result, there's an explosive and unstoppable proliferation of "holocausts" and "genocides." Only if you have become a successful victim and overcome this anesthetized layer will you be admitted into the field of distributed power and attention. If you lack real power but are authentically and uniquely powerless, at least you have touched on real power and have a sense of its other, dark side. You weren't empowered but unempowered. If so, you can still be a witness to power – only from a different angle. You can, therefore you are. Thanks to your unempowerment others can – once more you are, only in a different way.

Hence, the idea of double genocide widespread in Lithuania and beyond is based on the assumption of the symmetry in suffering of Eastern European Jews as victims of the Holocaust, and their non-Jewish compatriots and neighbors as victims of Stalinism and Communism. This says that the Holocaust was only about the Jews, whereas Stalinism was exclusively hostile only to the Balts and other non-Jews, as the Jews have enormously contributed to Communist causes.

Needless to say, the distortion of history is too obvious here to need emphasis, yet it throws more light on why and how the wave of the obfuscation and trivialization of the Holocaust became possible in Lithuania. Here an attempt was made to equalize the Holocaust as a major crime against humanity and the crimes of Communism; as if to say that we have experienced not one, but two Holocausts, two parallel realities of horror and hatred, a Holocaust of the Jews and a Holocaust of Gentiles, the former orchestrated by the Nazis, and the latter by the Communists.

Let me put aside all considerations about the moral and political aspect of this campaign or sinister tendency of memory politics. We have to understand how this mechanism works, as it is in the process of becoming a pattern of the rewriting of history, hijacking someone else's narrative, inflating the concepts, and then deliberately conflating the victims and the perpetrators within the framework of a symmetry theory or of a comparative martyrology perspective. It is too obvious to need emphasis that identity, memory, and victimhood tend to become deeply intertwined each time when it comes to a search for a plausible historical-political narrative within the framework of political self-legitimation, which is itself a pivotal aspect of the process of political legitimation.

Contrasting a success-centered history to a suffering-centered history, and tracing their political implications in terms of open-ended or self-contained modes of historical-political discourse, George Schöpflin suggests that:

> "A history that places success at its centre and legitimates a claim to power thereby is evidently future orientated, because it implicitly argues a linearity of success projected into the future because glory is repeatable and it is desirable that it should be repeated. Victimhood, by contrast, creates its polarity overwhelmingly around a non-repeatable event (it is really rather unlikely that a group would construct a historical narrative that actually seeks the experience of victimhood in the future). In this sense, glory creates open structures; victimhood closes them. Victimhood locks the identity in question into a discourse that focuses on past suffering, on a unique suffering, but offers a clarity of identity by delimiting it very emphatically from others in the same political or territorial space, by attempting to transcend both." (Schöpflin, 2010, 102)[1]

1. Schöpflin, George: *The Dilemmas of Identity.* Tallinn University Press, Tallinn, Estonia, 2010.

Schöpflin might have added that victimhood, as a mode of discourse and as a frame of meaning within a historical narrative, does not necessarily become a path to our sympathetic understanding of others, human compassion, and a sense of belonging. Instead, it strengthens our feeling of having been singled out by those representing power structure. If so, the world owes us something. And that something is a passport to power. As mentioned, successful victimhood is a prospective call to share power, to slice the cake of global attention, and to grant access to Realpolitik and established political vocabulary.

It would be difficult to imagine a more appropriate, sensitive, humane, and perceptive guide into the somber world of Eastern European traumas of history and memory than Robert van Voren's book *Undigested Past: The Holocaust in Lithuania.* The author of deeply original and rich books on the political abuse of psychiatry in the former Soviet Union and the regime's fierce struggle against dissent (see Van Voren, 2010; Van Voren, 2009),[2] Robert van Voren has unique qualifications to undertake such a study. Since I have had a privilege of introducing Van Voren's two books published by Rodopi, I am not going to repeat myself concerning the unquestionable academic merits and overall intellectual brilliance of the writer in question.

Yet a couple of remarks should be made here. Everybody more or less involved in a study of an ongoing process or of a politically sensitive and highly charged phenomenon knows what it means to end up finding themselves in the battlefield of fact and value. Even more problematic is to challenge, analyze, and expose a trauma deeply hidden and intertwined with a repressed aggression, a sense of guilt, and, consequently, the violent denial of one's past and history as it *is*, rather than as it *ought to be* presented and narrated to console us while healing our wounds and telling the world a story of our heroic struggle and victimhood.

A cosmopolitan citizen of Lithuania and a European straight out of Montesquieu's vision of Europe, Robert van Voren, with the breadth of his perspective and multiple identities, perhaps, will be long remembered as a scholar who combined the experience of an outsider and that of an insider. As regards Lithuanian society, he is an observer and a participant of societal life there. A Canadian-born Dutch political scientist and historian,

2. Van Voren, Robert: *Cold War in Psychiatry: Human Factors, Secret Actors.* Rodopi, Amsterdam & New York, 2010.

———.*On Dissidents and Madness: From the Soviet Union of Leonid Brezhnev to the "Soviet Union" of Vladimir Putin.* Rodopi, Amsterdam & New York, 2009.

who became a citizen of Lithuania, he has much to say about the mindset, political behavior, mentality, habits of the heart, and the disturbing legacy of totalitarianism and its aftermath still so manifest in the country which successfully joined the EU.

I will not allow myself to expose what is left for an intimate touch of the reader of this book; nor will I deprive the readership of the pleasure and delight of discovering the charms of this book. Suffice it to mention that the strength of this book comes from a warm and humane perspective of the author; to lecture an Eastern European society enlightening it on its own past is the last thing he would do. At the same time, Dr. Van Voren's book combines the richness of a well-documented, closely argued academic work and a lively narrative. He knows how to tell an exciting story. At this point, the book represents the best of interdisciplinary scholarship where beautiful academic prose uncovers archival data, oral history, testimonies of survivors, living memory, subtle psychological points, and theoretical insights. A comparative approach successfully employed by Van Voren, which allows a glimpse of the similarities and differences of Dutch and Lithuanian political experiences of the Holocaust as a central and pan-European moral, political, and historical event, is unique in world scholarship.

I believe that Robert van Voren's book, *Undigested Past: The Holocaust in Lithuania*, will become a marvelous read and a long-term companion for anyone interested in European studies, dissent studies, the study of the Holocaust, and especially in how the challenges of post-totalitarian era came to a small European country with a rich, albeit troubled and unkind, history.

Prof. Leonidas Donskis,
Member of the European Parliament (MEP ALDE 2009–2014), and
Recurrent Visiting Professor of Politics at Vytautas Magnus University in Kaunas, Lithuania

Introduction

Nothing in the national past could have prepared the Lithuanian people for these disasters, especially the extent of the violence, which had no historical parallels or precedents either in the quantitative or qualitative sense.

Christoph Dieckmann & Saulius Sužiedėlis[1]

The road to Auschwitz was built by hatred, but paved with indifference.

Ian Kershaw[2]

Genocide... is an exercise in community building.

Philip Gourevitch[3]

My first visit to the killing fields in the Paneriai forest outside Vilnius turned out to be something of an expedition. In this place, approximately one hundred thousand people, among them some seventy thousand Jews, were murdered during the Second World War. There were no road signs indicating where to go, and only after an hour of trying various inroads into the forest did we find a local resident able to show us the right direction. As we arrived at the site, we noticed the dead silence. No other visitors, just the sounds of the forest and, in the distance, cars rushing by. When entering the site, a strange sensation overtook us. The brilliant sunlight of a beautiful summer day was shining through the trees, yet it could not prevent a heavy feeling grabbing us by the throat. What we heard was not only the singing of the birds, but also the sound of death.

During subsequent visits, the number of people viewing the memorials marking the many execution sites was never more than a handful, and virtually all were foreign visitors. The victims in the forest, whose ashes are scattered all over the area, are as much avoided as the full story of their liquidation. And, yet, one of the most crucial and gruesome events in Lithuania's history took place here; an event that willingly or unwillingly continues to influence Lithuanian politics and thought today.

1. *The Persecution and Mass Murder of Lithuanian Jews*, p. 175
2. Kershaw, Ian: *The Persecution of the Jews and German Public Opinion in the Third Reich.* Leo Baeck Institute Year Book 26, 1981, p. 281
3. Gourevitch, Philip: *We Wish to Inform you that Tomorrow We will be Killed with our Families*, p. 95

The history of Lithuania in the twentieth century is marred with a sequence of promising and tragic events. While the country obtained independence at the end of the First World War, it soon found itself an object of political scheming by its neighbors: Poland, (Nazi-) Germany and the Soviet Union. In 1940, it fell victim to Soviet occupation, only to be occupied by German forces a year later. The war resulted in the almost total extermination of its large Jewish minority and the death of many of its Polish and Lithuanian citizens.[4] More than 95 percent of the Jewish population of Lithuania was massacred.[5] Vilnius was destroyed by at least half; most of its population (35% Jews, 62% Polish, Byelorussian and Russian and 3% Lithuanian)[6] killed or forced to emigrate. In 1944, the Soviets were back and continued their repressive regime, ending only at the beginning of the 1990s.[7] Since then, the dark pages of Lithuanian history hang as a Sword

4. In total, some 410,000 people lost their lives in Lithuania during the war. Apart from the Jews, some 170,000 Soviet prisoners of war died on Lithuanian territory between June 1941 and spring 1942; some 40,000 Soviet civilians died in camps and 10,000 Lithuanians and other civilians were killed. See Dieckmann, Christoph in *Holocaust in Litauen*, p. 63
5. Of the survivors, 7-8,000 Jews survived outside Lithuania in German captivity, in Lithuania itself only about 1,700 Jews survived, less than one percent of the Jews who lived within Lithuania's borders when the war started.
6. See Liekis, Šarūnas: 1939, p. 257. A census carried out in the Russian Empire in 1897 showed that the Vilnius population at that time consisted of 23.6% Orthodox Christians, 36.9% Catholics and 41.3% Jews (including some Muslims, Karaites, Lutherans and even two Mennonites). As native tongue, 40% named Yiddish, 30.0% Polish, 20% Russian, 4.2% Byelorussian and 2.1% Lithuanians. See Weeks, Theodore: *From Russian to Polish*, p. 2. Of course, the Russian component also included soldiers and civil servants who considered Vilnius as their home only temporarily, and probably quite a few Lithuanians were either Polonized or decided not to indicate that Lithuanian was their native language. In 1916/1917 a German census showed that 54% of the population was Polish, 41% Jewish and 2.1% Lithuanian. See Weeks, Theodore: *From Russian to Polish*, p. 15. According to census data on the eve of the Second World War, Vilnius had a population of 64.6% Poles, 28.2% Jews and the remainder others, including Lithuanian. In 1937, Vilnius region had a total population of 457,000, of which 39.37% were Poles, 34.16% Jews, 19.23% Lithuanians and the remainder Byelorussians, Russians, Tatars and others (Liekis, p. 298). In 1939-1940 al large group of refugees from Poland entered Vilnius (by December 2, 1939, already more than 18,000, see Liekis p. 298) and the Jewish population of 60,000 increased to 80,000 (a German demographical count even came to a total of 90,000) and so the balance changed. As Liekis points out, Lithuanian sources tend to increase the percentage of Lithuanians in the city, for obvious reasons, but even with such an increase it is clear that Vilnius was, in fact, a Polish-Jewish city.
7. One should not forget that many more Lithuanians died after the war than during the war, so for Lithuanians the "after war" is much more damaging than the war itself, so that very much colors the collective Lithuanian memory.

of Damocles over Lithuanian society, causing considerable of underlying tension, anger, aggression and discord.

Why? This question has been asked repeatedly, but so far no fully adequate answer has been provided. Many Lithuanians, including scholars, tend to avoid the question, look for external factors or find answers that cannot be considered adequate. In their landmark book, "*The Baltic States – Years of Dependence*," Romuald Misiunas and Rein Taagepera wrote in 1980: "Some outbreaks of indiscriminate killing of Jews occurred in Lithuania soon after the German attack. Several bands of *ad hoc* executioners are known to have perpetrated such massacres. The connection between their activity and the LAF's organized uprising is spotty, with no definite indication of any direct relationship except in time and circumstance."[8] Albertas Gerutis was even more limited in his reporting in the book "*Lithuania 700 Years,*" published in 1969 in the United States. The word "Jew" appeared in the book only once, whereas not one word was dedicated to the Holocaust in Lithuania.[9] Others acknowledge the scope of the issue, but are equally puzzled and not able to find an adequate answer.

The German historian Joachim Tauber writes in his foreword to the official report, "*Preconditions for the Holocaust,*" of the International Commission for the Evaluation of the Crimes of the Nazi and Soviet Occupation Regimes in Lithuania: "...it could seem that until the Soviet occupation in June 1940, the Lithuanian Jews, the *Litvaks*,[10] lived in a relatively quiet and secure environment... (...) Nonetheless, everything has ended in a crime that bears special significance even in the context of the Holocaust: nowhere else were the Jews killed with such vehemence, brutality, and "efficiency" as in Lithuania between June and July 1941."[11] And indeed, the "efficiency" of the extermination of Jews in Lithuania is striking – by the end of 1941, six months after the Nazi occupied the country, some 160,000-164,000 Jews had been killed, 80% of the total Jewish presence on Lithuanian territory.[12]

8. Misiunas, Romuald and Taagepera, Rein: *The Baltic States – Years of Dependence*, p.p. 58-59
9. Gerutis, Albertas: *Lithuania 700 Years*. Manyland Books, New York, 1969
10. The term "Litvak" refers to Jews with roots in the Grand Duchy of Lithuania: (present-day Belarus, Lithuania, Ukraine, and the northeastern Suwalki region of Poland). The term is sometimes used, especially in Israel, to cover all Orthodox Jews who follow a "Lithuanian" (Ashkenazic and non-Hasidic) style of life and learning, whatever their ethnic background
11. Truska, Liudas, and Vareikis, Vygantas: *The Preconditions for the Holocaust; Anti-Semitism in Lithuania*, p. 107
12. According to Yitzhak Arad, there were approximately 203,000-207,000 Jews in Lithuania when the Nazis invaded the country. See Yitzhak Arad in Nikžentaitis, Alvydas: *The Vanished World of Lithuanian Jews*, p. 176. Karen

On the other side of Europe, the Dutch were also very "efficient" in making the extermination of Dutch Jews an easy task for the German occupational forces. So easy, that even *SS-Obersturmbannführer* Adolf Eichmann later would say that the transports from The Netherlands went so smoothly that it was a pleasure to watch them.[13] The Dutch facilitated not as much by active participation, but especially through compliance and by continuing what they were told to do as police officers, civil servants, and railway employees – thereby contributing substantially to the virtual extermination of Dutch Jewry. Within a one-year period, between July 1942 and July 1943, as many as 100,000 Dutch Jews were deported to the transit camp Westerbork in the East of the country; more than 73,000 of those were sent on to their extermination.[14] Approximately 75% of the Dutch Jews did not live to see the end of the war.

The end result was similar in Lithuania. However, when discussing the issue of the Holocaust, there are very specific Lithuanian circumstances that need to be taken into account and analyzed. In his introduction to the report of the International Commission for the evaluation of the Crimes of the Nazi and Soviet occupation regimes in Lithuania, Joachim Tauber points at the crucial importance of the year 1940-1941, when the country was occupied by the Soviets. And he adds: "However, can this account for the developments in Lithuania that started on June 22, 1941? I believe, not."[15] Indeed, this would be far too simple an answer; the issue is far more complex. In fact, the deeper one examines what happened, the more one realizes that no simple and single answer can be found. It is the result of a clash of several historical developments and human weaknesses that led to this catastrophic orgy of violence that virtually ended the presence of Jewry on Lithuanian soil.

This study is primarily directed at Lithuanian society as well as those who wish to try to find an answer to the question as to why Lithuania acted so ferociously. This study is not focusing on finding those who are guilty. The issue of guilt, even though this issue very much blurs the discussions today, is not a helpful concept in finding reasons for what happened. The main purpose of this work is to understand and explain why these unbelievably tragic events took place in a country that for more than five hundred years harbored a large Jewish community and how these events still influence Lithuanian society almost seventy years later.

Sutton mentions a total of some 270,000 Jews, including refugees from Poland. See Sutton, Karen: *The Massacre of Jews of Lithuania*, p. 85.

13. Van der Heijden, Christ: *Grijs Verleden*, p. 286
14. Meershoek, Guus: *The Amsterdam Police and the Persecution of the Jews*, in Berenbaum, Michael: *The Holocaust and History*, p.296
15. Truska, Liudas, and Vareikis, Vygantas: *The Preconditions for the Holocaust; Anti-Semitism in Lithuania*, p. 112

Acknowledgements

This book would not have been possible without the editing of Ellen Mercer, to whom I am greatly indebted, and the Dutch Jewish Humanitarian Foundation that financially supported its development through the Jewish Culture and Information Center in Vilnius (LT).

Chapter 1 – Lithuanian Historical Background

Lithuania's National Anthem urges her sons to draw strength from the past.

Albertas Gerutis[16]

Lithuania! My fatherland! You are like health! Only he who has lost you may know your true worth!

Adam Mickiewicz[17]

Lithuanian history of the twentieth century is complex, a sequence of successes and failures, of victories and defeats. The shape of the country changed so many times in less than forty years; it does not take much imagination to understand that this had far-reaching consequences, leaving a proud nation traumatized and, clearly, with a strong sense of being a victim of history. Without going too much into detail with regard to Lithuania's history, it is important to point out some important moments in the country's past that help to explain what happened in the period 1941-1944.

The history of Lithuania, as a country, dates back to at least 1009, the first recorded written use of the designation. The area was at that time very sparsely populated consisting of wild forests, lakes, and rivers with only a few fortifications, no towns or cities. "Small groupings or tribes in semi-feudal organizations were under local rulers or dukes. Farming was conducted in forest clearings. The tribes were fierce and raided other groups in the area. The people were pagan, believing in demons and monsters and practicing human sacrifice."[18] After conquering neighboring lands, Lithuanians finally established the Kingdom of Lithuania in the 13th century and under the leadership of Mindaugas managed to withstand the threat by the Teutonic order to conquer the area. The Grand Duchy of Lithuania remained fiercely independent and was notably one of the last areas of Europe to adopt Christianity in 1387, as a result of which certain pagan traditions still remain in Lithuania.

In the 15th century, under the reign of Vytautas the Great (1392-1430), the country became the largest state in Europe and a formidable power reaching all the way to the Black Sea. This period is usually referred to as

16. Gerutis, Albertas: *Lithuania 700 Years*. Manyland Books, New York, 1969, p. xi
17. quoted in *The Reconstruction of Nations*, p. 28
18. Schoenburg, Nancy (et.al.): *Lithuanian Jewish Communities*, p. 4

the Golden Age. The country included not only Lithuania, but also Byelorussia and Ukraine. On this vast area of 390,000 square miles, a total population of 2 million people lived, of whom approximately only one-eighth were ethnic Lithuanians, who occupied the ruling positions. Most of the people living within the boundaries of the state enjoyed a relative autonomy, with their own identities, laws and customs. In the course of the fifteenth century, Lithuania and Poland merged into the Polish-Lithuanian Commonwealth.[19] In 1569, the union between the two countries was finally sealed in Lublin, and Lithuania practically became part of Poland.

In 1795, however, the country was erased from the political map as a result of the Partitions of Poland. The Lithuanians would live mostly under the rule of the Russian Empire until the 20th century. At times, Tsarist policies were very discriminatory towards Lithuanian culture and language, resulting in a nation determined to save its language and traditions and oppose the restrictions imposed by what was seen as foreign domination. Lithuanians proudly remember the so-called book smugglers, or *knygnešiai*, who, from 1864 till 1904, smuggled Lithuanian language books across the Prussian-Russian border into the country to counter the discriminatory language policy of the Tsars, which forbade the use of Lithuanian in Latin letters. However, at the same time, one should not forget that when Russia obtained Lithuanian lands at the end of the eighteenth century, it absorbed elites who spoke Polish, peasants who spoke mostly Byelorussian, and towns with mainly Jews who spoke Yiddish.[20] As Timothy Snyder writes in *The Reconstruction of Nations*, by the end of the nineteenth century, "The Lithuanian foundations were buried under a good deal of history. The Lithuanian language had not been considered a language of politics for centuries. The Lithuanian grand dukes had never published Lithuanian books. The last Lithuanian grand duke who even knew the Lithuanian language died the year Columbus discovered America."[21] According to the Russian imperial census of 1897, more people spoke Byelorussian in Vilnius province than all other languages com-

19. Although Lithuanians consider this to have been a Lithuanian-Polish State, in many or maybe even most other countries the state is referred to simple as Poland, and the name of Lithuania is not even mentioned. In secondary school, I was never even informed that Poland was originally a commonwealth of two states and Lithuania was never mentioned. Even in university, while studying history, the information remained vague. For instance, in *A History of the Modern World*, Palmer and Colton refer to the "submerged Lithuanians (p. 205) and the Republic of Poland" (p. 211), leaving no doubt who they consider to be the dominant nationality. See Colton, Joel and Palmer, R. R.: *A History of the Modern World*, Knopf, 1984.
20. *The Reconstruction of Nations*, p. 25
21. *The Reconstruction of Nations*, p. 32

bined. "In Vilnius, Minsk, Grodno, Mogilev and Vitebsk provinces, contiguous territories of historic Lithuania, speakers of Byelorussian were three-quarters of the population."[22]

Jews in Lithuania

Lithuania played also a very important role in the history of Jews in Eastern Europe. Jews began living in Lithuania as early as the 8th century. In 1388, they were granted a charter by Vytautas the Great under which they formed a class of freemen subject in all criminal cases directly to the jurisdiction of the grand duke and his official representatives, and in petty suits to the jurisdiction of local officials on an equal footing with the lesser nobles, boyars, and other free citizens.[23] As a result, the community prospered. In 1495, they were expelled by Alexander Jagella but allowed to return in 1503. The Lithuanian statute of 1566 placed a number of restrictions on the Jews, and imposed sumptuary laws, including the requirement that they wear distinctive clothing, including yellow caps for men and yellow kerchiefs for women.

The Polish Jews deeply suffered as a result of the Khmelnytsky Cossack Uprisings of 1648-1652, which were the result of a decaying Polish state that had entered a state of decline and stagnation. Pillaging Cossack troops set out to kill as many Jews as possible and it is estimated that some 100,000 were killed in the course of the uprising.[24] It also resulted in the destruction of the existing Jewish institutions, destroying the yeshivas and schools and killing the scholars and teachers. However, the Lithuanian Jews managed to escape much of the destruction by the Cossacks. Although they suffered heavily during the Russo-Swedish wars that ended only in 1661, they escaped the mass murders at the hands of the Cossacks. As a result, the Jewish population of Lithuania grew from an estimated 27,000 in 1578 to approximately 32,000 in 1676.[25] After the 1793 Second Partition of the Polish-Lithuanian Commonwealth, Lithuanian Jews became subjects of the Russian Empire.

At the end of the 19th century, over five million Jews were living in Russia.[26] Virtually all of them lived in the so-called *Pale of Settlement*, an area that corresponded to historical borders of the Polish-Lithuanian

22. *The Reconstruction of Nations*, p. 42
23. See Greenbaum, Masha: *The Jews of Lithuania*, p. 8
24. Schoenburg, Nancy (et.al.): *Lithuanian Jewish Communities*, p. 22
25. Schoenburg, Nancy (et.al.): *Lithuanian Jewish Communities*, p. 22
26. In 1820, there were 1.6 million Jews in Russia (including Poland). In 1851 that number had increased to 2.4 million and in 1880 it had reached 4 million. The census of 1897 showed that there were 5.2 million Jews in Russia, of which

Commonwealth and included much of present-day Lithuania, Belarus, Poland, Bessarabia, Ukraine, and parts of western Russia. Additionally, a number of cities within the Pale were excluded from giving permission to Jews to settle there. In the Pale, Jews constituted 11 percent of the total population; yet were often the majority in Byelorussian and Lithuanian cities.[27] Most of them were poor. In the 1890s, nineteen percent of Jewish families in Russia and over 22 percent in Lithuania lived in extreme poverty and had to ask for communal assistance to survive and be able to celebrate Passover.[28]

The major reason for the sudden surge of emigration of Jews, mainly to America, was the assassination of Tsar Aleksandr II on March 1, 1881, by a terrorist cell of the political movement "Narodnaya Volya." Although only one member of the group, Gesia Gelfman, was of Jewish origin, word soon spread that the Jews had killed the Tsar and a government inspired pogrom engulfed the country. One of the main instigators was the Chief Procurator of the Holy Synod, Konstantin Pobedonovtsev, also referred to as the "Grey Cardinal," who argued that the best way to deal with Russian Jewry was to force one-third into emigration, have one-third baptized and kill the remaining one-third.[29]

During the preceding decades, the Jews in Russia had actually gone through a period of relative tranquility. During the previous century, they had lived through cycles of relaxation and repression, often pressured by the Russian authorities to adapt and assimilate to their Russian environment. Within the Jewish community, various groups positioned themselves differently. The enlighteners, *maskilim*, wanted to bring the benefits of European culture to the Jews and advocated reforms in religion. They believed in the good will of the Tsar and thought he was working for their betterment. The *maskilim* were opposed by the more religious Jews, such as the *Hassidim*, who believed that the *maskilim* were undermining traditional authority in the Jew-

only 300,000 lived outside the Pale of Settlement. See Kochan, Lionel (ed.): *Jews in Soviet Russia since 1917*, p. 15.

27. According to the same census of 1897, over 50% of the population in towns in Lithuania and Belarus was Jewish. In Vilnius, about half of the city's population was Jewish.
28. *The Promised City*, p.31. Alas, the immigration wave of the late nineteenth century and early twentieth century did not improve the quality of life for those left behind. Although the number of Jews decreased, and one could assume this would decrease the economic pressure on those remaining, so did the number of consumers and potential clients for the remaining artisans and, thus, the result was further increased poverty.
29. Greenbaum, Masha: *Jews of Lithuania*, p. 187

ish community and were leading the Jews towards assimilation and integration into Russian culture.[30]

While the majority of Jews remained firmly rooted in their traditional Jewish identity, a growing number turned to enlightenment in an attempt to connect their Jewishness with modernity, with progress. Some converted to Christianity, others became Russian in their way of life, or turned to socialism or internationalism. A growing number became politically active, not only trying to change the position of the Jews but with the goal of changing society and the political system as a whole. Yet while this growing pluralism within Jewish society weakened its cohesion, it did not necessarily mean that the assimilation of Jews into the surrounding environment and culture was very much stimulated. "Given the fact… that almost every conceivable aspect of life could still take place within the boundaries of the Jewish community, the bulk of the Jews of East Central Europe continued to live separately from their non-Jewish environment," writes André Gerrits. "Even those Jews who had liberated themselves from the narrow margin of traditional, religiously defined Jewish life, did not need to merge into non-Jewish society."[31] And thus, again according to Gerrits, "even during the interwar years, the large majority of the East European Jews, those in Poland included, remained within their own, gradually more pluralistic society. The point however, is that these barriers were not exclusively, and perhaps not even primarily, the result of anti-Jewish sentiments among their Christian neighbors. Jewish isolation was also self-selected."[32]

Most of the Jewish socialists were "*narodniki*," and based their hopes on an enlightened self-liberating peasant class. But when they finally met the peasants, they were bitterly disappointed, because "they beheld the peasants as most of them really were: a brutish, crude, boorish, superstitious lot, influenced by an obscanturist reactionary clergy. Theirs was a social class in which individuals brimmed with hatred and bitterness towards each other, their feudal lords, and all strangers, especially if they were not Russian Orthodox. Their priests taught them to hate Catholics because of

30. See, among others, *The Jews in Soviet Russia since 1917*, pp. 18-19. More strict religious leaders such as the Vilnius Gaon, who feared that Hassidic leaders themselves would become objects of adulation, in turn, opposed the Hassidim. In particular they opposed the Hassidim's view that one could attain spiritual fulfillment not only through learning and intellectual efforts but also through sincere prayer and behavior expressive of the joy of drawing closer to God, including song and dance, often fueled by the use of alcohol. Slonim, coincidentally, was one of the centers of the Hassidim.
31. Gerrits, André: *The Myth of Jewish Communism*, p. 37
32. Gerrits, André: *The Myth of Jewish Communism*, p. 38

the authoritarian hierarchy in Rome, Protestants for their individualism, and above all Jews, who had 'killed Christ'."[33] Their political beliefs were further shaken when, during the 1881-82 pogroms, farmers actively participated in the witch-hunt against the Jews. Even more shocking to them was the fact that their fellow non-Jewish revolutionaries applauded the active participation of peasants as a first step towards political emancipation. The theory was that by striking at the Jews, the peasantry was learning to become self-assertive, to defend itself against its oppressors. They believed that eventually the peasants would learn that the Jews were not the real enemy, but, rather, the autocratic exploitative system. However, if some Jews had to be sacrificed in that process, so be it.[34] The *Narodnaya Volya* bulletin of 1882 summarized it quite directly: "Today the Jew, tomorrow the Czar and the kulaks."[35]

The pogroms of 1881-82 were followed by a set of laws of May 1882 in which it was stipulated that the Jews were no longer allowed to live outside the towns and shtetls. They were forbidden to do business on Sundays, and as Saturday was for them a holy day, it automatically meant that they were in an unfavorable position vis-à-vis their non-Jewish competition. In Russian schools a *numeris clausis* was introduced, stipulating that in the Pale, only 10 percent of students in secondary schools could be of Jewish origin and 5 percent outside. [36] In 1890, the Moscow police ordered that all Jewish shops were required to have the owners' names in Hebrew, and, a year later, all the Jews were expelled from Moscow altogether. The May Laws have also been described as a perpetual administrative pogrom that remained on the books until the October Revolution of 1917.[37]

The economic hardships, anti-Semitic pogroms and restrictive laws forced many Jews to leave their homes in search of a better life elsewhere. A mass migration started to develop, with many Jews from Lithuania and Byelorussia streaming south into Ukraine or westward to the industrialized cities of Poland. Urban centers developed almost over night. In 1897, Jews accounted for 52% of the urban population of Lithuania and Byelorussia, followed by Russians with 18.2%, Poles with 12.8%, Byelorussians with 11.8% and Lithuanians with 1.7%.[38] The Polish city of Lodz, a village with only 11 Jews in 1793, grew swiftly to a Jewish population of almost

33. *Jews of Lithuania*, p. 195
34. *Century of Ambivalence*, p. 7-13
35. *Jews of Lithuania*, p. 196
36. In Moscow and St. Petersburg it was a maximum of 3 percent, which was later reduced even further.
37. *Jews of Lithuania*, p. 190. The May Laws were introduced by Interior Minister Count Pavel Ignatiev.
38. Schoenburg, Nancy (et.al.): *Lithuanian Jewish Communities*, p. 31

100,000 in 1897 and 166,000 in 1910. Warsaw, which had 3,500 Jews in 1781, grew to have 219,000 in 1891.[39] In 1914, 51% of the population in Minsk was Jewish; in Gomel, the Jewish population totaled 55%; in Pinsk, 74%; and in Vitebsk, 51%.[40] By the time the Second World War started, one third of Poland's population was Jewish. In Vilnius, approximately 35% was Jewish by the time the Second World War started.

Because the restrictive laws banned Jews from owning or renting land, and later also from being innkeepers or restaurateurs, and the *numeris clausis* made access to educational institutions almost impossible, many tried to earn a living through artisanship. Workshops and sweatshops sprang up all over the towns and cities. Many Jews worked in the industries, thereby creating a new proletariat.[41] By the end of the 19th century, Jews constituted over 21 percent of the factory workers in the Pale, and in Poland the number was as high as 28 percent.[42] Jewish women had originally taken on many responsibilities in the family business in order to allow their husbands to devote time to religious study. In the 1870s, the introduction of the Singer sewing machine revolutionized Jewish homes, and wives and daughters were sent to work making garments. In larger towns, women started to work as tailoresses, seamstresses, and sock makers.[43]

Jews and socialism

The development of a Jewish working class in the cities also meant that Marxian Socialism achieved a much more widespread appeal. [44] As early as the 1870s, Jewish workmen resorted to sabotage and violence in strikes, driven by poverty and hardships. In 1888, the Social Democrats founded strike funds and strike treasuries in a variety of trades, setting off a more organized union activity.[45] Soon the first national trade union was organized in Russia,[46] with Jews forming the backbone of the organization.

Political activism among the Jews also resulted in higher numbers among political prisoners. Between 1901 and 1903, of the 7,791 persons imprisoned in Russia for political reasons, 2,269 were Jews. From March 1903 to

39. *The Promised City*, p. 24
40. *The Reconstruction of Nations*, p. 56
41. *The Promised City*, p.27
42. *The Promised City*, 28
43. *The Promised City*, p. 27
44. *The Promised City*, p. 43
45. In 1895, workers in the tobacco industry of Vilnius managed to win several victories with their strikes and, in Bialystok, thousands of textile workers set off a great labor upheaval.
46. The Universal Union of Bristle Workers in Russian Poland

November 1904, 54 percent of those sentenced for political reasons were Jews; of the women sentenced for political crimes, more than 64 percent were Jewish. In 1904, of an estimated 30,000 organized Jewish workers, 4,476 were imprisoned or exiled to Siberia.[47]

In 1897, a "General League – Bund – of Jewish Workingmen in Russia and Poland" was founded in Vilnius, forming a national organization of social democratic and Marxist labor organizations. In 1901, Lithuania was added to the name.[48] Between 1897 and 1900, the Bund led 312 strikes that led to higher wages and better working conditions.[49] In 1898, the Bund was instrumental in founding the Russian Social-Democratic Labor party (RSDLP) during a meeting in Minsk, and it entered this party itself as "an autonomous organization, independent only in matters which specifically concern the Jewish proletariat."[50] However, at the Second Congress of the RSDLP in 1903, the Bund was expelled from the party because of its "nationalistic positions."[51]

This expulsion only made the Bund even more Jewish in orientation. It formed self-defense groups against pogroms, and gradually the organization became a sort of "counter-culture," strongly promoting Jewish culture. This became even more so after the failed revolution of 1905, when political activity was heavily repressed. The Bund strongly promoted the use of Yiddish as a Jewish national language (and opposed the Zionist project of reviving Hebrew). It organized musical, literary and theatre societies, developed its own press, set up Yiddish schools, promoted Yiddish writers and was instrumental in developing a vibrant cultural life. Yet again, also in the case of Jews becoming communists, it did not automatically mean that this ended their isolation within society. In a way, Jews who became communist swapped one isolation for another; it was "not so much an act of assimilation as an act of exchanging one form of isolation, that of being a Jew, for another, that of being a communist (if not to add one to the other, becoming a Jewish communist). Jewish communists remained an embattled minority, at best willfully ignored by Jews and non-Jews alike, but more often vilified and attacked."[52]

47. *The Promised City*, p. 45
48. In Yiddish "Algemeyner Yidisher Arbeter Bund in Lite, Poyln un Rusland"
49. *The Promised City*, p. 45
50. *Century of Ambivalence*, p. 15
51. The Bund formally rejoined the RSDLP when all of its faction reunited at the Fourth (Unification) Congress in Stockholm in April 1906, but the party remained fractured along ideological and ethnic lines. The Bund generally sided with the party's Menshevik faction and against the Bolshevik faction led by Vladimir Lenin.
52. Gerrits, André: *The Myth of Jewish Communism*, p. 40

At the same time, Zionism was on the rise, based on the concept that for Jews there would never be a place in Europe, emigration was no solution, and socialism would not be able to solve the Jewish predicament. It was believed that the only solution was to establish a Jewish state where Jews would find a home, free of persecution and anti-Semitism. One of the first adherents of this view, Leon Pinsker, argued that anti-Semitism was endemic to Europe, that its fundamental irrationality made it immune to education and rational arguments and, therefore, the Jews had no option but to leave the continent. At the beginning of the twentieth century, attempts were made to combine the ideologies of Zionism and socialism, and in 1906 the Poalei Zion Party was formed, professing this combination.

The Bund strongly opposed Zionism, arguing that emigration to Palestine was a form of escapism. Nevertheless, many Bundists were also Zionists, and the Bund suffered from a steady loss of active members to emigration.[53] Still, there remained a considerable portion of Jews that refused the concept that Europe was a hopeless territory and should be left behind. They believed that there was a place for them in Russia, as long as the political order could be reformed and liberalized. In 1905, 6,000 Jews signed a "Declaration of Jewish Citizens," arguing that Jews were human beings with the same rights as other people and that their rights should be respected accordingly.[54]

Anti-Semitism continued, however, and regular pogroms shocked the Jewish community. In 1905, a wave of pogroms enveloped the country after the Tsar had issued a manifesto granting the people a constitutional government. His decision was the result of mass protests and a general strike during the 1905 Revolution in October of that year, and anti-Semitic organizations used the occasion as a pretext to blame the Jews and organize pogroms in over 300 towns and cities. The worst pogrom took place in Odessa, where over 300 people were killed and 600 Jewish children orphaned. These events gave, of course, an extra impetus to the emigration of Jews. As the historian S. Ettinger concludes, "...the situation of the Jews was desperate; clearly, only the fall of the tsarist regime could save them."[55]

When the First World War started, and Tsarist Russia was invaded by German troops, again the Jews suffered quite excessively. Some 200,000 Jews were deported from Kaunas, Kuršas and Grodno (now in Belarus)

53. Many Bundists became later active in forming socialist parties in Palestine and, subsequently, Israel.
54. *Century of Ambivalence*, p. 20-21
55. *The Jews in Soviet Russia since 1917*, p. 20

to the inner part of Russia because they were deemed to be unreliable and pro-German. The retreating Cossacks and Russian soldiers carried out pogroms and plundered the Jews.[56] A detailed description of the sufferings this brought upon the Jews can be found in Hirsz Abramowicz's *Profiles of a Lost World*.[57]

Lithuanian independence

During Russian Tsarist rule, Lithuanian society stagnated. The population consisted mainly of Lithuanian peasantry and Polish gentry (although part of them were, in fact, Polonized Lithuanian gentry), yet the most common languages were Polish for the elite and Byelorussian among the peasants, particularly in the East.[58] Only after serfdom was abolished in Russia in 1861, did a Lithuanian intelligentsia start to emerge, which had its founding in the now free Lithuanian peasantry. With it Lithuanian nationalism got a boost. "Lithuanians utilized this historic period as a base. This period of great military expansion was idealized and Vytautas was deified. The union with Poland was regarded as the great betrayal of Lithuania. Poland was regarded with hostility. Pagan origins were looked on with pride and contemporary manifestations of paganism were commented upon with enthusiasm. (...) These factors were utilized to bridge 400 years of societal non-existence, allowing Lithuanian intellectuals to talk of 700 years of Lithuanian history. This search for national identity led to calls

56. Truska, Liudas, and Vareikis, Vygantas: *The Preconditions for the Holocaust; Anti-Semitism in Lithuania*, p. 141. The experiences of the First World War, when the Germans replaced the Russians and behaved quite differently, created the impression among some Jews that life under German rule could not be all that bad. See also Van Voren, Robert: *Cold War in Psychiatry* (Rodopi 2010) discussing the German occupation of Slonim in 1915:

"Russian control lasted until 1915, when the German army captured the town. Moshe Eisenstadt, a local resident at the time, described how the Germans were welcomed by the population: 'What can I tell you? If we had seen the Messiah, the joy would not have been as great as when we saw the Germans marching through the town. Houses and stores immediately opened. People went out to walk in the streets, and everybody came out to greet the newly arrived Germans. In several parts of the town, old Jews came out of their houses and kissed the German soldiers. Everybody brought something to treat them with.' However, the joy did not last long as Slonim found itself right in the middle of the front. Long barrages of artillery bombing followed, turning much of the town into rubble. Also the Germans turn out to be less civilized than expected, and repeatedly were seen stealing property." *Cold War in Psychiatry*, pp. 24-25

57. Abramowicz, Hirsz: *Profiles of a Lost World*, p. 182-208

58. *The Reconstruction of Nations*, p. 46

for territorial autonomy and finally independence."[59] Yale-based historian Timothy Snyder views this from a somewhat different perspective: "Although the Lithuanian national idea involved extraordinary feats of historical imagination, it is much easier to invent history by writing massive tomes than it is to change tradition by changing elite behavior. (...) Lithuanian activists, often Russian-educated peasant sons, happily skipped over several centuries and spoke of rebirth."[60]

One should not forget that the ethnic "map" of Lithuania was much more complex than now often recalled, not the least of which was Vilnius. "By 1914, the old capital of the Grand Duchy of Lithuania was a desired political capital to Lithuanians, Belarusians and Poles wishing to lead nations; a spiritual capital to the Jews who were the city's most distinctive group; and an ancient Russian city to the officials who exercised power."[61] In Vilnius, Byelorussian speakers "far outnumbered Lithuanian speakers. In Vilna [Vilnius] province as a whole, speakers of Belarusian were more than half the population. In Vilna, Minsk, Grodno, Mogilev and Vitebsk provinces, contiguous territories of historic Lithuania, speakers of Belarusian were three-quarters of the population."[62]

During World War I, Lithuania was incorporated into *Ober Ost*, and ruled by the occupational German government. As the war progressed, it became evident that Germany would not reach an effective victory and would have to compromise peace with the Russian Empire. As open annexation could result in a public relations backlash, Germans planned to form a network of formally independent states that would in fact be completely dependent on Germany, the so-called *Mitteleuropa*. The Germans allowed the Vilnius Conference to convene in September 1917; however, they demanded that Lithuanians declare loyalty to Germany and agree to an annexation. Yet contrary to their plans, the Conference elected a 20-member Council of Lithuania and empowered it to act as the executive authority of the Lithuanian people and on February 16, 1918, the Council adopted the Act of Independence of Lithuania. It declared Lithuania to be an independent republic, based on democratic principles.

Following the Armistice of Compiègne, which was signed on November 11, 1918, ending the First World War, the Lithuanians quickly formed their first government, adopted a provisional constitution, and set up the first administrative structures. While the defeated German army retreated from

59. Schoenburg, Nancy (et.al.): *Lithuanian Jewish Communities*, p. 35
60. *The Reconstruction of Nations*, p. 48
61. *The Reconstruction of Nations*, p. 52
62. *The Reconstruction of Nations*, p. 54

the Eastern Front, the Soviet Red Army followed it in its wake. The Soviets created a number of puppet states, including the Lithuanian Soviet Socialist Republic, and by December 1918 the Red Army had reached the borders of Lithuania, starting the Lithuanian-Soviet War. The Lithuanian government evacuated from Vilnius to Kaunas, which became the temporary capital of Lithuania. The Red Army captured Vilnius on January 5, 1919.

While Lithuanian and Soviet troops were militarily engaged, problems also developed with Poland, which had its own territorial claims over Lithuania, especially regarding the Vilnius Region. These tensions led to a Polish-Lithuanian War. In mid-May, the Lithuanian army began an offensive against the Soviets in northeastern Lithuania and, by the end of August 1919, the Soviets had been pushed out of the country. Subsequently, the Lithuanian Army concentrated on fighting the paramilitary West Russian Volunteer Army, which invaded Lithuania from the north. By the end of 1919 they, too, had been defeated.

The Constituent Assembly of Lithuania was elected in April 1920 and met for the first time in May of that year. It soon adopted the third provisional constitution and signed the Soviet-Lithuanian Peace Treaty. The Soviet Union fully recognized Lithuanian independence as well as its claims to the disputed Vilnius region. However, the treaty incensed the Poles exactly because of this territorial dispute. To prevent further fighting, the Suwalki Agreement was signed in October 1920; but, before it went into effect, General Lucjan Zeligowski staged a mutiny, invaded Lithuania, captured Vilnius, and established the short-lived Republic of Central Lithuania. The League of Nations attempted to mediate in the dispute; however, the negotiations broke down as neither side agreed to compromise. The Republic of Central Lithuania held a plebiscite and was subsequently incorporated into Poland in March 1922. Lithuania broke off all diplomatic relations with Poland, refusing to recognize its control over Vilnius. The dispute would dominate Lithuanian foreign policy for the entire interwar period.

The Constituent Assembly, which adjourned in October 1920 due to threats from Poland, initiated many reforms needed in the new state and obtained international recognition and membership in the League of Nations. Lithuania became a democratic state, with a Seimas (parliament) elected by both male and female citizens for a three-year term. The Seimas in turn elected the president. The First Seimas was elected in October 1922, but could not form a government as the votes split equally 38-38, forcing it to resign. Its only lasting achievement was the Klaipėda Revolt in January 1923. Lithuania took advantage of the Ruhr Crisis and captured the Klaipėda Region, a territory detached from the East Prussia on the basis of the Treaty of

Versailles and placed under French administration. The region was incorporated as an autonomous district of Lithuania in May 1924.

The Second Seimas, elected in May 1923, was the only Seimas in independent Lithuania to serve the full term. The Third Seimas was elected in May 1926. It was sharply criticized for signing the Soviet-Lithuanian Non-Aggression Pact and accused of "Bolshevization" of Lithuania. As a result of growing tensions, the government was deposed during the December 1926 Lithuanian coup d'état. This coup, organized by the military, was supported by the Lithuanian Nationalists Union (*tautininkai*) and the Lithuanian Christian Democrats. They installed Antanas Smetona[63] as President and Augustinas Voldemaras[64] as the Prime Minister. Smetona suppressed the opposition and remained in power as an authoritarian leader until June 1940. This political development was very much in line with the general tendency in Europe: for instance, in Italy democracy ended in 1922, in Spain and Portugal in 1923 and 1926 respectively. Germany became a dictatorship with Hitler's ascent to power in 1933. Closer to home, the USSR was a dictatorship from 1917 onwards, with the exception of the two Baltic neighbors, Estonia and Latvia, who became a dictatorship in 1934.

When the Nazi Party came into power in the Weimar Republic, German-Lithuanian relations worsened considerably, as Nazi Germany did not accept the loss of Klaipėda Region. The Nazis sponsored anti-Lithuanian organizations in the region. In 1934, Lithuania put the activists on trial and sentenced about 100 people, including their leaders, Ernst Neumann and Theodor von Sass. That prompted Germany, one of the main trade partners of Lithuania, to declare an embargo of Lithuanian products.

As tensions were rising in Europe following the annexation of Austria by Nazi Germany, Poland presented an ultimatum to Lithuania in March 1938. Poland demanded the re-establishment of normal diplomatic relations, which were broken after the Zeligowski's mutiny in 1920, and threatened

63. Antanas Smetona (1874-1944) was one of the most important Lithuanian political figures between World War I and World War II. He served as the first President of Lithuania from April 4, 1919 to June 19, 1920. He again served as the last President of the country from December 19, 1926 to June 15, 1944.
64. Augustinas Voldemaras (1883-1942) was a Lithuanian nationalist political figure. He served as the country's first Prime Minister in 1918, and again from 1926 to 1929. He was the head of an organization called Geležinis Vilkas (Iron Wolf), whose honorary head was President Smetona. Although he and Smetona had formerly worked closely together and shared similar ideologies, their association was soon to be brought to an end, partly because of Voldemaras' intense involvement with Geležinis Vilkas.

military actions in case of refusal. Lithuania, having weaker military power and unable to enlist international support for its cause, had no choice but to accept the ultimatum. Lithuania-Poland relations somewhat normalized and the parties concluded treaties regarding railway transport, postal exchange, and other means of communication. Just a year after the Polish ultimatum and five days after the German occupation of Czechoslovakia, Lithuania received as oral ultimatum from the German Foreign Minister Joachim von Ribbentrop demanding to cede the Klaipėda Region to Germany. Again, Lithuania was forced to accept. This triggered a political crisis in Lithuania and forced Smetona to form a new government that, for the first time since 1926, included members of the opposition.

Even though the port of Klaipėda remained accessible for Lithuanian trade, the loss of the Klaipėda region was a major blow to Lithuanian economy. A considerable part of the country's industry had been situated here. The country shifted to the sphere of German influence and when Germany and the Soviet Union worked out the Molotov-Ribbentrop Pact in 1939 and divided Eastern Europe into spheres of influence, Lithuania was, at first, assigned to Germany. The loss of the Klaipėda region also showed the Lithuanians that the lenient policy of allowing a national minority to use their own language (German) instead of imposing the use of Lithuanian had failed; the result was that when in 1939 Vilnius and the Vilnius region was handed to them by the Soviets (see later), a policy of forced Lithuanization was implemented; however, with equally unpleasant effects and resulting in much resentment among the Jewish and Polish populations of the region.[65]

Sovietization

In August 1939, Nazi Germany and the Soviet Union signed the Molotov-Ribbentrop Pact, with secret clauses assigning spheres of influence in the area of the Baltic Sea. Lithuania, although initially assigned to the German sphere of influence, was now transferred to the Soviets in secret additional protocols of the German-Soviet Boundary and Friendship Treaty of September 28, 1939. The Red Army occupied the city of Vilnius during the invasion of Poland on September 19, 1939. Three weeks later, on October 10, the Russians announced that they would cede the Vilnius district to the Lithuanians, although it was not until October 27 that the Russians actually withdrew and the cessation was implemented. But it was not without a price: on the basis of a Soviet-Lithuanian Mutual Assistance Pact, one fifth of the Vilnius Region was handed over to Lithuania in exchange for stationing 20,000 Soviet troops within Lithuania. "Under the rule of the Lithua-

65. For more information on this policy see Liekis, Šarūnas: *1939*.

nians the people breathed more freely," wrote Israel Cohen in a guide to Vilnius published in 1943; "and the Jews enjoyed a feeling of comparative relief such as they had not known before. But this condition was destined to prove only transitory; for after eight months it came to a sudden end."[66]

The eight months between the Soviet invasion and the annexation of the country by the Soviets turned out to be the calm before the storm, in particular for the Jewish part of the population. From Poland, more than 25,000 refugees surged into the region, among who were some 15,000 Polish Jews.[67] During the days preceding the transfer of authority from the Soviets to the Lithuanians, in particular, many Jews tried to reach Vilnius as there was no border control and transportation was still functioning. Among the refugees were 1,500-1,600 rabbis, yeshiva students and their families from *yeshivot* in places like Mir, Kamenetz, Radin, Grodno, Bailystok and Slonim.[68] "Once the Lithuanian government was in undisputed control of the Vilna [Vilnius] district, systematic measures were taken for the relief of the refugees. Under its auspices a coordinating committee was formed, consisting of representatives of the American Jewish Joint Distribution Committee, the American Red Cross, the Commission for Polish Relief, and the Lithuanian Red Cross. (...) Nor was any discrimination shown on the grounds of race or religion; for a number of Polish refugee journalists, including some notorious anti-Semites, were housed and fed by the [Jewish] Joint Distribution Committee."[69] Among the refugees were also well known Jewish intellectuals such as Herman Kruk, whose diary of the Vilnius Ghetto would become a solid yet painful monument to the 80-90,000 Vilnius Jews killed during the war.[70] The flow of refugees stopped only after September 23-25, 1939, when the border with Lithuania came under Soviet control.[71]

An additional group of refugees came from a German-occupied territory to the south, the "Suwalki triangle." Starting in late October 1939, the Germans started pushing Jews from that region across the border. They were, however, sent back by the Lithuanian border guards, but when the Germans put up machine guns and threatened to shoot them all, the Lithuanians

66. Cohen, Israel: *Vilna*. Pp. 469-470
67. Greenbaum, Masha: *The Jews of Lithuania*, p. 289. Already by December 2, 1939, the Lithuanian authorities had registered 18,311 refugees from Poland, of whom 7,728 were Poles, 6,860 Jews and 3,723 Lithuanians. See Liekis, Šarūnas: *1939*, p. 298
68. Liekis, Šarūnas: *1939*, p. 301
69. Cohen, Israel: *Vilna*. P. 472
70. Kruk, Herman: *The Last Days of the Jerusalem of Lithuania*, Yale University Press, 2002
71. Liekis, Šarūnas: *1939*, p. 141

halted their efforts. Approaches to the German border police did not provide any solution and when the Lithuanian side told the Germans that they were unable to take the Jewish refugees in, the Germans suggested to them to put up machine guns as well and to shoot those who would cross the border.

In order to solve the issue, Lithuanian ambassador Kazys Škirpa met with the German Foreign Ministry in Berlin, where he was told bluntly by the responsible civil servant: "*Wie Sie wissen, wir haben keine Liebe zu den Juden*" (as you know, we do not love the Jews). "Škirpa replied, also as if he was joking, that Jews were not loved in Lithuania either, as there were too many in the country already. (...) Škirpa ended the conversation, saying that the Reich had the right to do what it pleased with its own Jews, but that it should not burden Lithuania, as thrusting one's Jews onto others was unacceptable."[72] Still, all Lithuanian protests were in vain and in the end some 1,500-2,000 Jews from the Suwalki region wound up in Lithuania.

"Within the brief period from the capture of the city [of Vilnius] by the Russians in September 1939, until they retook it in the following June, the Jews underwent a medley of emotions and experiences, in which anxiety alternated with hope, and relief with despair" wrote Israel Cohen in 1943.[73] Indeed, the attitude of the Lithuanian government was much more favorable to them than that of the previous Polish authorities. The Polish authorities had been increasingly anti-Semitic and gradually Jews had been banned from all spheres of public life. At university, so-called "ghetto benching" was enforced in October 1938, a boycott of Jewish shops started that same fall and Vilnius radio had been "Aryanized" and Jewish singers and musicians were no longer welcome on radio. Shortly after, the total removal of Jews from the film industry was demanded.[74] Cohen continued: "The attitude of the Lithuanian government itself, however, was one of gratifying tolerance. It issued a manifesto in Yiddish to the Jews of Vilna, guaranteeing them equality of rights. It formally recognized the legal status of the Jewish Kehillah.[75] It approved the appointment of a Jew as vice-mayor. It allowed the *Vilner Tageblatt* and two other Jewish newspapers to resume publication. Four streets in the city were renamed in honor of the popular Jewish writers, Mendele Micher Seforim, Perez, Dick and the distinguished Jewish communal worker, Dr. Shabad. (...) And for the first time in Lithuanian history a government official was tried on charges

72. Liekis, Šarūnas: *1939*, pp. 207-212
73. Cohen, Israel: *Vilnius*. P. 470
74. See Dawidowicz, Lucy: *From that Place and Time*, pp. 168-173. Lucy Dawidowicz, an American Jewish girl living in Vilna at that time and working at YIVO, vividly describes the climate in Polish-dominated Vilna in her book.
75. A Kehillah (plural: Kehillot) is a Jewish elected local community council that had both secular and religious administrative powers

of anti-Semitism made by fourteen non-Jewish colleagues."[76] The American Jewish newspaper *Di Yiddishe Velt* wrote in October 1939: "The Jews of Vilnius had God to thank for their lucky fate, knowing that the Jews in Lithuania were not complaining about their situation and were not being badly treated by the Lithuanian government. The Jews of America had to be sure that Jewish cultural and religious institutions and YIVO would be able to work freely. The city was destined to preserve its historically important name, 'the Jerusalem of Lithuania'."[77] I will later return to the position and daily life of the Jewish population of Vilnius, but here it is important to note that Lithuanian rule was actually a relief after twenty years of Polish dominance.

For the Polish population of Vilnius, however, life was far from ideal. The Lithuanian authorities immediately commenced a forced Lithuanization and within days the language used on advertisement boards, signs of businesses and other public displays had been changed from Polish into Lithuanian, making a population live in a totally alien environment. Lithuanian became a mandatory language for all civil servants and state employees, and those who were unable to communicate in Lithuanian lost their jobs immediately. Civil servants from Kaunas were brought in to fill the empty spaces. All public business had to be done in Lithuanian, and as a result people suddenly found themselves in a foreign country. The Stefan Batory University of Vilnius was closed in December 1939 and replaced by the Lithuanian University of Vilnius, as a result of which the number of students plummeted by two-thirds. Persons receiving Lithuanian citizenship were pressurized into reporting their nationality as being Lithuanian rather than Polish, all part of the attempt to Lithuanize the region as quickly as possible. A complaint by a group of Polish intellectuals to the Lithuanian authorities, explaining that they were alienating 90% of the population with their policies, had no effect whatsoever. In fact, it seems that many Lithuanian officials had no previous understanding of how foreign the region actually was. A sanitary platoon of the Lithuanian army that traveled for two weeks through the countryside to combat unsanitary situations and contagious diseases "did not encounter any Lithuanian-speaking villagers in the country side, though initially the mission was to help 'the true sons and daughters of Lithuania'."[78] In the end, the Lithuanization policy quickly antagonized many citizens in the region, which did not help the Lithuanian cause at all and also tarnished the image of the country internationally.

76. Cohen, Israel: *Vilna*. P. 474
77. Liekis, Šarūnas: *1939*, p. 294
78. Liekis, Šarūnas: *1939*, p. 176

In June 1940, the Soviets presented an ultimatum to Lithuania. The ultimatum demanded the formation of a new pro-Soviet government and to admit an unspecified number of Russian troops. President Smetona proposed armed resistance against the Soviets, but the majority of the government and the commanders of the army did not concur with this proposal. In their view, effective military resistance was impossible with Soviet troops already stationed within the country.[79] In fact, during the whole preceding period, the Lithuanian government had excelled in the inability of mobilizing public opinion, resources or the military in order to be able to defend the country if that were necessary.[80] The public at large was quite unaware of what was happening behind the scenes, right to the last moment.[81] "The government itself and the State Defense Council ... several times discussed the measures to be taken in light of the possible encroachment and aggression by Soviet forces in the country and from outside." writes Šarūnas Liekis. Yet "The discussions in essence were not about how the country should be defended, but how to ensure ... the successful evacuation of the Government abroad. None of the discussions ever reached the operational planning stage..."[82] Facing an unwilling government and an equally unwilling military, who seem not even to have understood that the country was actually about to loose its independence altogether, Smetona turned over the duties of President to Prime Minister Antanas Merkys, and on June 15 he and his family fled to Germany. Attempts by Merkys, probably pressured by the Soviets, to convince him to come back and legalize the transfer of government failed.[83] Later the Smetona family continued to Switzerland and from there to the United States.[84] On the

79. Liekis, Šarūnas: *1939*, pp. 330-331. Smetona was supported in his proposal by Defence Minister Kazys Musteikis who, on June 15, fled with Smetona to Germany.
80. In fact, the military never made any plans in case of an attack by the USSR as, until the Soviet invasion of Poland, the countries had no common border and thus the Lithuanian military never perceived the Soviet Union as a potential enemy. See Liekis, Šarūnas: *1939*, pp. 317-318. However, Liekis concludes, the Lithuanian Army would have had no chance against a Soviet attack, as it lacked equipment (some units lacked up to 85% of the helmets!) and was an army of World War I standard. See Liekis, Šarūnas: *1939*, p. 325
81. Liekis, Šarūnas: *1939*, p. 311. This fact also contributed to the complete shock among Lithuanians when the Soviet troops overtook the country on June 15 and strengthened the conviction that they had been helped by a Fifth Column, being the Jews.
82. Liekis, Šarūnas: *1939*, p. 309
83. Maslauskienė, Nijolė et.al.: *Occupants and Collaborators*, p. 415
84. In 1941, Smetona emigrated to the United States and lived in Pittsburgh and Chicago before settling in Cleveland, Ohio in May 1942 with his son Julius's family. While in exile, he began work on a history of Lithuania and on his memoirs. Smetona died in a fire at his son's house in Cleveland, on January 9, 1944, and was buried there.

next day, Antanas Merkys announced on national radio that he had removed Smetona from the position of President, and had taken over the Presidency himself. Soviet military forces (15 divisions with 150,000 soldiers) crossed the Lithuanian border on June 15, 1940. On several occasions, acting President Merkys declared that the army of a friendly state had entered Lithuania in the interests of the USSR and of Lithuania itself for the purpose of preserving peace and security in this region of Europe. The same day, June 15, Merkys approved the new People's Government and resigned. Two days later he was arrested by the Soviets.[85] Lithuania lost its independence.

Lithuanian historian Liudas Truska sees this "giving away" of the country as one of the main reasons for Lithuania's moral crisis, and one of the factors that made the Lithuanians scapegoat the Jewish population, to compensate for their own inability to at least resist or protest. In fact, the transfer to Soviet rule went very smoothly, much more so than in the case of Latvia and Estonia, and Lithuanian authorities assured the world that the new government was legitimate, that it reflected the will of the Lithuanian people. The Minister of the Interior, Mečys Gidvilas, assured the people in a speech that the Red Army did not intend to revise the country's social and economic structure, but rather "to protect us from the danger of war and help us maintain our independence."[86] Army Commander General Vincas Vitkauskas ordered Lithuanian troops to greet the Soviet Army as a friendly force, and also the head of the Riflemen's Union, Colonel Pranas Saladžius, instructed the same to his members. From Moscow, Foreign Minister Juozas Urbšys instructed officials at his ministry in Kaunas to inform the world that the Soviet demands had not been an ultimatum but merely a series of requests.[87] Hence most countries accepted the transfer of power and recognized the new government. The Dutch, however, did not; not because they were very principled, but because of the sheer fact that by then the Dutch had not yet recognized the USSR and, thus, there was a technical obstacle to recognizing Lithuania as part of the USSR.

Elections for the new People's Seimas were organized on July 14-15, 1940. With only Communist-approved candidates running, official results showed over 90% of voter turnout and support for the Communists. During its first session on July 21, the People's Seimas unanimously decided to convert Lithuania into the Lithuanian Soviet Socialist Republic and to petition to join the Soviet Union. Naturally, the Supreme Soviet of

85. Merkys was deported with his family to Saratov, Russia, and died in 1955 in exile in Vladimirskaya Oblast, Russia. See Anušauskas, Arvydas, *Terror and Crimes against Humanity*, p. 69
86. Sutton, Karen: *The Massacre of the Jews in Lithuania*, p. 79
87. Truska, Liudas, and Vareikis, Vygantas: *The Preconditions for the Holocaust; Anti-Semitism in Lithuania*, pp. 203-204

the Soviet Union approved the petition on August 3, 1940. Thus legitimization of the occupation was complete. Yet, at the same time, it is important to note that, technically speaking, the occupation and annexation of Lithuania by the Soviet Union had taken place fully in accordance with the Lithuanian constitution and other Lithuanian legal acts, making the whole process even more painful for the Lithuanians and deeply hurting their national pride.

Immediately following the occupation, Soviet authorities began a rapid Sovietization of Lithuania. All land was nationalized. To gain support for the new regime among peasants, large farms were distributed to small landowners. However, in preparation for the eventual collectivization, agricultural taxes were dramatically increased hoping to bankrupt all farmers. Nationalization of banks, larger enterprises, and real estate caused disruptions in production causing massive shortages of goods. The Lithuanian *litas* was artificially undervalued and withdrawn by spring 1941. The standard of living plummeted. All religious, cultural, and political organizations were banned leaving only the Communist Party of Lithuania and its youth branch.

Also for the Jewish population, the Soviet occupation was a period of repression and fear. In spite of the fact that, on paper, the Soviets guaranteed equal rights to all citizens, in reality, the Jews suffered heavily under Soviet totalitarian rule. The fact that a Jew, Solomon Gavenda, was elected to be vice-mayor, and that the offices of the Jewish committee were allowed to continue functioning in the interest of social welfare, did not change the general picture. On July 6, 1940, the Communist oriented daily *Lietuvos Aidas* made clear in a report that Jewish organizations could also count on being curtailed or banned: "During the Smetona period, the Jewish reactionaries were trustful collaborators of the Lithuanian plutocrats. The Jewish bourgeoisie was an ally of Smetona: its representatives made a fool of the Jewish labor masses. The Jewish capitalists worked together with the Lithuanian capitalists."[88] Jewish religious, social and cultural life was severely curtailed. "Its elaborate religious organization, which had flourished for centuries, was disrupted. All forms of expression of Jewish nationalism were banned and suppressed. All Zionist societies and community organizations were dissolved. Among the organizations that had to deliver their membership lists and archives on September 3, 1940, were six Jewish organizations (a.o. the A. Mapu Society, Kneset Izroël, the Gorodnija Zionist Youth Society).[89] The members were put on lists of people to be arrested. Also

88. As quoted in Sutton, Karin: *The Massacre of the Jews of Lithuania*, p. 81
89. Anušauskas, Arvydas, *Terror and Crimes against Humanity*, p. 71

Jews who fought for Lithuanian independence were to be arrested, as well as leaders of Zionist organizations, of the Betar Jewish national association, and the Union of Jewish Combatants.[90] The Palestine Immigration Office was closed. Even the Yiddish newspapers had to cease publication, though a successor was soon provided in the shape of a Communist daily."[91] Still, many Jews compared their situation to those in Nazi occupied territories and, in spite of the hardships of Soviet rule, were grateful that they managed to escape that ordeal.

Following the Soviet annexation of the country, a total of 6,606 "enemies of the people" were arrested. During the night of June 14-15,1941, just one week before the German invasion, some 17,000 people (mostly former military officers, policemen, political figures, intelligentsia and their families, but also a large number of Jews) were deported to Siberia, where many perished due to the inhumane living conditions.[92] Of the 6,606 people imprisoned in Lithuania in 1939 (when Vilnius and Vilnius region was shortly in Soviet hands) and in 1940-1941, 334 were Jews (5.1%). Of those deported and exiled to the Soviet Union the percentages of Jews were respectively 13.5% and 11.8%, considerably more than their percentage among the total population.[93] Paradoxically, the Jews that were deported to Siberia as part of this group thus escaped the Holocaust and those who survived formed a sizeable part of Lithuanian Jewry that returned to the country in 1944.[94]

German occupation

On June 22, 1941, Nazi Germany invaded the Soviet Union. The German forces moved rapidly, encountering only sporadic Soviet resistance and within a week controlled the entire country. The retreating Soviet forces massacred Lithuanian political prisoners, among others in the Rainiai forest near Telšiai, where the NKVD murdered 76 Lithuanian political prisoners during the night of June 24-25, 1941.[95] It was one of many massacres that Soviet forces carried out in June 1941, like in other parts of the USSR. In Lithuania, several thousand people were killed in these mass killings.

90. Anušauskas, Arvydas, *Terror and Crimes against Humanity*, 73
91. Cohen, Israel: *Vilna*, p. 475
92. According to Arvydas Anušauskas, in total 23,000 Lithuanians were deported in the period 1939-1941. See Anušauskas, Arvydas, *Terror and Crimes against Humanity*, p. 94
93. Anušauskas, Arvydas, *Terror and Crimes against Humanity*, p. 85
94. According to Yitzhak Arad, of the 15,000 Jews deported and exiled to the USSR or who managed to escape during the first days of the Second World War, 12,000 survived.
95. See Anušauskas, Arvydas, *Terror and Crimes against Humanity*, p. 99

The Rainiai massacre was far from the largest of these massacres, but it is one of the best known, due to the brutality and torture inflicted on the victims by the perpetrators.[96] When the Soviets were gone and the bodies discovered, local police forced Jews to bury the corpses in a common grave.[97] Tragically, less than three weeks later, on July 15-16, in the same forest, Lithuanian partisans would kill about 1,000 Jewish men.[98]

The Lithuanians generally greeted the Germans as liberators from the oppressive Soviet regime and hoped that Germany would restore some autonomy to Lithuania. The Lithuanian Activist Front organized an anti-Soviet June Uprising, declared independence, and formed the Provisional Government of Lithuania with Juozas Ambrazevičius as Prime Minister. The attempt to restore independence proved futile, as it did not correspond with the German plans. All the attempts to show its pro-German attitude to the Nazis and, by doing so, change the hearts of the Germans proved to be in vain. It is regretful that as a result of the collaborationist positioning of the Provisional Government, which in fact was no different than the government of Jozef Tiso in Slovakia and Marshal Pétain in Vichy-France,[99] the issue of a Lithuanian re-institution of independ-

96. Because they were unable to evacuate the political prisoners incarcerated in Telšiai prison, the Soviets called in a punishment squad of the Red Army to liquidate them. Most of the prisoners were put into trucks during the night of June 24, brought to the Rainiai forest where they were tortured and killed. Many of the victims were so mutilated that only twenty-seven bodies could be identified after they were exhumed three days later. According to the coroner's examination after the exhumation, both the report and the testimonies of witnesses concurred that the Soviets cut off tongues, ears, genitals, scalps, put genitals into mouths, picked out eyes, pulled off fingernails, made belts of victims' skins to tie their hands, burned them with torches and acid, crushed bones and skulls, all done while the prisoners were still alive.
97. Gitelman, Zvi: *Bitter Legacy*, p. 187
98. Gershon Greenberg in Nikžentaitis, Alvydas: *The Vanished World of Lithuanian Jews*, p. 235. The 2,000 women and children who belonged to the same families were killed a few days later in Geruliai.
99. Jozef Tiso (1887-1947), a priest, headed the Slovak government during the years 1939-1945. His regime was pro-German, anti-Semitic and under his rule a large proportion of Slovak Jews were deported, mainly to Auschwitz for extermination. He was convicted after the wear and hanged. Marshal Henri Pétain (1856-1951), the "Hero of Verdun" (one of the main battles against the Germans during the First World War), headed a collaborationist government in the southern half of France during the years 1940-1944. The government was fairly reluctant to deport French Jews, but had no problem deporting non-French Jews who had sought refuge in France. After the war, he was sentenced to death but pardoned by General Charles de Gaulle. He died at the age of 95 in imprisonment. The last years of his life, he was fully demented.

ence was tainted and although some Lithuanians look at the events with a certain sense of national pride, others see it as another dark page in the country's history.

During its short existence, the Provisional Government was increasingly ignored and stripped of any actual power. It met for the last time on August 5, 1941.[100] On August 13, *Generalkommissar für Litauen* Theodor-Adrian von Renteln dismissed the government by decree, stating that "after taking over the civil government of Lithuania, I hereby declare the activity of the Provisional Government of Lithuania as ended from August 5 onwards, and I release the members of the Provisional Government of Lithuania from their functions."[101] Most members of the Provisional Government later refused to join the Nazi-sponsored Council headed by General Petras Kubiliūnas.[102]

This civil administration, known as the *Reichskommissariat Ostland* and headed by the Baltic German Adrian Von Renteln as *Generalkommissar* for Lithuania, had already been established on July 17, 1941. The country was subdivided into five districts, with a commissar in charge of each of them: Hans Hingst (Vilnius city), Horst Wulff (Vilnius district), Hans Gewecke (Šiauliai), Hans Kramer (Kaunas) and Karl Lentzen (Kaunas District).[103] The Germans did not have enough manpower to staff local administrations; therefore, most local offices were headed and staffed by Lithuanians. While there were only 660 German civil servants working in Lithuania in 1944, there were 20,000 Lithuanian civil servants. Policy decisions would be made by high-ranking Germans and actually implemented by low-ranking Lithuanians. The former ministries were led by so-called *Generalräte* (General Councilors), all of Lithuanian nationality. The First *Generalrat* was, as mentioned, General Petras Kubiliūnas, who was also responsible for Internal Affairs. Of the nine *Generalräte*, six seats were filled by representatives of the *Lietuvių nacionalistų partija* (Lithuanian Nationalists' party, LNP), a right wing and extremely anti-Semitic political group.[104] All in all, local self-government was very much developed in Lithuania and, as many apologists for the Provisional Gov-

100. Sutton, Karen: *The Massacre of Jews of Lithuania*, p. 139. The Provisional Government was also opposed by a group of Voldemarists from Tilsit in East Prussia, who had been recruited by the Gestapo. This group was headed by a lieutenant of the SD named Kurmis and when entering the country, it excelled in killing 5,500 Jews. See Sutton, Karen: *The Massacre of Jews of Lithuania*, p. 135
101. Brandišiauskas, Valentinas in *Holocaust in Litauen*, p. 51
102. Sužiedėlis, Saulius: *The Burden of 1941*
103. Sutton, Karen: *The Massacre of Jews of Lithuania*, p. 138
104. See Dieckmann, Christoph in *Holocaust in Litauen*, p. 69

ernment assert, in the end this helped to sabotage or hinder several German initiatives, including the establishment of a Lithuanian *Waffen-SS* unit or providing men for forced labor in Germany. In that sense the argument is no different than in The Netherlands (see the chapter on Compliance and Collaboration).

As we will see later in more detail, the cooperation and collaboration between the German forces and part of the Lithuanian population went much further and was quite extensive. The Lithuanian Activist Front helped form a volunteer police force, known as *Tautinio Darbo Apsaugos Batalionas* (Defence of National Labor Battalions, TDA), hoping that it would be later transformed into a regular army of independent Lithuania. Instead the Germans employed these units as helpers in killing of Jews.[105] Another infamous unit was the Lithuanian Security Police (*Saugumo policija, SP*), headquartered in Kaunas under the direction of Vytautas Reivytis and in Vilnius headed by Aleksandras Lileikis. In the fall of 1941, some 250 persons worked for the SP in Kaunas and another 130 in Vilnius.[106] A number of other police battalions also were formed. Part of this auxiliary force was later employed outside Lithuania and either involved in killing operations (in particular in Byelorussia) or tasked with securing communications, guarding prisoners, delivering supplies, etc. In addition, in other occupied territories such auxiliary forces were set up and by the end of 1941, a total of 33,000 men manned the various Estonian, Latvian, Lithuanian (8,400) and Ukrainian police battalions. These forces proved to be an essential addition to the 3,000 men of the *Einsatzgruppen* in exterminating the Jews.[107]

Harsh German policies of settling ethnic Germans in Lithuania, collecting large war provisions, gathering people for forced labor, conscripting men into the German army, etc., soon produced a resistance movement. The most notable resistance organization, the Supreme Committee for the Liberation of Lithuania, was formed in 1943. Despite German pressure a *Waffen-SS* division was never established in Lithuania. Eventually, the Lithuanian general Povilas Plechavičius agreed to form the Lithuanian Territorial De-

105. For a detailed analysis of the TDA see Stang, Knud: *Kollaboration und Massenmord.* Frankfurt/Main, 1996
106. MacQueen, Michael in *Holocaust in Litauen*, p. 104. Aleksandras Lileikis (born in 1909) was found to be living in the United States and eventually denaturalized on May 24, 1996 by a US Federal District Court in Boston. Subsequently he was returned to Lithuania to stand trial. However, the trial dragged on endlessly and was in spite of massive international protests eventually suspended indefinitely by the court for reasons of ill health. Lileikis died in Lithuania in 2000.
107. Christopher Browning in Cesarani, David: *The Final Solution*, p. 140

fense Force (LTDF), which was to operate solely in the Lithuanian territory and be commanded by Lithuanian officers.[108] When Germans did not honor the agreement and attempted to subordinate LTDF to the German army, Plechavičius disbanded it in May 1944.[109]

108. Povilas Plechavičius (1890-1973) was an Imperial Russian and then Lithuanian military officer and statesman. In the service of Lithuania, he rose to the rank of General of the Army in the interwar period. He is best known for his actions during the Lithuanian Wars of Independence, for organizing the 1926 Lithuanian coup d'état and for leading a Lithuanian self-defense force during the German occupation of Lithuania.
109. On April 6, 1944, the Germans ordered Plechavičius to mobilize the country. Plechavičius responded that the mobilization could not take place until the formation of the detachment was complete. After a failed offensive against Polish Armia Krajowa, Jackeln demanded that Plechavičius' troops take an oath to Hitler. After Plechavičius rejected the demand, Jackeln ordered the detachment units in Vilnius to revert to his direct authority. All other units of the detachment were to come under the command of the regional German commissars. Furthermore, the detachment was to wear SS uniforms and use the "Heil Hitler" greeting. Again Plechavičius refused and, instead, issued a declaration for his men to disband and disappear into the forests with their weapons and uniforms. The Lithuanian headquarters directed the units in the field to obey only the orders of the Lithuanian commanders and told its Officer School in the city of Marijampole to send the cadets home. The men from the detachment would form the core of the armed anti-Soviet resistance in Lithuania for the next eight years.

Chapter 2 – Origins of Anti-Semitism

The identification of Jews with communism colored the perceptions of Jews... It turned traditional, often religiously inspired anti-Jewish sentiments into a murderous, politically motivated rampage.

André Gerrits[110]

In the past the Jews were envied because of their money, qualifications, positions, and international contacts – today they are envied because of the crematoria in which they were burned.

Witold Kula[111]

Although anti-Semitism itself is as old as the presence of a Jewish community on European soil, "modern" anti-Semitism was formed by the development of natural sciences, which in turn led to an interest in racial differences. Social Darwinism had created racial hierarchy, and, on the basis of this concept, the Jewish race found itself at the bottom of the hierarchy.[112] They were seen as something alien, hostile, and a threat to racial purity. On top of that they were suspected of a plot to dominate the whole world. The Tsarist police made very effective use of this growing fear of a Jewish conspiracy when compiling the notorious "*Protocols of the Elders of Zion,*" the publication of which sparked off a whole series of pogroms that shook the Jewish world and led to a sharp increase in emigration to America.[113]

110. Gerrits, André: *The Myth of Jewish Communism*, p. 9
111. Quoted in Dean, Carolyn: *Aversion and Erasure*, p. 1
112. For instance, in 1853-1855 Arthur Graf Gobineau published "*Die Ungleichheit der Menschenrassen*" (The Inequality of People's Races), which even though it was not directed towards the Jews, formed one of the cornerstones of racial theory and, later, of scientific anti-Semitism.
113. The Protocols of the Elders of Zion is a fraudulent anti-Semitic text purporting to describe a Jewish plan to achieve global domination. The text was fabricated by the Russian Tsarist secret police on the basis of two mid 19th century texts trying to prove the Jewish intent to strive for world domination. The Protocols purports to document the minutes of a late 19th-century meeting of Jewish leaders discussing their goal of global Jewish hegemony. Their proposals to engender such include subverting the morals of the Gentile world, controlling the world's economies, and controlling the press. The text was translated into several languages and widely disseminated in the early part of the twentieth century. In 1921, a series of articles printed in *The Times* revealed that the text was a fraud. The Protocols is still widely available today on the Internet and in print in numerous languages.

Because of this concept of racial inferiority and being alien, in the view of anti-Semites, neither assimilation nor conversion to Christianity could alter the situation: once a Jew, always a Jew. As a result, the only answer was found in the development of regulations to keep the Jews from "infecting" the superior race, such as bans on inter-racial marriage, birth control, forced sterilization or forced emigration. Between 1900 and 1914 alone, 1.5 million Eastern European Jews emigrated to the United States mainly to escape anti-Semitism and resulting poverty.[114] At the same time, ideas about the superior "Aryan" or "Nordic" race found a very fertile breeding ground, particularly among the petty bourgeois circles.

During the last three decades of the nineteenth century, anti-Semitism became a regular feature in European politics. As Wolfgang Benz writes, it was "the expression of the tension and crisis that had very diverse grounds: national conflicts, social upheavals, economic crisis, fight for the political power, and rapid and cultural changes."[115] Very often, anti-Semitic claims were completely outlandish, having no bearing on reality whatsoever. As George Orwell said, "one of the marks of anti-Semitism is an ability to believe stories that could not possibly be true" and, for instance, Fyodor Dostoevsky filled his novels with anti-Semitic stereotypes, including that Jews were rich, even while, in reality, he was living in St. Petersburg among Jews who were extremely poor.[116]

Anti-Semitism resulted in a wave of publications on "solving the Jewish question," and soon, for many, the only solution to the "Jewish question" was either expulsion or destruction. In November 1879 in Berlin, *Reichstag* member and historian Heinrich von Treitschke published an article in which he protested the mass immigration of Jews from Eastern Europe and blamed the German Jews for having assimilated themselves insufficiently. Treitschke became one of the principal advocates of anti-Semitism and has often been misquoted (predominantly by the National Socialists and contemporary leftists) as having coined the phrase "*Die Juden sind unser Unglück*!" ("The Jews are our misfortune!") adopted as a motto by the Nazis. He actually remarked, "Everywhere in Germany you hear the same phrase, 'The Jews are our misfortune'."[117]

The First World War proved to be a turning point. In Germany, Jews were accused of being cowards and profiteers, even though the number of Jew-

114. *The Promised City*, pp. 5-8
115. Truska, Liudas, and Vareikis, Vygantas: *The Preconditions for the Holocaust; Anti-Semitism in Lithuania*, p. 113
116. Carmichael, Cathie: *Genocide before the Holocaust*, p. 73
117. Truska, Liudas, and Vareikis, Vygantas: *The Preconditions for the Holocaust; Anti-Semitism in Lithuania*, p. 115

ish volunteers joining the Army was extraordinary high. Anti-Semitism increased further because of the Communist October Revolution in Russia, which was by many seen as part of the "Jewish conspiracy" and Bolshevism and Jewishness were often equated. Everything bad that was the result of communism was blamed on the Jews, who were said to be behind it all. In Germany, anti-Semitism soared, and even though the country only had a Jewish minority of 500,000 persons (0.8% of the population), the ineffective Weimar Republic was scolded as being a "republic of Jews" and two politicians of Jewish origin, Matthias Erzberger and Walther Rathenau, fell victim to political assassination.[118] In the 1920s, a new generation grew up, which openly discussed "the Jewish question" in a very factual and "unemotional" way, considering them to be an "eternal enemy" that in one way or another had to be disposed of.

Anti-Semitism in Lithuania

In Lithuania, anti-Semitism found itself a base also in a number of other aspects. First of all, the country was strictly Catholic, and it was the Catholic Church that was the main driving force behind the popular belief that the Jews had not only killed Jesus Christ and needed to be punished for that, but also that the Jews maintained the ritual of using fresh blood of Christian children in preparing matzos. Secondly, the Jewish community in Lithuania, which formed approximately 6-7% of the total population, was seen as an alien element in society and many Lithuanian nationalists considered Jews to be "unfaithful" to the young independent Lithuanian republic. They did not speak Lithuanian but Yiddish, their shops had Yiddish signs and not Lithuanian ones (if they had signs in a different language, it was usually Russian and not Lithuanian), they purposely remained a rather closed and separate community and integrated into Lithuanian society only to a certain level. Remaining outsiders, they unwillingly contributed to the concept of being alien, and thus Lithuanian nationalists and anti-Semites found fertile soil in the country.

With the ascent to power of the National Socialists in Germany, a new impetus was given to those who favored an irreversible solution to the "Jewish problem." In his main political tractate, "*Mein Kampf*," Hitler showed how much the ideas of racial anti-Semitism were part of his own worldview. He spoke of "the black-haired Jewish youth" who "lurks in wait for the unsuspecting girl whom he defiles with his blood, thus stealing her

118. Truska, Liudas, and Vareikis, Vygantas: *The Preconditions for the Holocaust; Anti-Semitism in Lithuania*, p. 110. The assassin of Walter von Rathenau confessed that he committed the assassination in the belief that Von Rathenau was one of the 300 Elders of Zion.

from her people. With every means he tries to destroy the racial foundations of the people he has set out to subjugate. Just as he himself systematically ruins women and girls, he does not shrink back from pulling down the blood barriers for others, even on a large scale."[119] He blamed the Jews for the existence of contingence of black soldiers in the French occupational army in the Rhineland, against which the Nazi's vehemently protested.[120] He added: "And so he tries systematically to lower the racial level by a continuous poisoning of individuals. And in politics he begins to replace the idea of democracy by the dictatorship of the proletariat. In the organized mass of Marxism he has found the weapon which lets him dispense with democracy and, in its stead, allows him to subjugate and govern the people with a dictatorial and brutal fist." In other words, Communism was merely a tool of the Jews to poison other races and eventually dominate the world.

Lithuanian anti-Semitism, to a great extent, originated from the Catholic Church and never underwent the change as in Germany, resulting from Social Darwinism. As mentioned earlier, the Jews were, from early on, considered to be the murderers of Jesus Christ and ritual murderers who used fresh children's blood for the preparation of matzos. These caricatures were fed to children from an early age and, thus, became standard "knowledge" in people's heads. For instance, a 1908 Catechism stated: "priests and elderly Jews hated Christ the Lord. His enemies agreed to destroy him… He suffered terrible physical pain and death, because Pilot, wanting to please the Jews, ordered that the Savior be severely flogged." In his analysis of anti-Semitism in Lithuania, Vygantas Vareikis points out that in nineteenth century prayer books and catechisms, based on texts of the 18th and even 17th century, as well as in writings by Lithuanian priests, there were references to the murder of God and the torture of Christ by the Jews.[121]

Also in Lithuanian literature, anti-Semitism was a frequent issue, and many well-known and respected Lithuanian writers and intellectuals such as Simonas Daukantas, Motiejus Valančius, and Vincas Kudirka professed quite rabid anti-Semitic views in their writings. Kudirka, for instance, wrote in 1890 about "the blight of Jews with their dirt and self-

119. As quoted in Truska, Liudas, and Vareikis, Vygantas: *The Preconditions for the Holocaust; Anti-Semitism in Lithuania*, p. 116

120. Later, after the French capitulation in June 1940, approximately 3,000 African French prisoners of war were executed by the German Wehrmacht. See Scheck, Raffael: *Hitler's African Victims: The German Army Massacres of Black French Soldiers in 1940*. Cambridge, Cambridge University Press, 2006

121. Truska, Liudas, and Vareikis, Vygantas: *The Preconditions for the Holocaust; Anti-Semitism in Lithuania*, p. 126

neglect polluting the air with secrets of the Talmud, with the dirty and virtuous morale distorted by the harm made to Christians."[122] In an article in *Varpas* (The Bell), Kudirka rallied against "the Jews… our most terrible enemies… the most vicious wolves dressed in sheep's clothing."[123] At the end of the nineteenth century, the Lithuanian clergy started linking Jews also to Masonry and Socialism; Jews were considered to be enemies of Catholicism, accused of seeking power as the main goal in all their actions.

122. Truska, Liudas, and Vareikis, Vygantas: *The Preconditions for the Holocaust; Anti-Semitism in Lithuania*, p. 130
123. Saulius Sužiedėlis in Nikžentaitis, Alvydas: *The Vanished World of Lithuanian Jews*, p. 122

Chapter 3 – Jewish Life in Lithuania between World Wars

The colors are somber, the horizons dark, but I fear that there is still worse to come; the last act of the tragedy is not yet upon the stage.

James Parks (1939)[124]

Jewish communists were very visible, especially for those who wanted to see them.

André Gerrits[125]

The establishment of Lithuania as an independent state was an enormous step forward for the Jewish community. From being curtailed by repressive laws of Tsarist Russia, Jews were now propelled into a position as equal citizens in the newly established country. Lithuanian Jews took active part in the fight for Lithuania's independence. When on December 29, 1918, Lithuania's government called for volunteers to defend the Lithuanian state, among the 10,000 volunteers responding, there were more than 500 Jews. All in all, some 3,000 Jews served in the Lithuanian army in 1918-1923.[126] Not less than 23 of them were awarded the highest decoration - the Cross of Vytis - for their outstanding service.[127]

According to the "Paris Declaration" that was concluded by a Lithuanian delegation to the Paris Peace Conference led by Augustinas Voldemaras and *Comité des Délégations Juives* (Committee of Jewish Delegates) under the leadership of Leon Motzkin, Jews would have full autonomy in independent Lithuania. This was based on a concept authored by the Russian-Jewish historian Simon Dubnow, who believed that segregation and ghettoization of Jews was not beneficial to either side and that providing them with autonomy could make then active citizens within a country

124. Quoted in Gerrits, André: *The Myth of Jewish Communism,* p. 45.
125. Gerrits, André: *The Myth of Jewish Communism*, p. 197.
126. For instance, the later head of the Vilnius ghetto, Jacob Gens, had been an officer in the Lithuanian Army, maintained friendly relations with Lithuanian officers right up to the German occupation and considered himself to be both a Jewish nationalist and a Lithuanian patriot who had to serve both nations.
127. According to incomplete data, 73 Jews perished in battles. In 1933, former soldiers founded the Union of Lithuanian Jewish soldiers. In 1935 the Union began publishing its Lithuanian language newspaper "*Apžvalga*" ("Review") with the prime purpose of informing Lithuanians about Jewish life.

and thus able to participate in the economy and other fields.[128] Dubnow strongly favored the coexistence of Jews and non-Jews in Eastern Europe; however, by living together yet apart.[129] On the basis of the Paris Peace Conference agreement, there would be a Minister for Jewish Affairs, as well as proportional representation in Parliament (Seimas), in the bureaucracy and in the judiciary. Jews would have full civil rights and autonomy in all internal matters such as social services, education and culture. Local governing councils, *kehillot*, would impose taxes and issue instructions regarding religion, education and welfare. Complete autonomy in religious affairs was granted, with the right to celebrate Sabbath, as well

128. Simon Dubnow was born in the Belarusian town of Mstsislaw. A native Yiddish speaker, he received a traditional Jewish education in a heder and a yeshiva, where Hebrew was regularly practiced. Later Dubnow entered into a kazyonnoe yevreyskoe uchilishche (state Jewish school) where he learned Russian. In the midst of his education, the May Laws eliminated these Jewish institutions, and Dubnow was unable to graduate; Dubnow persevered, independently pursuing his interests in history, philosophy, and linguistics. In 1880 Dubnow used forged documents to move to St Petersburg. In 1890, the Jewish population was expelled from the capital city and Dubnow, too, was forced to leave. He settled in Odessa and continued to publish studies of Jewish life and history, coming to be regarded as an authority in these areas. Throughout his active participation in the contemporary social and political life of the Russian Empire, Dubnow called for modernizing Jewish education, organizing Jewish self-defense against pogroms, and demanding equal rights for Russian Jews, including the right to vote. Living in Vilnius, during the early months of 1905 Russian Revolution, he became active in organizing a Jewish political response to opportunities arising from the new civil rights that were being promised. In 1906, he was allowed back into St Petersburg, where he founded and directed the Jewish Literature and Historical-Ethnographic Society and edited the *Jewish Encyclopedia.* After 1917 Dubnow became a Professor of Jewish history at Petrograd University. He welcomed the first February Revolution of 1917 in Russia, which brought the long anticipated liberation of the Jewish people. Yet he felt uneasy about the increasing profile of Lenin. Dubnow did not consider such Bolsheviks as Trotsky (Bronstein) to be Jewish. "They appear under Russian pseudonyms, because they are ashamed of their Jewish origins (Trotsky, Zinoviev, others). But it would be better to say that their Jewish names are pseudonyms; they are not rooted in our people." In 1922 he emigrated to Kaunas and later to Berlin. His magnum opus was the ten volume World History of the Jewish people, first published in German translation in 1925-1929. In August 1933, after Hitler came to power, Dubnow moved to Riga, Latvia. There his wife died, yet he continued his activities, also writing his autobiography Book of my Life. Then, in July 1941, Nazi troops occupied Riga. Dubnow was evicted, losing his entire library. With thousands of Jews he was transferred to the Riga ghetto where he was executed in the city on December 8, 1941.

129. Gerrits, André: *The Myth of Jewish Communism*, p. 42

as other Jewish holidays. In the 1930s, the number of rabbis reached 160. They registered births, weddings, divorces, and deaths, issued metrics. On January 5, 1920, the delegates of the *kehillot* set up the highest body of autonomy, a 34 member National Council (*Va'ad ha-Arets*), which people called the Jewish parliament and whose task it was to provide oversight.

All these points were included in the Lithuanian Constitution of August 6, 1919. Among the members of the Government were, apart from the Minister of Jewish Affairs, two Jewish Deputy Ministers: those of Foreign Affairs and of Trade & Industry. The Jews had their factions in all four sessions of the Seimas.[130] There were also quite a few Jews in local administrations; some of them were the vice-mayors of towns. Another important document that guaranteed the rights of Jews in Lithuania was the Minorities Treaty that was ratified by the Lithuanian government in 1922. The minority treaties were drawn up between the Allied Powers on one side and the newly created or expanded states on the other side.[131] The Treaty governed eligibility for citizenship and granted citizens belonging to racial, religious, or linguistic minorities certain collective rights. Among the provisions granted by the treaties were the right to equal treatment and protection by the state for their members; the right to use minority languages for specified public purposes, including in courts and elementary schools; the right to establish and control educational, religious, and social welfare institutions for their groups and, finally, receipt of a proportional share of state expenditures for educational, religious, and welfare services.

The first Minorities Treaty signed was the Polish treaty, in June 1919, which served as the template for the subsequent ones.[132] Specific provisions varied from treaty to treaty and not all guarantees were specified in each agreement. In the case of Lithuania, as in some other countries, the minorities' clauses were part of the treaties by which the Allies recognized independence and frontiers. The agreements stipulated that each state would incorporate the clauses' provisions in its constitution. The League of Nations was to guarantee implementation and the agreements were not to be modified without the consent of a majority of the League Council.

130. In the Constituent Seimas, 6 delegates out of 112 were representatives of the Jewish community; in the first Seimas - 3 out of 78, in the second - 7 out of 78, and in the third - 3 out of 85.
131. The allied states were the United States, the British Empire, France, Italy, and Japan; the new states were Albania, Austria, Bulgaria, Czechoslovakia, Estonia, Greece, Hungary, Iraq, Latvia, Lithuania, Poland, Romania, Turkey, and Yugoslavia.
132. The Polish Minority Treaty is often referred to as either the Little Treaty of Versailles or the Polish Minority Treaty.

However, as with most of the principals adopted by the League, the Minorities Treaties were part of a rather idealist approach to international relations, and as with the League itself, the Minority Treaties were increasingly ignored by the respective governments. In the course of the 1930s, the entire system ground to a halt. In Lithuania, by 1924 a process of undermining and curbing Jewish self-rule had already started and by the early 1930s, basically nothing was left of it.[133]

Jews were initially also very active in civil service, although they never managed to get even close to an equal representation within the state bureaucracy.[134] The tragedy was that when their representation in civil service became substantial during the Soviet regime, it was immediately perceived as proof that all Jews were Bolsheviks. Had their representation been more equal during Lithuanian independence, probably this sudden change in their presence would not have been so noticeable.

From the mid-1920s onwards, an active policy of "Lithuanization" was implemented, both in politics and trade, and as a result the presence and influence of Jews at all levels waned. Jews had historically been the middle-class of society, dominating the fields of trade, industry and medicine. Almost 70 percent of the middle-class Jews were merchants and artisans, the remainder mainly active in the fields of medicine and law. However, by the mid-1920s a growing Lithuanian middle-class was pushing Jews out of these positions and programs to 'Lithuanize" these parts of the economy were strongly supported both by the Catholic Church and by the government. The programs were very successful indeed and, step by step, the Jews were pushed out of their dominant positions.[135]

In general, Jewish culture continued to be tolerated. A wide range of cultural, sport, and educational clubs existed; there were Jewish theatres which performed in Yiddish, and more than 200 Jewish school and public libraries existed. Quite a number of Jewish newspapers were published. In 1930s in the capital Kaunas alone there were four dailies, two of them having separate evening editions.

Vilnius, or Wilna (Polish) or Vilne (Yiddish), was considered by Jews to be a center of Jewish cultural, intellectual and religious life. "During the final decade of the nineteenth century and the first forty years of the

133. The portfolio of Jewish Affairs was annulled in 1924; the last Jewish judge was unseated in 1933. See Sutton, Karen: *The Massacre of the Jews of Lithuania*, pp. 44-45
134. In 1934, only 1.35 % of 31,091 state employees were Jews. See Sutton, Karen: *The Massacre of the Jews of Lithuania*, p. 50
135. See Sutton, Karen: *The Massacre of the Jews of Lithuania*, pp. 47-51

twentieth, it was a treasure trove for research in Jewish knowledge, literature and religious studies," wrote Hirsz Abramowicz in one of his essays published in "*Profiles of a Lost World.*" "If Vilna rightfully came to be known as the 'Jerusalem of Lithuania,' this was due in part to the Strashun Library. (...) The library served rabbis and preachers as well as writers, historians, and students attending Jewish secular schools. The founder of the library, Matthias Strashun, was a great scholar and typical of Vilna's pious maskilim. He was also a great bibliophile who purchased and collected rare books, old manuscripts, and every publication of Jewish content. He bequeathed this treasure, which at his death consisted of some 6,000-7,000 volumes, to the Vilna Jewish community."[136]

Another important Jewish institution in the city was the YIVO, or *Yidisher Visnshaftlekher Institut*, which was established with the goal to collect and preserve everything that was related to the Jewish culture and the Yiddish language. In the late 1930s, it held over 220,000 items, including some 40,000 books, 10,000 volumes of Jewish newspapers from many countries and in many languages, as well as a large archive of manuscripts, autographs, leaflets, pamphlets and Jewish communal records. It had been founded in 1925 in Berlin, but set up its headquarters in Vilnius as this was considered to be the right environment for such a center. "Everything about the YIVO – its location [on Wiwulskiego/Vivulskio 18], its landscaped setting, its modern design, the gleaming immaculateness of the place – delivered a message. I interpreted it to mean that the YIVO had class, was no moldering institution, but a place from which distinction and excellence would issue. Even more: the YIVO was no seedy relic of the past; it belonged to the future."[137]

However, between 1919 and 1939 Vilnius was under Polish rule, together with a long stretch of land that went all the way up to the Latvian border. This position turned the city somewhat into an outpost. "After Vilna became part of independent Poland, it lost its geographical advantage and

136. Abramowicz, Hirsz: *Profiles of a Lost World*, p. 260. The Strashun Library was partially destroyed during the Second World War and its remains later razed by the Soviet authorities.
137. Dawidowicz, Lucy: *From that Place and Time*, p. 79. The German advance into Eastern Europe caused YIVO to move its operations to New York, with a second important center established as the Fundacion IWO in Buenos Aires, Argentina. A third active center of activities today is situated in Chicago. Part of the YIVO archives and leadership fortuitously survived the war. The Nazis carried the bulk of YIVO's archives to Berlin, where the papers survived the war intact and eventually ended up in New York. All four directors of YIVO's research sections were already in the Americas when the war broke out or were able to make their way there.

became instead a geographical dead end. To the north, the Lithuanian border had been closed since 1919, because of the conflict over Vilna... The border with the Soviet Union was closed to travel and trade. Industrially, Vilnius was outclassed even by Białystok, whose population was less than half of Vilna's..."[138] Poland was at that time a poor country, and the combination of being situated at a dead end and part of a poor country did not help to improve the quality of life of its population. "Over 30 percent of the Polish population was illiterate. In rural areas, the illiteracy rate was even higher, with the highest proportion to be found in the eastern border regions, including the Vilna area."[139]

Being increasingly outcasts in a poor country, the situation for the Jewish population in the city gradually worsened. Poverty was widespread, and the funds provided by the American Jewish Joint Distribution Committee were insufficient to stem the tide. In 1939, 24,000 of the 60,000 Jews in Vilnius received relief during the Passover holiday, while 9,000 schoolchildren received free lunches every day.[140] "Every day the Jews in Vilna grew poorer. Their pauperization was accelerated by the government's anti-Jewish policies, which were intended to improve the economic opportunities of the Poles by depriving the Jews of theirs."[141] The result was a paradoxical situation: anti-Jewish policies resulted in a lot of poverty, and yet this poverty fuelled anti-Semitic sentiments, as people were walking around in rags and unable to care for themselves. In her memoirs, Lucy Dawidowicz describes the image of the babies in a clinic financed by the American Rockefeller Foundation: "I'd never seen such babies in my life – ashen, skinny, withered, sad-eyes, cheerless, cranky, coughing, wailing, unbelievably filthy. Children were swaddled in old dirty rags. One tot, with frail spindly legs, wore a pair of oversized coarse woolen stockings whose feet were full of holes."[142] No wonder the Jews in Lithuania felt privileged living there and not under Polish rule, even though anti-Jewish policies in the economy also gradually started to affect their well being.

At the turn of the century, an estimated 124,000 Jews lived in Lithuania, approximately 7.5% of the Lithuanian population. By 1923, the Lithuanian Jewish population had grown to 154,000 persons, 7.6 % of the total population. Two-thirds of them lived in cities, with the largest Jewish communities living in Kaunas (35,000), Šiauliai (13,000), Panevežys (12,500),

138. Dawidowicz, Lucy: *From that Place and Time*, p. 151
139. Dawidowicz, Lucy: *From that Place and Time*, p. 150
140. Liekis, Šarūnas, *1939*, p. 278
141. Dawidowicz, Lucy: *From that Place and Time*, p. 149
142. Dawidowicz, Lucy: *From that Place and Time*, p. 148

Utena (8,000), Ukmergė (8,000), Raseiniai (7,000), Klaipėda (1,000).[143] In Vilnius, at that time part of Poland, out of a population of approximately 196,000 in 1931, 28% or 55,000 were Jewish. This figure has been estimated to have risen to 57,000 by September 1939. Due to an influx of refugees (mainly from Poland), the Jewish population had swollen to at least 80,000 by June 1941 (approximately 35%).[144] In total, Lithuania had therefore some 203,000-207,000 Jewish inhabitants by the time the Germans invaded the country.

Approximately 40,000 Lithuanian Jews lived in the countryside, in closely-knit communities in villages, called *shtetls*. The map of Lithuania was covered with shtetls, with a large concentration in the southern and eastern parts of the country (which was partially under Polish control between 1919 and 1939). The communities lived relatively peacefully with their Lithuanian, Polish and Byelorussian neighbors, and anti-Semitism was not a frequent feature. Most anti-Semitic outbursts took place in the cities, or were exported to the countryside by anti-Semitic activists. Vygantas Vareikis writes: "The values, lifestyles, and businesses of Lithuanian Jews were to a large extent different than those of the Lithuanians, usually villagers, surrounding them. Lithuanian scholars … in describing Lithuanian-Jewish relations, pointed out that the two nations lived alongside each other for centuries as two closed communities linked by almost no mutual relations, except for economic contacts."[145] This factor is also stressed by the famous Lithuanian writer Tomas Venclova, who writes that "We Lithuanians knew little about Polish culture, something about German and Russian culture, but about Jewish culture which was being created under our very eyes, in our country, we had not the slightest idea. The religion, language, alphabet, and customs were too great a barrier. The Jewish community was considered an exotic inclusion unconnected to us spiritually."[146]

A very vivid description of daily life in a Jewish shtetl was authored by the late Joseph Narotzky, an inhabitant of Pabradė (Podbrodz), who emi-

143. Truska, Liudas, and Vareikis, Vygantas: *The Preconditions for the Holocaust; Anti-Semitism in Lithuania*, p. 144. Also in The Netherlands a large part of the Jewish population lived in cities. Of the 140,000 Jews in the country, 97,497 lived in Amsterdam, 14,646 in The Hague and 8,835 in Rotterdam. See Van der Heijden, Chris: *Grijs Verleden*, p. 212
144. According to a demographic study carried out by the Germans in mid-July 1941, the number of Jews in Vilnius was 90,000, out of a total population of 258,000. See Priemel, Kim in *Holocaust in Litauen*, p. 34
145. Truska, Liudas, and Vareikis, Vygantas: *The Preconditions for the Holocaust; Anti-Semitism in Lithuania*, p. 124
146. From an article of Tomas Venclova, published in 1976 in the Moscow Jewish samizdat journal *Evrei v SSSR*, issue 12.

grated to South Africa in 1934 and committed his memories to paper in the 1980s. As Narotzky describes, Pabradė was inhabited by 300 Jewish families and 350 Polish families. There were two synagogues or *Shuls* in Pabradė. Narotzky writes: "One was an old wooden *Shul*. It looked quite old; it could have been about a hundred years old. There was a new Shul built of bricks, and that Shul was built about five years before we left for South Africa. It took about two years to build it, on account of the shortage of funds. Podbrodz had seven streets. Every street was named after an adjoining town – like Vilna Street, Swienciany Street – except the main street in the centre of the town that was called Pilsudski Street, named after the Polish hero and Prime Minister, Marshall Pilsudski. There were three two-story buildings on the main street. The others were just wooden houses with shops attached to them – shops in front and living quarters behind. There was even some empty ground in the main street where things grew, so the ground in the main street couldn't have been expensive."

Narotzky describes vividly the weekly market and its role in the community: "Monday was market day in Podbrodz and nearly everybody in Podbrodz depended on that market. Every Monday morning early, nearly all the smallholders from the adjoining villages brought their produce by horse and cart to sell at the market. (…) There was a large variety of goods available … for example vegetables, fruits, eggs, butter, live chickens, turkeys, wool, mushrooms, dry beans, and many other things – all things that weren't sold in shops in those days. They could only be bought at the market. In turn, the smallholders bought in town what they required, like groceries, paraffin. It could have been a padlock, a piece of glass or grease for their wheels. (…) There used to be stalls at the market. Gypsies would come and tell you your fortune for a few *grozsy*,[147] even magicians and fire-eaters would show their skill for just a few grozsy."

As Jews had been banned by the Tsarist government from owning or renting land, many tried to earn a living through trade or artisanship. "At least ninety percent of all shops in Podbrodz were owned by Jews." Jews were also allowed to work in industry, but no Jews were accepted in public service, at the railways in the police or the armed forces. "The Jews had to make their living mostly as tradesmen, shopkeepers and dealers in whatever they could."

On the whole, in 1923, 25,000 Jews in Lithuania were working in the retail business, 14,000 in industry and only 5,000 in agriculture. At the same time, 77 of the trade enterprises in Lithuania were controlled by Jews, and

147. As the region was part of Poland in those days, Polish currency was used.

the same counted for 22 of the industrial enterprises. In contrast, 90% of the Lithuanians were related to agriculture.[148]

Narotzky also describes the level of anti-Semitism in his hometown. His recollections clearly show that anti-Semitism did not originate from neighbors in the community itself, but rather from the big city – in this case Vilnius, some 45 kilometers down the road. "In the Vilna University, there were proportionately more Jewish students than Polish students. The Polish Students Organization, called *Endecks*, demanded quotas, that the percentage of Jewish students at the university should be based on the percentage of the Jewish population.[149] They also divided the class into two sections, in order for the Jews to sit separately. In about 1933, Polish students from Vilna demonstrated against the Jews, whom they hated. They broke windows in Jewish shops and held anti-Semitic meetings. While it was soon after Hitler came to power, they had no chance of doing anything serious because of the large Jewish population in Vilna. One of the meetings was dispersed by an organized group of Jews. One of the student leaders named Wlotzlavsky[150] ran away and hid in a toilet. A Jewish fellow caught him there and hit him so hard that he died. Since then, the Polish Endeck students held demonstrations every year on the day of Wlotslavsky's death. (…) There was talk of self-defense to be organized in Podbrodz, as a pogrom was expected when Polish students were seen walking into the main bottle store of Podbrodz. (You could recognize students by the caps they wore). As no bottle stores could be owned by Jews, that's where they went, but nothing came of it. Perhaps the reason was that the owner of the bottle store, Grunievitz, had a Jewish mistress."

Anti-Semitism on the rise

In 1923, when the influence of Christian Democrats gained strength, the autonomy of Jews was gradually limited and eventually discarded completely. In 1924, the office of the Minister of Jewish Affairs and the *Va'ad ha-Arets* (National Council) were abolished, and, after the coup, all the remaining elements of autonomy were annulled. Nonetheless, in the field of religion some of the elements remained; for example, in the army a

148. Truska, Liudas, and Vareikis, Vygantas: *The Preconditions for the Holocaust; Anti-Semitism in Lithuania*, p. 144
149. The Polish National Democrats (the nationalists, Endeks, or Endecks) believed that Poland's Jews were an inimical factor in Polish life owing to the non-assimilated state of most of them, along with their dominance of the economy.
150. The student was actually called Stanislaw Waclawski, who had died on November 10, 1931, in the aftermath of a Polish student rampage against the Jews. See among others Dawidowicz, Lucy: *From that Place and Time*, p. 168

chief rabbi attended to the spiritual needs of Jewish soldiers. From the early 1920s onward, anti-Semitism became stronger, resulting in regular outbursts.

In his contribution to the report on *The Preconditions for the Holocaust*, published by the International Commission for the Evaluation of the Crimes of the Nazi and Soviet Occupation in 2004, Klaipėda-based historian Vygantas Vareikis extensively sums up the growing number of anti-Semitic expressions and excesses in Lithuania from independence in 1919 onward until the Soviets annexed the country in 1940. And there are many. Some were based in century old beliefs that Jews were the killers of Christ and were involved in barbaric rituals in which Christian children were slaughtered (and which interestingly became much more prevalent in the 1930s and led to many tense situations when children disappeared and the Jews were immediately blamed).[151] There was the inextinguishable conviction that Jews were a sly people, extorting honest and hard-working Lithuanians, untrustworthy and only interested in material gain. Jokūbas Blažiūnas, for instance, in a 1922 article in the journal *Trimitas* of the Lithuanian Riflemen's Union described the Jews as a "degenerate nation" that lived on what others created: "while not creating anything itself nor having any inclination to do so. A Jewish craftsman is a rarity and a good-for-nothing as well; a Jewish farmer is even worse and even much rarer [...] The Jews have lived in Lithuania for ages but have not created anything that would be a reminder of their existence here if fate made them clear off. If the Jews moved out of Lithuania, only dung would be left after them in Kaunas as it is left in the cattle-shed after sending the cattle to the fallow."[152] This belief that nothing would be left if the Jews would one day disappear has, of course, a very bitter aftertaste if one thinks how much these words were almost prophetic, much more than Blažiūnas ever could imagine in 1922.

The stereotype that Blažiūnas painted, repeated by many Lithuanian leaders, clergymen and intellectuals, was maybe not as much based on Social Darwinism as in Nazi Germany, but it definitely had an increasingly racial undertone. As Blažiūnas worded in the quote above, more and more frequently were Jews depicted as being filthy, of a lesser culture, parasites. Associate Professor Jonas Aleksa compared in 1933 the Lithuanian farmer with the Jew; the former was "a producer, creator of new riches" while the Jews were nomads. "Nomad Jews, being gifted with rhetoric and talented

151. Truska, Liudas, and Vareikis, Vygantas: *The Preconditions for the Holocaust; Anti-Semitism in Lithuania*, p. 130
152. Truska, Liudas, and Vareikis, Vygantas: *The Preconditions for the Holocaust; Anti-Semitism in Lithuania*, p. 150

persuaders, seek to enslave other nations, and the entire world, if they are lucky." Aleksa maintained that "because of certain defects of their nature, they are being destructive rather than constructive to... Western life."[153] So here we see that there is a racial undertone, a "defect" that is ascribed to the Jews, and at the same time a complete denial of the rich Jewish culture that existed right next to the Lithuanian communities but, yet, remained so distant to the Lithuanians.

The almost total separation of the two communities very much strengthened this inability to understand Jewish life and to know that in Jewish culture, study and creativity took, in fact, a very prominent position. As Kaunas resident S. Ginaitė-Rubinsonienė writes in her memoirs: "Like the majority of the Jews in Kaunas, our family had no Lithuanian friends and no close relations with them. My father's contacts with the Lithuanians were limited to business and commercial ties. My mother had no contacts with Lithuanians at all."[154] Also Lithuanian President Antanas Smetona repeatedly lamented that "no closer" economic and cultural ties existed between Jews and Lithuanians yet, at the same time, he also expressed the belief that even though the Jews lived a "closed" life totally separated from Lithuanians and, as a result, could not comprehend Lithuanian aims, both communities were founded on the same democratic principles.[155]

Until Lithuanian independence, this total separation had not been so important, as a sort of "buffer" existed between the two communities, consisting of either the Tsarist bureaucracy, or the Polonized aristocracy or the German military administration. Both communities had their grudges against these three dominant "external" powers, but now with them gone they had to deal with each other directly. Among the intelligentsia of both communities, there was also a different cultural outlook, with the Jewish upper layer of society focusing mainly on Russian culture, whereas Lithuanians were more prone to assimilate with Polish culture.

153. Truska, Liudas, and Vareikis, Vygantas: *The Preconditions for the Holocaust; Anti-Semitism in Lithuania*, p. 158
154. Ginaitė-Rubisonienė, S.: *Atminimo knyga*, p. 17
155. Vladas Sirutavičius in Nikžentaitis, Alvydas: *The Vanished World of Lithuanian Jews*, pp. 64-65. Smetona was widely revered among Jewish circles, and was often seen as the main or even sole guarantee against anti-Jewish excesses. And indeed, as Saulius Sužiedėlis writes, "The allegedly 'fascist dictator' had not only protected the country against the most egregious political extremes of left and right, but had, by and large, contained anti-Semitic violence, allowed cultural diversity, condemned Nazi racism and rejected official discrimination... See Sužiedėlis in Nikžentaitis, Alvydas: *The Vanished World of Lithuanian Jews*, p. 136, 144

In general terms, it seems that even though anti-Semitism clearly increased during the *interbellum*, in Lithuanian politics the "Jewish issue" did not play a major role. The main reason for this was the fact that the Jews were not perceived as a direct danger to Lithuanian cultural and political aims. For Lithuanians, the Polish issue was far more important and even during the beginning of the German occupation of Lithuania, the Germans complained that the Lithuanians in Vilnius were much more concerned with the Polish issue than the Jewish one; as a result the number of killings remained relatively limited. A nationalist memorandum of 1926 stressed the need for an "ethnic national state" for Lithuanians; yet, at the same time, pointed out that the Jews were the only minority which should be "allowed to participate in the government... without harm to the state's independence" since, contrary to Poles and Germans, they did not pose a threat of territorial claims or foreign sponsors."[156]

As mentioned earlier, after the 1926 coup, Jews were blocked from employment by state institutions. As a result, they engaged in so-called freelance occupations, such as trade. Also the enrollment of Jews in university at the faculties of medicine and law was restricted by a *numeris clausus*. University students organized anti-Semitic demonstrations; the majority of the faculty condemned them, but the demonstrations continued nonetheless. With the growth of economic competition, Lithuanian businessmen became increasingly anti-Semitic and called for a boycott of Jewish shops. An increasing number of scholars agree that the major reason for the growing anti-Semitism was in fact economic and professional competition. By the mid-1930s, almost half of the Lithuanian population lived in urban areas and wanted jobs that the rather weak economy was not able to create, especially because Lithuania was hard hit by the worldwide economic crisis. As a result, Lithuania's new educated middle class inevitably came into professional conflict with its Jewish rivals. The traditional Jewish role in business and the professions became a cause for envy and resentment. The step to anti-Semitism was not difficult to take.

The Lithuanian Businessmen's Association (*Lietuvių verslininkų sajunga*), established in 1932 to further Lithuanian presence in industry and trade, initially focused its attacks on the German minority, but soon changed their focus to the Jewish businesses. A program of "affirmative action" was promoted to change the economic landscape and make sure that Lithuanians had "their share" of the economy. Since the Lithuanian economy did not expand very much, it meant that Jews would be pushed out of business and their positions would be taken over by Lithuanians. Publicly,

156. Saulius Sužiedėlis in Nikžentaitis, Alvydas: *The Vanished World of Lithuanian Jews*, p. 125

though, the *verslininkai,* as the members were called, rejected violence against Jews and believed that the Lithuanians should obtain their rightful share through "natural evolution." Yet their newspaper, "*Verslas*" ("Business"), published increasingly vitriolic anti-Jewish articles, which resembled the style of the Nazi press, and in 1935-1936 the Kaunas mayor, Antanas Merkys, criticized the verslininkai and cautioned the Businessmen's Association to observe the principles of "moral competition" and to avoid "low-brow chauvinism."[157] Also President Smetona repeatedly denounced anti-Semitism; however, with his power weakening, his influence became gradually less and even the semi-official newspaper "*Lietuvos Aidas*" began publishing anti-Semitic articles.

Part of the Lithuanian criticism towards the Jews was caused by the fact that Jews not only used Yiddish as their main language of communication, but also their second language was very rarely Lithuanian. Many used either Polish or Russian as a second language, also in pubic places, and this repeatedly led to outbursts of violence. For example, during one night in 1923 in Kaunas the Yiddish signboards of shops and offices of doctors and lawyers were painted over with tar. Later this was repeated in Šiauliai and elsewhere. There were some Jews who understood this irritation; for instance, in 1937 Jewish organizations sponsored a meeting in Kaunas, which ended with a resolution condemning "the use of Russian in public places" and reminding the audience that this behavior "really does intensely irritate Lithuanians." The resolution was welcomed by the *verslininkai*: "We can only welcome such an attitude on the part of the Jewish society."[158]

Judeo-Bolshevism

After 1917, an additional factor added fuel to anti-Semitism in the country: the Bolshevik Revolution and the establishment of Soviet power in the Soviet Union. Being "Jew" became almost synonymous with being "Communist" and whether that was true or not was irrelevant. Of course, as we have seen earlier, socialism held a special attraction for Jews in Tsarist Russia, as it promised a world without restrictions, without being ostracized, without the eternal fear of pogroms and vandalism. Yet among the Jews there were also many who opposed socialism and, instead, sought refuge in religion and maintaining Jewish rituals and traditions. On top of that, the Jewish membership of the Bolshevik Party was actually very small, not more than 4%.

157. Saulius Sužiedėlis in Nikžentaitis, Alvydas: *The Vanished World of Lithuanian Jews*, p. 127
158. Saulius Sužiedėlis in Nikžentaitis, Alvydas: *The Vanished World of Lithuanian Jews*, p. 127

After 1917, Jews had very little reason to support the Bolsheviks because it was anti-religious, anti-nationalist and anti-bourgeois. According to a census of 1922, only 958 Jews had joined the Party before 1917 and not more than an additional 1,175 had joined in 1917.[159] The Mensheviks and the Bund had a far greater Jewish membership. However, this concept of "Jew-Communist" was one that was used as a tool during the Civil War in Russia, and the Whites used it as a means to denounce the Soviet government, as it was purely a government of "Jews-Communists." More than 30,000 anti-Communist Jews who fled to territories held by the Whites were killed during pogroms in White-held territory and in Ukraine, where the armed forces of Simon Petlyura excelled in cruelty and barbarism.[160] It was further fueled by the rabid anti-Semitism coming from Germany, not only in Lithuania but also elsewhere in Europe. Anti-Semitism and equating being Jewish with being Communist became *bon ton* on the European continent.

In Lithuania, the general argument is, even today, that during the Soviet annexation and occupation, cadres of communist Jews assumed significant roles in the NKVD and local communist nomenklatura.[161] This view was repeated over and over again, almost as a mantra, and it is still widely accepted as the truth. American political scientist Roger Petersen repeats many of these allegations without much criticism in his book "*Resistance and Rebellion*," mainly basing himself on outdated Lithuanian émigré sources, yet he makes one important remark while doing so: "During my own fieldwork, I heard several interviewees refer to the 1940-1941 period of Soviet rule as 'the Jewish occupation'."[162] However, later he adds that "It is not the number of Jews who occupied these positions that is critical. Rather, the fact that any of them occupied these positions of authority at all changed Lithuanian thinking about the nature of the ethnic hierarchy. Clearly, many Lithuanians believed that they had become subordinate to

159. Sutton, Karin: *The Massacre of the Jews in Lithuania*, p. 35
160. Gitelman, Zvi: *A Century of Ambivalence*, p. 65-70
161. This argument does not only count for Lithuania, but for Eastern Europe as a whole, leading to the myth of Jewish Communism. A detailed study of this myth can be found in Gerrits, André: *The Myth of Jewish Communism*, in which Gerrits lists four observations (p. 119): not only Jews but ethnic minorities as a whole were over-represented in Communist parties in the region (e.g. Armenians, Georgians, Latvians); Jewish participation in the communist movement varied considerably; more significant that the actual number of Jews in the communist movement was their conspicuousness; the number of Jews in prominent positions often diminished as soon as Communist rule was firmly established.
162. Petersen, Roger: *Resistance and Rebellion*, p. 93

Jews."[163] According to Vygantas Vareikis, the number of Jews in Communist Party structures was not higher than the percentage of Jews in Lithuanian society, yet in Kaunas the situation was slightly different: between 1935 and 1940 Jews constituted 60.25% of the members of the Lithuanian Communist Party in Kaunas District as opposed to 36.3% Lithuanians and 3.45% other nationalities. As a result, Vareikis concludes, "The persons of Jewish nationality involved in Communist activity [in Kaunas] constituted a higher percentage than average in Lithuania, and that could have created the impression that the Jews prevailed in the Soviet and Party structures."[164]

However, Liudas Truska analyzed the Jewish presence in government, Party and NKVD-NKGB structures in much more detail, and comes to quite a different conclusion. According to the data provided by Truska,[165] of the five members of the Chief Electoral Commission that falsified the results of the election to the new People's Seimas on July 6, 1940, none was a Jew. Among the members of the People's Seimas who on July 21 declared Lithuania to be a Soviet Republic, 67 were Lithuanians, three were Poles, two Byelorussians, one Russian, one Latvian and four Jews. According to data of the Lithuanian pre-Communist intelligence agency, VSD, from 1939, of the 1,120 members of the Lithuanian Communist Party, 670 were Lithuanians and 346 were Jews (35%).[166] Of the 263 most active Young Communists, 81 were Lithuanians and 165 Jews. However, during the first half year of Soviet rule, many Jews were expelled because they belonged to the exploiters' class, and so the situation changed quite dramatically. On January 1, 1941, of the 2,500 members of the Party, 67% were Lithuanians and only 16.6% Jews (in all cases, the remaining members belonged to other nationalities, notably Russian and Byelorussian). Five months later, in June 1941, of the 4,703 members and candidate members of the Party, 46.6% were Lithuanians and 12.6% were Jews. In Kaunas the percentage was still higher: here 21.7% were Lithuanians and 25.9% Jews. Among the Communist youth, 17.5% were Jews by nationality.

163. Petersen, Roger: *Resistance and Rebellion*, p. 94

164. Truska, Liudas, and Vareikis, Vygantas: *The Preconditions for the Holocaust; Anti-Semitism in Lithuania*, p. 169. On the same page, he further adds: "Nevertheless, Jewish communist activity caused fears among the Lithuanian authorities, which, naturally, were reflected in the moods of society, which, in turn, contributed to the establishment of the 'Jewish Communist' stereotype among Lithuanians."

165. See Truska, Liudas, and Vareikis, Vygantas: *The Preconditions for the Holocaust; Anti-Semitism in Lithuania*, pp. 182-186

166. On the eve of the Communist takeover in Lithuania, of the 1,261 members of the Communist Party, 30.61% were Jews. See Maslauskienė, Nijolė et.al., *Occupants and Collaborators*, p. 504

Within the Party's Central Committee, of the 13 members in the summer of 1940, four were Jews; in February 1941, after elections, of the 47 new members, 24 were Lithuanians and five were Jews. In June 1941, of the 56 secretaries of city and counties committees, only three were Jews. Of the 119 Party organizers in the regional administration, five were of Jewish nationality. Of the 35-member Kaunas City Party Committee of January 1941, 19 were Lithuanians and four were Jews.

The Presidium of the Supreme Soviet of the Lithuanian Soviet Socialist Republic (LSSR) contained no Jews whatsoever and, in June 1941, 26 of the 49 People's Commissars were Lithuanian and five were Jews. Also at middle governmental level, the role of Jews was limited. In the media the role was slightly more significant: out of 32 censors, 9 were Jews.

Another claim is that many of the NKVD and NKGB officers were of Jewish background and that, hence, Jews played a major role in the terror that was unleashed against the Lithuanian population. Indeed, as Truska points out, the role of Jewish officials in the beginning of the first Soviet period was "significant."[167] The new service director, Antanas Sniečkus, established a team to set up the new service, consisting of an equal number of Lithuanians and Jews. Of the 12-member committee established to put together arrest lists, half were Jewish. Among the 254 newly employed staff in late August 1940, 36.2% were Russians, 17.3% Jews and the remainder (46.5%) were Lithuanians. However, the ranks were soon filled with new people brought in from the USSR proper and by May 1941, of the 138 members of the executive central staff, 72 were Russians, 42 were Lithuanians and 23 were Jews. Of the 44 NKVD city and county chiefs and their deputies, only one was a Jew. In Kaunas, the NKGB (State Security People's Commissariat, mostly involved in torture and repressions) had a staff of 208 persons, of which 60 were Lithuanians and 35 Jews. In Vilnius, the NKGB consisted even more of outsiders: among the 21 directors and deputy directors of its departments and sections, there were no locals

167. Truska, Liudas, and Vareikis, Vygantas: *The Preconditions for the Holocaust; Anti-Semitism in Lithuania*, p. 184. André Gerrits discusses this issue in his book The Myth of Jewish Communism and points out that not only Jews were disproportionally represented in the ranks of the Cheka and NKVD, but also Latvians and Poles. In the Moscow Cheka in September 1918, of the 781 officials more than 35% were Latvians, 6.3% Poles and 3.7% Jews. Also later the percentage of Jews in the top of the NKVD remained relatively high, yet suddenly decreased quickly in 1938 due to the purges, in the course of which many Jews were repressed. While in 1934 38.5% of the top officials in the NKVD were Jews, this number was decreased to 31.9% in July 1937, 21.3% in January 1938, 3.9% in September 1938 and 3.5% in January 1940. See Gerrits, André: *The Myth of Jewish Communism*, p. 125

whatsoever and among the 137 field agents, only 4 were Lithuanian and 2 were Jews. Of the NKGB country departments, almost all directors were Lithuanians with Russians being their deputies; not one was a Jew. Of the 15-member Supreme Court, two were Jews and of the 36 county judges, 4 were Jews. And so on, and so on…

All in all, on the basis of the above mentioned figures, one can conclude that proportionally, there were more Jews among the members of the ruling bodies in the LSSR; whereas the Jewish population consisted of 8% of Lithuania's inhabitants while in quite a few services, the percentage of their presence was double that figure. However, one cannot speak of an "overdose" of Jews among Communist formations.

Interestingly, on the basis of Truska's research, one can also conclude that, in fact, the Jewish presence within the ranks of the Communist Party damaged the Party's position and was a barrier for Lithuanians to join or support the new regime. For instance, on July 2, 1941, a pro-government demonstration was held in Šakiai, in which apparently a considerable number of Jews participated. Local farmers were unhappy, according to a report by the Marijampole Country State Police, and remarked "if not for the Jews, then we could have marched too." In Kalvarija, at a July 7 rally, many farmers and others left as soon as a Jew mounted the stage to speak. The same happened on July 11 In Trakai: "As soon as a Jewish individual started speaking, the crowd immediately began to laugh and make fun of him…" Anti-Jewish slogans were also heard on July 12 in Išlaužas.[168]

In reality, the number of Jews in government positions could have been much higher, Truska notes, if not for the fact that Lithuanians did not want to have Jews in their offices. As in most cases, a Lithuanian would remain the director with a trusted Party member as deputy to keep a check on everything; instead of the unwanted Jews, deputies were very often Rus-

168. Truska, Liudas, and Vareikis, Vygantas: *The Preconditions for the Holocaust; Anti-Semitism in Lithuania*, p. 180. The same negative effect of the prominence of Jews in the Communist Party is reported from Central European countries after the war, where this led to anti-Semitic outbursts and riots. For instance in Poland, where the Kielce pogroms were followed by massive protests on Łodz against the prominence of Jews in the Party ("Poland is ruled by Jews"), the later Party leader Władisław Gomulka wrote to Stalin in December 1948 in which he complained about the irresponsibly large number of Jews within the Party. In the late 1940s the Jewish dominance was countered by purges of the Party cadres leading to, for instance, the openly anti-Semitic Rudolf Slánský trial in 1952 in Czechoslovakia. In Poland, a wave of anti-Jewish trials was being prepared in the early 1950s, which never took place due to Stalin's sudden death in March 1953.

sians "imported" from the USSR proper. There were many other instances when Lithuanians expressed their dissatisfaction about the presence of Jews in leading positions, sometimes leading to a walkout of the Lithuanians altogether.[169] In July 1940, the chief of Tauragė County informed the NKVD that "anti-Semitism is increasing very swiftly, and it is visible not only among farmers but also among workers."[170] Shortly after, on August 7, a bulletin of the NKVD on the situation in Tauragė reported: "Emergent and widespread anti-Semitism has not receded. Because the county Communist party is led by persons of Jewish nationality, the majority of Lithuanian workers and peasants are unhappy. The same is true about other counties. This is the most important cause of the Communist party's unpopularity."[171]

Whereas during the first month of Soviet occupation, anti-Jewish demonstrations were frequent, tactics soon shifted because of the Soviet repressive machinery starting to function. The main tool of expression became the dissemination of anti-Semitic leaflets, in which Jews were equated with Communism and were branded as slave drivers, oppressors and people who had betrayed Lithuania, even though the country had treated them kindly and liberally. Already in late June 1940, a leaflet surfaced in Šiauliai titled "Sons and Daughters of Lithuania!" that called for the removal of all Jews from Lithuanian territory: "And let us endeavor to eliminate completely these Jewish parasites from Lithuanian land, so that no one ever stands in our way again."[172] Also a pro-Soviet "Lithuanian anti-Jewish Committee" shared these anti-Semitic stereotypes and made clear that among the "ranks of honorable Communists" there was no place for "Jewish oppressors": "We call for the nationalization of Jewish assets… We call for the nationalization of all Jewish houses in cities… We want to see those rich Jews toiling hard next to us, doing the physical labor that they have shunned and feared their whole life."[173]

Looking at the above, an interesting picture emerges. It seems that prevailing anti-Semitism among the Lithuanian population, caused by a combination of factors to which I shall turn later, led to the need to find a stick

169. Truska, Liudas, and Vareikis, Vygantas: *The Preconditions for the Holocaust; Anti-Semitism in Lithuania*, p. 187
170. Truska, Liudas, and Vareikis, Vygantas: *The Preconditions for the Holocaust; Anti-Semitism in Lithuania*, p. 192
171. As quoted in Truska, Liudas, and Vareikis, Vygantas: *The Preconditions for the Holocaust; Anti-Semitism in Lithuania*, p. 187
172. Document reprinted in Truska, Liudas, and Vareikis, Vygantas: *The Preconditions for the Holocaust; Anti-Semitism in Lithuania*, p. 234
173. Document reprinted in Truska, Liudas, and Vareikis, Vygantas: *The Preconditions for the Holocaust; Anti-Semitism in Lithuania*, p. 235-237

to hit the culprit – to find an argument that would confirm once again that the Jews were to blame for the nation's misfortune. Sure, the reported outbursts of happiness of groups of Jews when seeing the Soviet Red Army enter their towns must have deeply hurt the proud Lithuanians, who saw their country occupied. Yet one cannot escape the impression that the picture had already been fixed – that misfortune was "of course" caused by the Jews (just as in one of the favorite Nazi slogans: "*Die Jüde sind under Unglück,*" the Jews are our misfortune), and thus the presence of Jews among government, party and NKVD officials only confirmed that image, whether correct or not. The Jews had to pay the price, and this was just an additional reason.

Also in Poland the Jews tended to consider the Soviets a lesser evil than Nazi domination. At least in theory, there was no anti-Semitism under Communism, and Jews were able to fill government positions. Hence, at the beginning of the war, many Jews tried to make their way to the East, rather than to the West. Non-Jews viewed this with much suspicion. To them it was proof that Jews were not to be trusted, that they side with the Communists. "Anti-Semites had long accused Jews of being Communists; here they could claim to have found proof. Some Christians had always charged Jews with trying to destroy Christianity; now they could say they had evidence of an atheist conspiracy. We tend to assume that shared hardships draw people together; often, however, quite the opposite occurs. In the early stages of World War II, the tribulations faced by all Poles tended to drive wedges between Christians and Jews."[174]

Soviet repressions

The one-year period of Soviet rule from June 1940 to June 1941 resulted not only in a never-ending wave of repressive measures, arrests, and executions and, a week before the German invasion, mass deportations. In total some 52,000 Lithuanians were killed, injured or disappeared, of whom some 9,000 political prisoners were killed by the Soviets right after the German invasion.[175] The repressions also deepened all the conflicts within Lithuanian society to such an extent that it resulted in an orgy of violence and murder as soon as the Soviet regime collapsed. As Zenonas Ivinskis[176] wrote in his diary at the end of June 1940: "Most of the people

174. Bergen, Doris: *War & Genocide*, p. 124
175. Sutton, Karen: *The Massacre of the Jews in Lithuania*, p. 94
176. Zenonas Ivinskis (1908-1971) was a Lithuanian historian. In 1925, he entered the University of Lithuania to study philosophy, but later changed the subject to history. In 1929, he continued his studies in Germany where he received a Ph.D. After returning to Lithuania, he was drafted into the army. During his free time, he gave lectures at the Vytautas Magnus University and, in 1940,

(at least those whom I meet) are simply craving for the Germans to come. And then the real slaughtering of Jews would start. Fury at the Jews for their outrageous sympathies to the Bolsheviks, for their internationalism, and for their arrogance is great."[177]

Whereas some of the Jews in Lithuania proper saw the Soviets as their salvation from Nazi domination with all its foreseeable consequences, the Jewish population in Vilnius already had their share, and, thus, their enthusiasm was notably less. All in all, the Soviet regime did not bring much good to the Jews in Lithuania and many suffered, proportionally more than their Lithuanian fellow countrymen. Already in early July 1940, almost all Jewish newspapers and periodicals were banned, leaving only two periodicals in Yiddish out of 17 prior to the Soviet invasion. All educational institutes that used Hebrew as their language were closed, as Hebrew was a language of the bourgeoisie and reactionary Zionists; of 23 Jewish schools, only 12 remained. Tainted Jewish books were removed from libraries (because they were in Hebrew, Zionist in nature or "valueless") only to be followed by "tainted" books in Lithuanian. The Museum of Jewish History and Ethnography and the Strashun Library in Vilnius were handed over to the institute of Lithuanian Philology. The Sabbath as a free day was canceled and children had to attend school on Saturday. Also one synagogue after the other was closed and used for other purposes.[178]

Jews fell also victim to repressions and deportations. Of the political activists arrested in July 1940, more than 10% were Jews. By January 5, 1941, in Vilnius alone 548 Poles, 63 Lithuanians and 66 Jews had been arrested. The total number of Jews that suffered repressive measures amounted to 2,600, which is 8.9% of the total number of people who suffered repression. Of the people who were deported a week before the German invasion, 13.5 % were Jews.[179] In March 1941, the Vilnius NKGB

became an extraordinary professor. In that year he was invited to work at the Vilnius University. He served as the dean of Faculty of Theology-Philosophy at the Vytautas Magnus University from 1941 to 1942. For his active public defense of university autonomy, the Nazis listed him among other prominent public figures to be transferred to Stutthof concentration camp. Ivinskis was saved from death because he was ill and was hospitalized for half a year. In 1944, Ivinskis moved to Germany, where he died in 1971.

177. Truska, Liudas, and Vareikis, Vygantas: *The Preconditions for the Holocaust; Anti-Semitism in Lithuania*, p. 191
178. Truska, Liudas, and Vareikis, Vygantas: *The Preconditions for the Holocaust; Anti-Semitism in Lithuania*, pp. 188-189
179. Truska, Liudas, and Vareikis, Vygantas: *The Preconditions for the Holocaust; Anti-Semitism in Lithuania*, p. 189

had files on more than 1,400 Jews, many of them linked to the various Jewish organizations that either had their original base in Vilnius, such as the Bund, or had fled to the city from other regions, such as Poland, Western Belarus and Western Ukraine.[180] In their report on the illegal activities in the city, the NKGB concluded: "The nationalistic Jewish elements in Vilnius are carrying out anti-Soviet activities by maintaining contacts with counter-revolutionary Western Byelorussian, Western Ukrainian and foreign organizations that are receiving financial assistance from the American Jewish Joint Distribution Committee Organization."[181] In other words, the wheels of terror did not spare the Jewish population of Lithuania; even though the two communities were living side by side, it was almost as if they were on separate planets and, thus, this knowledge did not reach the Lithuanians. Since their views were already formed by old stereotypes, much more would have been necessary to steer it to a more positive attitude.

The role of the LAF

After Lithuania was established as the LSSR, the views of the Lithuanian population on their Jewish neighbors were pushed in an even more negative direction by a new organization that was established in Berlin on November 17, 1940, with the primary task of preparing Lithuania for a Nazi German takeover. The *Lietuvos Aktivistų Frontas* (Lithuanian Activists Front (LAF) was established by representatives of all Lithuanian political groups, but was dominated by representatives from three radical factions: the followers of former Prime Minister Augustinas Voldemaras[182]

180. Of the 1,400 people, 78 were members of the Bund, 854 were Zionists, 193 Zionist-Revisionists, 174 members of other "contra-revolutionary organizations" and 124 clericals. See Truska, Liudas, and Vareikis, Vygantas: *The Preconditions for the Holocaust; Anti-Semitism in Lithuania*, p. 191
181. March 29, 1941 NKGB document "On the Counterrevolutionary Activities of the Nationalistic Jewish Organizations"
182. Augustinas Voldemaras (1883-1942) was a Lithuanian nationalist political figure. He served as the country's first Prime Minister in 1918, and again from 1926 to 1929. He was the head of an organization called Geležinis Vilkas (Iron Wolf), whose honorary head was President Smetona. Although he and Smetona had formerly worked closely together and shared similar ideologies, their association was soon to be brought to an end, partly because of Voldemaras's intense involvement with Geležinis Vilkas. The dynamic personality of Professor Voldemaras continued to attract adherents among the younger nationalist officers, who were favorably impressed by emerging fascism, and who were displeased with what they perceived as Smetona's more moderate course. While attending a meeting of the League of Nations in 1929, he was ousted in a coup by President Smetona, who now ruled as dictator alone until the Soviet invasion in 1940. Upon Voldemaras' removal from office, Geležinis Vilkas

(*voldemarininkai*), the younger Nationalists (*tautininkai*)[183] and younger Catholics, who, by the end of 1938, had moved into the political orbit of the followers of Voldemaras.

Berlin was, at that time, the center of a wide variety of nationalistic, fascist, neo-fascist, national-socialist and other groups fighting for political change in their home countries. Since the Soviet occupation of Berlin, more than a thousand government officials, army officers, political party leaders and members of the Lithuanian Security Police had flocked together in the German capital.[184] From this group, the LAF was formed

went underground and received aid and encouragement in its activities from Germany.

Geležinis Vilkas planned and executed a coup in 1934, flying Voldemaras in from Zarasai to take over as head of the government. However, the coup was unsuccessful and Voldemaras was imprisoned for the next four years. During this time he wrote another major work, a historical account of the life of Christ, which was banned in Lithuania because of its controversial nature. In 1938, Voldemaras was pardoned and released from prison and exiled. He attempted to return in 1939, but was arrested and sent back to Zarasai. He tried to return on several more occasions, but each time was sent back to his place of exile. In June 1940, a few days after the Soviet Union invaded and occupied Lithuania, Voldemaras made another attempt to return from exile. He was arrested at the border by the Bolsheviks and was not heard from again. It was only learned much later that he had died while in a Moscow prison on May 16, 1942

183. The Lithuanian National Union (Lithuanian: *Lietuvių tautininkų sąjunga* or *Tautininkai*) was a nationalist, right-wing political party in Lithuania, founded in 1924 when the Party of National Progress merged with the Lithuanian Farmers' Association. It was the ruling party of Lithuania from the 1926 Lithuanian coup d'état in December 1926 to the Soviet occupation in June 1940. The party did not enjoy popular support and, in the May 1926 parliamentary elections, managed to win only 3 seats out of 85. However, its leaders, Antanas Smetona and Augustinas Voldemaras, were popular and influential public figures. The party was conservative and nationalistic; it stressed the need for a strong army and a strong leader.

The party was re-established when Lithuania declared independence in 1990. On March 11, 2008, the Lithuanian National Union merged into the Homeland Union.

184. Sutton, Karen: *The Massacre of the Jews in Lithuania*, p.100. According to researcher Michael MacQueen, some 52,000 persons were "repatriated" to Germany from Lithuania after the signing of the Molotov-Ribbentrop Pact in September 1939, whereas there were only 35,000 Germans living in Lithuania at that time. MacQueen asserts that the other 17,000 included actually many Lithuanians, who either "Germanized" themselves or were allowed in because the Germans thought they would come in handy. See Gitelman, Zvi (ed.): *Bitter Legacy*, p. 96

with the clear objective of reestablishing Lithuanian independence. It was clear, however, that this would only be possible after the Germans had attacked the Soviet Union and, thus, a delicate political game ensued to get the Germans to agree with Lithuania being an independent state within the German sphere of influence. The LAF was to be the organization to bring that goal within reach; in order to present itself as a broad political movement, it kept the door open to virtually everybody. "Any Lithuanian, without distinction, regardless of his political persuasion, can become a member of the Activist Front if he is determined to fight for the deliverance of Lithuania."[185] However, this formulation automatically excluded anybody who was not Lithuanian, meaning Poles and Jews. Those who joined the LAF were linked together by their nationalism, xenophobia, anti-Semitism and anti-Communism (with the latter two being automatically linked anyway).

The leader of the LAF was a former Lithuanian Army volunteer from 1918, Kazys Škirpa, who had participated in the wars for independence in 1918-1920 and who had become a National-Socialist by the end of the 1930s.[186] And even though the movement had as its primary aim to restore the independence of Lithuania, from the very first moment, they aligned themselves totally with the Nazi regime, which had clear plans for the future of the country.[187] In that sense, they found themselves in the same position as other political movements from the former Soviet

185. Sutton, Karen: *The Massacre of the Jews in Lithuania*, p. 101

186. Kazys Škirpa (1895-1979) was mobilized into the Russian army during World War I and attempted to form Lithuanian detachments in Petrograd. After Lithuania declared independence in 1918, he returned and volunteered during the Lithuanian Wars of Independence. In 1920 he, as a member of the Lithuanian Peasant Popular Union, was elected to the Constituent Assembly of Lithuania. After that he decided to pursue a military education in Kaunas and Brussels. Upon graduation in 1925, he worked as chief of the General Staff but was forced to resign after the 1926 Lithuanian coup d'état because he was actively refusing it and was trying to gather military force to protect the Government. Later he served as a Lithuanian representative in Germany (1927-1930), at the League of Nations (1937), in Poland (1938), and again Germany (1938-1941). After the Soviet Union occupied Lithuania in 1940, Škirpa formed the Lithuanian Activist Front. After Nazis invaded the Soviet Union, he was named as Prime Minister in the Provisional Government of Lithuania. However, Germans placed him under house arrest and did not allow him to leave for Lithuania. In 1944, he was sent to a concentration camp in Bad Godesberg. After the war he went to Paris, Dublin and, in 1949, to the United States. He worked at the Library of Congress in Washington D.C.

187. Škirpa is said to have burst in tears when he went to the German Ministry of Foreign Affairs and asked for assistance against the Soviet invasion and was told that Germany would not intervene.

Union, who hoped that alliance with the Nazis would bring them freedom (e.g. the OUN of Stepan Bandera, the *Narodno-Trudovoe Soyuz* (NTS) and later, after 1942, the Russian Liberation Army of Andrei Vlasov, etc.).[188]

Gradually their political statements became more and more radical, their anti-Semitism convictions stronger and stronger and, in that sense they outdid the *Banderovtsy* and *Vlasovtsy*; they became very obedient servants of their German hosts. In March 1941 in a leaflet titled "Dear Brothers in Slavery," they warned the Jews to get out of Lithuania before it was too late: "Inform the Jews that their fate has been sealed and that those who are able to flee should start leaving Lithuania now to avoid unnecessary harm."[189] Five days later in "*Instructions for the Liberation of Lithuania*" the LAF expanded on this theme by making clear that when the country would be liberated from the Soviets "it would be very important to take advantage of this occasion to get rid of the Jews. Therefore, there must be such an anti-Jewish climate in the country that not a single Jew would even dare to imagine that the Jews would have any minimal rights or any chance for subsistence in the new Lithuania. Our aim is to compel the Jews to flee Lithuania together with the Red Army troops and Russians. The more Jews who abandon Lithuania under these circumstances, the easier it will be later to achieve complete liberation from the Jews. The hospitality that Vytautas the Great offered to the Jews in Lithuania has been revoked for all times for the ongoing betrayal of the Lithuanian nation."[190]

188. The Russian Liberation Army (*Russkaya Osvoboditelnaya Armiya*; ROA) was founded by former Soviet general Andrei Vlasov in 1942-1943 and fought alongside the Nazis at the Eastern front. ROA was not very much trusted by Hitler, who suspected a second agenda and an obstacle to German supremacy in the East. And indeed, in the end, ROA turned against their German masters and was involved in the liberation of Prague, at a moment when the ROA leadership already understood that they had been engaged on the "wrong side" and that a harsh fate was awaiting them. How harsh, nobody could really imagine: most of the ROA soldiers were handed over by the British and Americans to the Soviet Army, and most were subsequently either shot or perished in the Gulag. General Vlasov himself was executed in Moscow in 1946. For more information on the ROA see Andreyev, Catherine: *Vlasov and the Russian Liberation Movement.* Cambridge University Press, Cambridge, 1987
189. Leaflet reprinted in Truska, Liudas, and Vareikis, Vygantas: *The Preconditions for the Holocaust; Anti-Semitism in Lithuania*, pp. 264-265
190. The complete document was reprinted in Truska, Liudas, and Vareikis, *Vygantas: The Preconditions for the Holocaust; Anti-Semitism in Lithuania*, pp. 245-263. Interestingly, Kazys Škirpa deleted the anti-Semitic and anti-Jewish parts of the document when he published it in 1973 in his book "*Sukilimas Lietuvos suverenumui atstatyti*," in an apparent attempt to hide LAF's

This revoking of the hospitality extended by Vytautas the Great became a regular feature in LAF publications. For instance, in a leaflet published in the spring of 1941 the LAF made clear that Jewish presence "in Lithuanian land that has lasted for five hundred years is now over. Have no hopeful illusions! There is no place in Lithuania for you anymore! The Lithuanian people, arising for a new life, consider you traitors and will treat you as traitors should be treated."[191] The document also listed the steps that would be taken: all Jews who committed crimes against Lithuania and Lithuanians would be arrested and court-martialed; all Jews would be expelled from Lithuania and Jewish property would be confiscated; any Jew that would try to destroy property would be punished "most severely on site," in other words: shot. Also in the pamphlet "*Let us Free Lithuania from the Yoke of Jewry Forever,*" published by LAF in spring 1941, these actions against the Jews in Lithuania were mentioned. Clearly, the grounds were prepared for a total end to the Jewish presence in the country and one can be quite certain that the LAF leaders in Berlin understood that a Nazi invasion (or liberation) of their country would not bode well for the Jews. How much they prepared the excesses that took place in the country the moment German troops set foot on Lithuanian soil and the Soviets started their hasty retreat and how willing they were to be involved in carrying out these plans, one can only guess. But there can be no doubt that preparatory work was being done in advance of the German invasion, at least psychologically.

While there was no mercy for Lithuanian Jews and their fate had been sealed, whether communist or not, whether involved with the Soviet authorities or not, LAF was quite different in its attitude towards Lithuanian communists. They invited those who had "erred" or had "been misled by others" to support the anti-Soviet rebels, and their changing sides would not be forgotten and they would not have to fear for themselves nor for their families' safety. Even soldiers and officers of the Red Army were addressed in a special pamphlet titled "*Boitsy i kommandiry Krasnoi Armii*" (fighters and commanders of the Red Army) and urged to be "real patriots of Russia" and liberate Russia from the "unprecedented slavery of the communists and Jews."[192]

blatant anti-Semitism after the war. Also other Lithuanians tried to conceal these aspects, both in emigration and later, after the end of the USSR, in Lithuania itself, see Leaflet reprinted in Truska, Liudas, and Vareikis, Vygantas: *The Preconditions for the Holocaust; Anti-Semitism in Lithuania*, p. 198

191. Leaflet reprinted in Truska, Liudas, and Vareikis, Vygantas: The *Preconditions for the Holocaust; Anti-Semitism in Lithuania*, pp. 309-311
192. Truska, Liudas, and Vareikis, Vygantas: *The Preconditions for the Holocaust; Anti-Semitism in Lithuania*, p. 197

According to Liudas Truska, the effect LAF pamphlets had in the minds of the Lithuanians was considerable.[193] The main action points mentioned above became official decrees of the Provisional Government once the German invasion has started. Still, Truska is convinced that the LAF never planned the killing of all Jews in Lithuania, but "merely" wanted them to get out of the country forever. He points out that on August 5, Juozas Ambrazevičius, head of the Provisional Government, told *Generalkommissar Litauen* Adrian von Renteln that his government did not have "the means to restrain excesses, for example, the executions being carried out in Kaunas and in the countryside" and thereby indirectly expressing his government's disapproval of the mass killings.[194] Yet at the same time, it is clear that Lithuanians were trained in Germany for infiltration into Lithuania on the eve of the German invasion and were later involved in the mass killings of Jews. For instance, Pranas Lukys, who was convicted by a West German court in 1957 for the murder of Jews and communists near Tauragė, was trained in 1940 with a group of 50 men first near Tilsit (Telšiai) and later stationed near Memel (Klaipėda) and eventually sent across the border on the night of June 21-22, 1941.[195]

Indeed, the goals of the LAF and of the Germans did not fully coincide. Whereas they shared anti-Jewish sentiments, the LAF continued to focus on a Lithuanian independent state and informed the Germans of their intentions. The Germans, however, never took these announcements seriously and made quite different plans for the region.[196] The tragedy is that, while the LAF tried to please the Nazis so much that it took on a rather pathetic quality, the Germans remained totally unaffected by this courting. The Lithuanians were, in their view, of a lesser race and although they still had a chance of being "Germanized," the Germans also planned to deport large numbers of them to the East and use Lithuanian land for colonists with a real "Aryan" background (e.g. Volga Germans from the Soviet Union they were planning to occupy). Two months prior to the invasion, institutions for the *Germanization* of the Baltic region were established, with Alfred Rosenberg appointed on April 20, 1941 as *Reichsminister für die Besetzte Ostgebiete*.[197]

193. Truska, Liudas, and Vareikis, Vygantas: *The Preconditions for the Holocaust; Anti-Semitism in Lithuania*, p.200
194. Leaflet reprinted in Truska, Liudas, and Vareikis, Vygantas: *The Preconditions for the Holocaust; Anti-Semitism in Lithuania*, p. 201
195. See Gitelman, Zvi (ed.): *Bitter Legacy*, pp. 96-97
196. Sutton, Karen: *The Massacre of the Jews in Lithuania*, p. 107
197. Alfred Rosenberg (1893 -1946) was born in Tallinn as the son of Baltic Germans. He was an early and intellectually influential member of the Nazi Party. He is considered one of the main authors of the Nazi racial theory, the concept of "Jewish Bolshevism," the persecution of the Jews, the concept of

All Lithuanian plans were thwarted by the Germans. The proposal to form a Lithuanian military brigade under the leadership of Colonel Oskaras Urbonas was turned down by the Germans and, instead, Lithuanians were added to German units as guides and interpreters. Lithuanian leaders remained unaware of the plans for the German invasion and were excluded from high-level meetings on military, political, economic and ideological goals of the invasion.[198] They did not even know the exact date the invasion would take place, although in November 1940, they had been informed by the German Army that the attack on the Soviet Union would take place in 1941.[199] In the country itself, LAF cells were unaware of the timing of the German invasion, or the extent of the military operations.[200] LAF leader Kazys Škirpa was kept under house arrest in Berlin and was not allowed to return to Lithuania even after the outbreak of the war.[201]

In spite of the impending invasion, the LAF prepared itself carefully for the day they would have the chance to reinstate Lithuanian independence. When the Germans arrived in Lithuania, the LAF orders on how to behave were carried out quite meticulously. Their "*Directions for Liberating Lithuania*" instructed that "units of the German army shall be welcomed everywhere as the army of a state friendly to Lithuania. Officials of the local authority and representatives of local communities shall greet the commanders of these units, shall introduce themselves and shall inform them about the local situation; they shall provide all the information at their disposal about the enemy and, if necessary, they shall offer their services."[202] And that is what happened, almost to the letter. A former Nationalist, Vincas Rastenis, is mentioned by Truska as

Lebensraum, the abrogation of the Treaty of Versailles, and opposition to "degenerate" modern art. As the Nazi Party's chief racial theorist, Rosenberg was in charge of building a human racial ladder that justified Hitler's genocidal policies. He considered blacks and Jews to be at the very bottom of the ladder, while at the very top stood the white or "Aryan" race. Rosenberg promoted the Nordic theory that considered Germans to be the "master race," superior to all others, including other Aryans (Indo-Europeans). Following the invasion of the USSR, Rosenberg was appointed head of the *Reichsministerium für die besetzten Ostgebiete*. Alfred Meyer served as his deputy and represented him at the Wannsee Conference where the Final Solution of the "Jewish question" was decided. In 1946 Rosenberg was tried at the War Crimes Tribunal in Nürnberg, sentenced to death and executed by hanging.

198. Sutton, Karen: *The Massacre of the Jews in Lithuania*, p. 104
199. See Dieckmann, Christoph in *Holocaust in Litauen*, p. 72
200. Sutton, Karen: *The Massacre of the Jews in Lithuania*, pp. 102-103
201. Sutton, Karen: *The Massacre of the Jews in Lithuania*, p. 103
202. Leaflet reprinted in Truska, Liudas, and Vareikis, Vygantas: *The Preconditions for the Holocaust; Anti-Semitism in Lithuania*, pp. 245-263

having expressed his astonishment as to how diligently the Lithuanians were willing to carry out orders from the Germans and carry out criminal acts.[203]

In the end, the LAF would become disenchanted with the German unwillingness to consider any form of autonomy or independence for the Lithuanian state. On September 15, 1941, it sent an angry memorandum to Adolf Hitler, complaining that in spite of its active support for the German cause, the Germans continued to treat Lithuania as an occupied territory. The response was swift: The headquarters of the LAF were stormed and its leader Leonas Prapuolenis was arrested. He disappeared until April 1942 in the Dachau concentration camp and was later not allowed by the Germans to come to Lithuania.[204] The movement disintegrated and fell apart in a variety of groups but with a common demeanor of a strongly nationalist, anti-Soviet and anti-Semitic stance.[205]

203. Truska, Liudas, and Vareikis, Vygantas: *The Preconditions for the Holocaust; Anti-Semitism in Lithuania*, pp. 200
204. Leonas Prapuolenis died in 1972 in Chicago, USA
205. Sutton, Karen: *The Massacre of Jews of Lithuania*, p. 139

Chapter 4 – The Holocaust in Lithuania

I was willing to eliminate these Jewish workers and their families, but the Reichskommissar and the Wehrmacht objected firmly, asking to leave these Jews and their families alive. The aim – to cleanse Lithuania of the Jews – was achieved only by the formation of the Rollkommando of selected men led by the Obersturmführer Hamann who fully understood my goals and could ensure cooperation with Lithuanian partisans and responsible civil authorities.

Franz Walter Stahlecker[206]

What happened during the first days of the war was a catastrophe for the Jews, but was a far worse catastrophe for the Lithuanians.

Tomas Venclova[207]

For me one of the most moving reports about the first days of the war in Lithuania comes from the diary of Grigory Szur, a Vilnius Jew who himself perished in the Holocaust but whose diary was hidden under the floor of the University Library and published in 1997.[208] He describes the fear of the first days of the war, when Soviet troops had already fled Vilnius and the Germans had not yet settled in. Szur writes: "With the appearance of the first German units in the city, the Lithuanian activists, many of whom had held important positions during Soviet rule, started their hunt for Bolsheviks and Jews. The activists appeared to be well armed and, on their arms, were bands with the swastika. In the streets of the city and at the station, they beat up everybody and apprehended anybody they wanted; some of them were shot to death without any trial. A number of citizens used the situation to enrich themselves by plundering the houses of Jews, robbing them of their money and looking for

206. As quoted in *The Persecution and Mass Murder of Lithuanian Jews*, p. 115
207. From an article of Tomas Venclova, published in 1976 in the Moscow Jewish samizdat journal *Evrei v SSSR*, issue 12.
208. Szur was among the last Vilnius Jews deported to the Stutthof concentration camp after the liquidation of the HKP camp in Vilnius. He was among the Jews that were loaded on a ship by the Germans and sunk in open seas.

gold and other valuables. Immediately during the morning of June 24 in the garden of the Franciscan Church at the Trocka [Trakų] street (where Lithuanian activists and soldiers had prepared an ambush during the night) they started the execution of Jews and Soviet military, who had been apprehended in the street or through denunciation. The first person apprehended was a young Jewish girl. Apparently she was on her way to her work, unaware of the danger. She was put in front of the machine gun that was positioned in the garden, and immediately shot..."[209]

The image of an innocent girl, pulled from the street by a group of thugs and shot without any other reason than her race, sums up the horrors that befell the country and, in particular, its Jewish community.

The persecution and killing of Jews in Lithuania started almost from the very moment German troops crossed the border on June 22, 1941. During the night, armed Lithuanian groups crossed the border to carry out sabotage acts against the Soviet Red Army and to prepare for the arrival of the German forces. The same groups would also be involved in the "spontaneous self-cleansing operations" on Lithuanian soil. This was fully according to plan. On June 29, 1941, the head of the Reich Security Main Office (RSHA) *SS Obergruppenführer,* Reinhard Heydrich, issued clear deployment orders, in which he stated: "The self-cleaning efforts (*Selbstreinigungsbestrebungen*) of anti-communist or anti-Jewish circles are not to be obstructed. On the contrary, they are to be unleashed, to be intensified when necessary and to be steered in the right direction. This must proceed without a trace, so that later the local 'self-defense circles' may not point to any decrees or political assurances. Since such actions are possible only in the first period of military occupation for obvious reasons, the *Einsatzgruppen* and *Einsatzkommandos* of the Security police and SD, in cooperation with the military authorities, are to send advance squads into the newly occupied territories as quickly as possible to make the necessary arrangements... The formation of permanent self-defense units under central leadership is to be avoided at first; in place of these, it makes sense only to unleash popular pogroms, as outlined above." [210]

The Einsatzkommandos were sub-groups of the four *Einsatzgruppen,* formed in early 1941, which were sort of mobile killing squads with a

209. Szur, Grigori: *De Joden van Wilno*, p. 40
210. Quoted in Gitelman, Zvi: *Bitter Legacy*, p. 95

membership of approximately 3,000 men.[211] Their mission was to carry out "cleansing operations" in the captured territories. In total, five *Einsatzgruppen* were formed and trained in the police school of Pretzsch (Saxony-Anhalt, Germany) and the surrounding areas.[212] *Einsatzgruppe A*, attached to the Army Group North, was assembled in Gumbinnen, East Prussia, June 23, 1941, the day after the start of operation "Barbarossa," and led by *SS-Brigadeführer* Franz Walter Stahlecker. On 25 June, *Einsatzgruppe A* entered Kaunas with the units of the German army. Among the German leadership of *Einsatzgruppe A,* which consisted of seventeen persons, eleven were lawyers, of whom nine had PhDs. All of them had long records of service with the SS and the police.[213] In short, their rabiate anti-Semitic worldview was combined with a legal education, resulting in a deadly force keen to fulfill its tasks in a well-organized and efficient manner. In the course of the war, the *Einsatzgruppen* were responsible for the murder (by shooting and gassing) of approximately one million Jews.[214]

During the first wave of "spontaneous" killings, mostly able-bodied men were targeted. Women and children were, for the time being, spared that fate. Less than one month into the occupation, the Germans halted the spontaneous and sporadic killings and replaced them with the first systematic mass murders in occupied Europe.[215] A report by *Einsatzgruppe A* of October 15, 1941 clarifies this point: "... It was obvious from the beginning that only the first days after the occupation would offer the opportunity for carrying out pogroms. After the disarmament of the partisans, the self-cleansing *Aktionen* necessarily ceased."[216] The same document also shows that the Germans deliberately had locals auxiliaries participate in the "spontaneous" killings in order to have documented proof "that the first spontaneous executions of Jews and Communists were carried out by Lithuanians and Latvians."[217] *Einsatzgruppe A* commander

211. The Einsatzgruppen consisted mainly of members of the Order Police and the *Waffen-SS*, supported by local collaborators and led by officers from the SD, Gestapo and Criminal Police.
212. Heine, Eric in *Holocaust in Litauen*, p. 92
213. Heine, Eric in *Holocaust in Litauen*, p. 92. Hilary Earl comes to slightly different figures: of the fifteen Einsatzgruppen commanders who worked in Russia between 1941 and 1943, six had a PhD. Of the sixty-nine leaders of the Einsatzkommandos, sixteen had a PhD. See Earl, Hilary: *The Nuremberg Einsatzgruppen Trial*, p. 100. Whatever the figures, it is clear that they were all above average in intelligence and ambition.
214. Earl, Hilary: *The Nuremberg SS-Einsatzgruppen Trial*, p. 7
215. Sutton, Karen: *The Massacre of the Jews in Lithuania*, p. 13.
216. Gitelman, Zvi: *Bitter Legacy*, p. 266
217. Gitelman, Zvi: *Bitter Legacy*, p. 266

Franz Walter Stahlecker wrote in his report: "...Within a few hours of our entering the city [Kaunas], local anti-Semitic elements were induced to engage in pogroms against the Jews, despite the extremely difficult conditions. In accordance with orders, the security police were bent on solving the Jewish question with extreme firmness using all the ways and means at its disposal. It was thought a good idea for the security police not to be seen too involved, at least not immediately, in these unusually tough measures, which were also bound to attract attention in German circles. The impression had to be created that the local population itself had taken the first steps of its own accord as a natural reaction to decades of oppression by the Jews and the more recent terror exerted by the Communists."[218] In other words, the Germans kept a low profile, steered the process from behind the scenes and made use of the local activists to create the impression that all the excesses were the result of spontaneous outbursts of rage against the "Jews-Communists." But all documents show that, in fact, it was the Germans who orchestrated most of the killings, staying in the background like a prompter watching the play on stage and intervening only when really necessary.

Why Lithuania became a sort of pilot for the systematic annihilation of Jewry on its soil is still a matter of debate. The Wannsee conference, where the plans for the *Endlösung* (Final Solution) were discussed and the fate of European Jewry was sealed, had not taken place yet.[219] Some argue that it was the result of the plans to "Germanize" the Baltic countries and fill them with German colonialists, whereby the Lithuanians and Latvians would be moved further East (the Estonians were in German eyes almost "Aryan"), and, thus, the Jews were very much in their way.[220] Earlier plans to create a *Judenreservat* (Jewish reservation) around Lublin and, when that did not materialize, in Africa had been abandoned in 1940 as

218. Klee, Ernst: *The Good Old Days*, p. 24
219. The Wannsee Conference was held on 20 January 1942. Originally the conference was supposed to take place on December 9 and invitations had been sent out on November 29, but it was subsequently postponed. The purpose of the conference was to inform administrative leaders of Departments responsible for various policies relating to Jews, that Reinhard Heydrich had been appointed as the chief executor of the "*Endlösung*" of the "Jewish question." In the course of the meeting, Heydrich presented a plan, presumably approved by Adolf Hitler, for the deportation of the Jewish population of Europe and French North Africa to German-occupied areas in Eastern Europe, and the use of the Jews fit for labor on road-building projects, in the course of which they would eventually die; the surviving remnant was to be annihilated after completion of the projects.
220. Arūnas Bubnys in Nikžentaitis, Alvydas: *The Vanished World of Lithuanian Jews*, p. 212-214

it proved to be too complex to organize.[221] And thus killing the Jews *en masse* seemed the only solution.[222]

Others, such as German historian Christoph Dieckmann, argue that it was for more practical reasons, as the German troops needed to be fed and, in order to avoid food shortages, the number of "useless mouths" needed to be reduced.[223] Dieckmann believes that when in the summer of 1941 it became clear that the *Blitzkrieg* against the Soviet Union was failing and the war would last much longer than planned and anticipated, the military commanders faced the immediate threat of not being able to feed both their troops and the civil population. As a result, choices had to be made,

221. The district of Lublin was not only supposed to house all Polish Jews but eventually all Jews from the rest of the Third Reich. When the Lublin Plan was abandoned, Heinrich Himmler (who apart from *Reichsführer SS* was also Reich Commissioner for the Strengthening of Ethnic Germandom (*Reichskommissar für die Festigung des deutschen Volkstums*) suggested Africa to Hitler. This gradually developed into the plan to ship all Jews to Madagascar, but when Germany lost the Battle of Britain and the occupation of Britain failed, and thus control of the seas remained a fata morgana, that plan was also abandoned. The Germans then had a major problem, because in Poland already big ghettos had been created in Warsaw and Lodz, in anticipation of the deportation. When that did not materialize, the situation in the ghettos became untenable and mortality skyrocketed. There only two solutions were either to let the Jews starve or to create a ghetto economy through which they would earn their own living. The choice fell on the latter. See Browning, Christopher: *Fateful Months*, pp. xvii-xix, and Browning in Cesarani, David: *The Final Solution*, p. 137

222. This is related to the ongoing discussion when Hitler and his team decided to exterminate all Jews. One of the most renowned experts in the field, Christopher Browning, writes in *Fateful Months* (p. 8): "The intention of systematically murdering the European Jews was not fixed in Hitler's mind before the war, but crystallized in 1941 after previous solutions proved unworkable and the imminent attack upon Russia raised the prospect of yet another vast increase in the number of Jews within the growing German empire. (...) In the spring [of 1941] Hitler ordered preparations for the murder of Russian Jews who would fall into German hands during the coming invasion. That summer, confident of military victory, Hitler instigated the preparation of a plan to extend the killing process to European Jews." In other words, while the decision had been reached to kill the Jews in the USSR, this did not automatically mean that the same counted for the European Jews. And, in fact, the policy of forcing German Jews into emigration lasted until October 1941, when emigration was finally banned and instead Jews were cornered in order not to let them escape. The Madagascar Plan was officially abandoned in February 1942. See Browning, Christopher: *Fateful Months*, p. 21

223. See Dieckmann, Christoph: *Deutsche und litauische Interessen*, in *Holocaust in Litauen*, pp. 63-76. This argument is strongly rejected by Yizhak Arad in Nikžentaitis, Alvydas: *The Vanished World of Lithuanian Jews*, p. 125

and the choice fell on getting rid of the racial subspecies: Jews and Soviet prisoners of war. Indeed, at least 170,000 Soviet prisoners of war died in Lithuania, the majority between June 1941 and spring 1942.[224] In total, more than half of the 5.7 million Soviet prisoners of war died in German captivity due to forced labor, starvation or outright murder.[225]

According to Yitzhak Arad, the decision to go for an all-out annihilation of the Jews was taken during a meeting at Hitler's headquarters on July 16, 1941. The reason was that, at that moment, the collapse of the Soviet Union still seemed imminent and an optimistic outcome. Hitler felt it would be only a matter of time before the country would be under German rule. The success of the military operation allowed the Germans to make use of the situation and deal with the Jewish enemy, because it was clear that after the war it would be much more difficult to carry out mass killings without an international outcry. At that moment, the United States had not yet entered the war and, thus, not triggering any reaction on their part was still a factor of importance.[226] Yet Richard Breitman argues in his chapter *Plans for the Final Solution in Early 1941* that, in fact, the Nazi leadership (in particular Hitler, Himmler and Heydrich) had already decided on the Final Solution, the *Endlösung*, and that only the date of its implementation was dependent on the fortunes of war.[227]

Finally, there are those who argue that the main factor causing the smooth extermination of the Jews was that Lithuanians very eagerly participated and thereby greatly facilitated the implementation of the extermination plans. Donald Bloxham even suggests that the Lithuanian and Romanian nationalists gave the Germans a "policy guide in extremism, since, at brief but seminal moments, non-Germans showed how murder could be expanded in scope."[228] Arūnas Bubnys points out that at the beginning of 1944 in Lithuania, not more than 660 German officials worked in the civilian administration, while in the Lithuanian administration, no less than 20,000 ethnic Lithuanians were employed. In the police itself, similar differences between German and Lithuanian presence existed. During the war period, there were some 60-100 Germans in the political and criminal police, as opposed to 800-900 Lithuanians. In the ordinary police, 550

224. See Dieckmann, Christoph in *Holocaust in Litauen*, p. 63 and p. 68, and also Heine, Eric in *Holocaust in Litauen*, p. 98
225. Kühne, Thomas: *Belonging and Genocide*, p. 105
226. Yizhak Arad in Nikžentaitis, Alvydas: *The Vanished World of Lithuanian Jews*, p. 183. The United States entered the war on December 7, 1941, when the Japanese attacked the US Fleet at Pearl Harbor, Hawaii.
227. Breitman, Richard: *Plans for the Final Solution in Early 1941.* in Berenbaum, Michael: *Holocaust and History*, pp. 187-196
228. Bloxham, Donald: *The Final Solution*, p. 8

Germans served, while the Lithuanian police force was a total of 12,000 men, with 3,700 in the Lithuanian ordinary police and 8,000 in police battalions.[229]

The Lithuanian Police Department, headquartered in Kaunas, was supervised by Colonel Vytautas Reivytis. Reivytis had a career of fifteen years in the police force by the time he was appointed to this position. During his career, he studied criminology in Kaunas and Berlin and eventually became a high-ranking officer in the railroad security service; when the Soviets invaded in June 1940, he fled to Germany.[230] In the summer and fall of 1941, Vytautas Reivytis supported the *Rollkommando* of Joachim Hamann by issuing instructions to round up and guard the unfortunate Jews. "Whenever problems arose," writes Saulius Sužiedėlis, "Reivytis was quick to implore Hamann for instructions, even on the minutest details of the operation."[231] For instance, on August 16, 1941, Reivytis sent a secret circular No. 3 to the Chief of Kaunas County Police: "Upon the receipt of this circular, arrest all the Jewish men over 15 years of age and the women who during the Bolshevik occupation were distinguished for their Bolshevik activities or are still distinguished for this activity or their impertinence, as detailed in the notes. The detainees have to be gathered on the main roads and information about them has to be sent to the Police Department immediately with special means of communication. This communiqué should specify the place and the number of detainees and the kind of detained Jews. Arrangements should be made to supply the detainees with food and appropriate protection; auxiliary police can be employed to this end. This circular has to be carried out within two days from its receipt. The detained Jews will be guarded until they are taken and transferred to the camp."[232] Sužiedėlis continues: "There is no way to know whether the colonel was galled by his humble subordination to a lowly SS lieutenant, but there was no doubt about his subservience and loyalty to the German cause throughout the occupation. Thus, while the Holocaust was, above all, a German project, the servile Reivytis and many of his policemen did a great deal to implement and assist the murders."[233] "The successful implementation of Nazi policy (including their Jewish policy) was inconceivable without the support of the ethnic Lithuanian

229. Data provided by Christoph Dieckmann at a symposium in London, February 7, 2011.
230. Saulius Sužiedėlis further adds that he was an accomplished target shooter and ju-jitsu expert who competed internationally with some success. An aviation enthusiast, Reivytis fit the self-image of the voldemarininkai, the hard right-wing "men of action." See Sužiedėlis, Saulius: *The Burden of 1941.*
231. Sužiedėlis, Saulius: *The Burden of 1941*
232. Bubnys, Arūnas: *The Holocaust in the Lithuanian Provinces 1941*
233. Sužiedėlis, Saulius: *The Burden of 1941.*

administration."[234] Yet at the same time, one can say with confidence that without the Germans, no mass extermination of Jews in Lithuania would have taken place. It proved to be a devilish combination.

The Holocaust in Lithuania can be divided into three stages: the period of mass executions (June-December 1941), the ghetto period (1942 - March 1943), and the final liquidation (April 1943 - July 1944).

Mass executions

From the onset, the Germans had been preparing for "special treatment" of the Jews they would find on their way when attacking the Soviet Union. Already on March 13, 1941 (that is, more than three months prior to the attack on the USSR), SS and Gestapo Chief Heinrich Himmler had been authorized by Adolf Hitler to carry out "special duties" in the Soviet Union. Two months later, on May 13, 1941, still more than a month before the attack on the USSR, a special decree of immunity was passed for acts that normally would have been subjected to severe military discipline. According to this "Decree on the Conduct of Court-martials in the District of 'Barbarossa' [the code name for the invasion of the Soviet Union] and for Special Measures of the Troops," German troops were immune from prosecution: "For offenses committed by members of the Wehrmacht and its employees against enemy civilians, prosecution is not compulsory, not even if the offense is at the same time a military crime or violation."[235] Members of the Wehrmacht were instructed to shoot "guerillas" ruthlessly in battle, during pursuit or even after having been captured. Also "collective punitive measures" were to be carried out immediately against villages from which the Wehrmacht was "insidiously and maliciously attacked." The decree not only "protected members of the armed forces and their "ancillary services" who engaged in summary executions of unarmed enemy civilians and established an unprecedented legal basis for

234. Arūnas Bubnys in Nikžentaitis, Alvydas: *The Vanished World of Lithuanian Jews*, p. 125

235. Quoted in Kühne, Thomas: *Belonging and Genocide*, p. 99. Interestingly, the Nazi leadership felt compelled to find a legal justification for this decree and did so by referring to the fact that the Soviet Union had not ratified the Geneva and Hague Conventions. See Bloxham, Donald: *The Final Solution*, p. 283. As Jürgen Försters shows in *Complicity or Entanglement? Wehrmacht, War and Holocaust* (published in Berenbaum, Michael et.al.: *The Holocaust and History*, already during the campaign in Poland in the fall of 1939, Hitler granted a general amnesty for those who violated military law during the Polish campaign, thereby setting a precedent. See p 271

such actions,"[236] it also fundamentally altered the conduct of war. The war had now been turned into a "war of extermination," as Hitler called it, a "clash of ideologies."[237] For the members of the German armed forces and the ancillary forces, it basically meant an "open hunting season" in which they could do everything imaginable and unimaginable. In the course of the war, between 300,000 and 500,000 civilians were killed in the Soviet Union during the Wehrmacht's anti-partisan war.[238]

The "ancillary services" were the four *Einsatzgruppen*, of which *Einsatzgruppe A* led by Franz Walter Stahlecker, was responsible for the whole Baltic region and a sub-division, *Einsatzkommando* 3 (EK3) led by Standartenführer Karl Jäger, was responsible for Lithuania.[239] Until August 9, 1941, Vilnius fell under the authority of *Einsatzkommando 9* (EK9), led

236. Sutton, Karen: *The Massacre of the Jews in Lithuania*, p. 7. Participation in the mass killings of Jews was not obligatory and German military had, in fact, the right to refuse orders if they went against their conscience, as we can see from the case of Klaus Hornig that I will discuss later in this book. Also Thomas Kühne in *Belonging and Genocide* mentions a considerable number of instances when German officers refused to participate or discontinued their involvement, see pp. 83-87. However, he wrongly asserts that none of those who refused were ever jailed or arrested, see page 85.
237. Kühne, Thomas: *Belonging and Genocide*, p. 99
238. Kühne, Thomas: *Belonging and Genocide*, p. 126. The role of the Wehrmacht has been subject to much debate and for many decades the image remained that soldiers in the Wehrmacht had merely defended their fatherland and had not been involved in mass murder and other atrocities. The change came in the 1990s and only in 1997 did German Defence Minister Volker Rühe openly dissociate the Bundeswehr from the German Wehrmacht. As Jürgen Förster writes: "With regard to the Holocaust, the Wehrmacht acted in many roles. It was perpetrator, collaborator, and bystander. Only after the war did it claim to be victim." See Förster, Jürgen: *Complicity or Entanglement in: Berenbaum, Michael: The Holocaust and History*, p. 267 and p. 280.
239. Born in 1900, Stahlecker was trained as a lawyer. In 1932 he joined the Nazi Party. Two years later he was appointed head of the Gestapo in the German state of Württemberg and soon assigned to the main office of the *Sicherheitsdienst SD* in Berlin. After the incorporation of Austria in the German Reich in 1938, Stahlecker became SD chief of the Danube district (Vienna), a post he retained even after being promoted to *SS-Standartenführer*. After differences of opinion with SD-Chief Reinhard Heydrich, he moved to the Ministry of Foreign Affairs (Foreign Office), after which he held posts in the Protectorate of Bohemia and Moravia and Norway, where he was promoted to *SS-Oberführer*. In June 1941, Stahlecker was promoted to *SS-Brigadeführer* and *Generalmajor der Polizei* and took over as commanding officer of *Einsatzgruppe A*. Stahlecker was eventually killed on March 23, 1942, during a fight with partisans near Krasnogvardeysk. See Arad, Yitzhak: *The Holocaust in the Soviet Union*, p. 126

by *SS-Obersturmbannführer* Alfred Filbert. EK9 belonged to *Einsatzgruppe B,* which was attached to the Army Group Center. After that date, also Vilnius fell under EK3, and on October 2 also Šiauliai (and with it, the north of Lithuania) was transferred to the operational region of EK3.

As said earlier, the persecution and killing of Jews started almost immediately after the German troops arrived, yet the actual mass killings commenced only in mid-August 1941.[240] Until then, at least 95% of the Jewish population of Lithuania was still alive. The mass executions were carried out in three main locations: Kaunas (Ninth Fort), Vilnius (in the Paneriai forest, 6 kilometers outside the city), and in the countryside (e.g. the Kužiai Forest outside Šiauliai, the Pajuostė Forest near Panevėžys, the Polygon near Pabradė) by the *Rollkommando* Hamann. This *Rollkommando* consisted of 8-10 members of *Einsatzkommando 3* (EK3) and a Lithuanian police battalion commanded by Lieutenant Bronius Norkus, consisting of eighteen Lithuanian officers and 450 men.[241] The leader of the *Rollkommando*, Joachim Hamann, was a 28-year old dynamic and fiercely anti-Semitic SS officer. An orphan of Baltic German parentage, he was trained as a chemist but could not find a job. In 1931, he joined the SA and seven years later the SS, where he made his career. He studied law on the side. He served with the Wehrmacht in Poland and France, in 1940, and subsequently returned to Berlin in service of the Gestapo and SD. In 1941, he was promoted to the position of commissioner of the criminal police. Just before the start of the war, he was promoted to the position of *SS Obersturmführer.*[242] He would sometimes be present during the killings, always with a whip in his hand. He was formally subordinate to Karl Jäger, yet the difference was clear: Hamann was more a man of action, while Jäger preferred to handle the bureaucratic side of the job, working with the numbers of killed Jews provided by Hamann.[243] As we will see later, Jäger had

240. In some places, such as Gargždai on June 24, Kretinga on June 25, Palanga on June 27, Darbėnai on June 29, Kybartai on June 30, and of course in Kaunas itself, mass killings took place earlier. See Bubnys, Arūnas: *Holocaust in the Lithuanian Provinces 1941*, p. 37

241. The unit headed by Major Antanas Impulevičius was the 2nd (and later 12th) Police Battalion, which participated in several mass killings in Belarus, in which a total of 46,000 Jews perished. See Bubnys, Arūnas: *Lithuanian Police Battalions and the Holocaust (1941-1943)*, p. 16 and later in this book. Impulevicius was tried by the Soviets in absentia in 1962. In 1948, 14 former members of this unit were tried and sentenced to 25 years imprisonment. In 1979, another member was identified as living under a pseudonym in the Soviet Union. He was sentenced to death and executed. See Martin Dean in Nikžentaitis, Alvydas: *The Vanished World of Lithuanian Jews*, p. 291

242. Heine, Eric in *Holocaust in Litauen*, p. 93

243. Heine, Eric in *Holocaust in Litauen*, p. 93

nightmares because of his work; the question is whether the same counts for Joachim Hamann.

The police battalions or *Tautinės darbo apsaugos batalionas* (Defence of National Labor Battalions; TDA), sometimes also referred to as *Schutzmannschaften*, stood under the command of Colonel Andrius Butkūnas and had been formed by decision of the Lithuanian Provisional Government on June 30, 1941. The main objectives of the TDA were to perform guard duties, but also to assist the Nazi's in rounding up Jews and either killing them or handing them over for transport to execution sites.[244] In total, twenty-five Lithuanian police battalions were formed. Of these, some were based in Kaunas, others in Vilnius (and named *Vilniaus atstatymo tarnyba*, Vilnius reconstruction unit) and some in other cities such as Šiauliai and Panevežys.[245] Lithuanian historian Arūnas Bubnys concluded after extensive research that, of these 25 battalions, ten took part in the Holocaust in one way or another, 14 did not and the role of one is still subject to research. "Data available at present [2004] allows one to state that there were about 1,000 policemen who directly performed the executions or guarded the victims of the 'operations' who served in the battalion, and their actions inside and outside of Lithuania resulted in approximately 78,000 executed Jews, not including victims of other nationalities and members of other groups as well as Soviet prisoners of war."[246]

From the very start, the Germans happily documented the participation of Lithuanian "auxiliary groups": the plan seemed to work perfectly well. On June 30, 1941, a report mentions the fact that "during the last three days, Lithuanian partisan groups have already killed several thousand Jews." On July 4, 1941, the Germans report the shooting of 200 persons in Telšiai as well as the formation of two groups of partisans in Kaunas totaling 300 men under the leadership of the right-wing journalist Algirdas Klimaitis,[247]

244. Shneidman, N.N.: *The Three Tragic Heroes of the Vilnius Ghetto*, p. 12
245. In November 1941, there were five police battalions formed in Kaunas, with a total number of 3,470 members. The Vilnius police battalions were formed after an order to that effect by the commander in Vilnius, Zehnpfennig and, in October 1941, there were five such units with a total membership of 2,014 men and officers. The Lithuanian police battalions were numbered 1-15, and later new numbers were allotted: 251-265 and 301-310. However, units 260-265 were never formed. See Bubnys, Arūnas in *Holocaust in Litauen*, p. 118
246. Bubnys, Arūnas: *Lithuanian Police battalions and the Holocaust (1941-1943)*
247. Klee, Ernst: *The Good Old Days*, p. 26. Stahlecker reports: "This group, as it proved itself satisfactory, was deployed not only in Kaunas itself but also in numerous parts of Lithuania, where it performed duties, in particular preparation of and participation in the execution of large liquidation actions, under the

and 200 men under the leadership of a physician with the name Zigonys. On July 11, *Einsatzgruppe A* commander Franz Stahlecker reported that "a total of 7,800 Jews have been liquidated so far, partly through pogroms and partly through shootings by Lithuanian commandos." And on August 3, the same *Einsatzgruppe* reports remarked how "easy [it was] to convince the Lithuanian circles of the need for self-purging actions to achieve a complete elimination of the Jews from public life. Spontaneous pogroms occurred in all towns."[248]

However, in reality things were not as easy as the Germans had hoped. Stahlecker's report of October 15, 1941, mentions clearly: "It was initially surprisingly difficult to set a fairly large-scale anti-Jewish pogrom in motion there." In other words, as indicated earlier, it was the German intention to stay in the background and pretend that it were spontaneous outbursts of anti-Jewish feelings that resulted in the mass killings. "[It was important] to establish as unshakable and provable facts for the future that it was the liberated population itself which took the most severe measures, on its own initiative, against the Bolshevik and Jewish enemy, without any German instruction being evident."[249] Also an extensive report by Arūnas Bubnys on the murders in the provinces clearly shows the German intention to remain in the background and record the shootings as carried out by the local Lithuanian population.[250] According to the historian Dina Porat, up to two-thirds of the Lithuanian provincial Jews were killed by locals, without any Germans around.[251] However, from all evidence it is clear that the German mastermind behind the scene was an essential factor in the overwhelming success of the operation and, without their planning, the killing spree would not have been so all encompassing. Thomas Kühne writes: "It required the Nazi occupiers to stimulate and orchestrate local collaboration. Only the German occupiers could integrate indigenous pogroms into systematic genocide."[252]

constant supervision of the Einsatzkommando with no significant problems..." See pp. 26-27. Algirdas Klimaitis was most likely a former officer from the Lithuanian Army and became later a right-wing journalist. According to his sister he became anti-Communist and anti-Semitic in the 1930s, and was later said to have been a Voldemarist. He died in Hamburg on August 29, 1988. See *The Persecution and Mass Murder of Lithuanian Jews*, p. 139

248. Sutton, Karen: *The Massacre of the Jews in Lithuania*, p. 10, quoting Ereignismeldungen UdSSR, published in Arad, Yitzak (et.al.): *The Einsatzgruppen Reports*, New York, 1989. Some are reprinted in Gitelman, Zvi: *Bitter Legacy*, pp. 265-269
249. Rislakki, Jukka: *The Case for Latvia*, p. 119
250. Bubnys, Arūnas: *The Holocaust in the Lithuanian Provinces 1941*
251. Dina Porat in Cesarani, David: *The Final Solution*, p. 163
252. Kühne, Thomas: *Belonging and Genocide*, p. 82

It is interesting to note that in Latvia, organizing these "spontaneous" outbreaks of public hatred towards the Jews proved to be even more difficult than in Lithuania. Franz Stahlecker complained in the same October 15 report: "It proved to be considerably more difficult [than in Kaunas] to set in motion similar cleansing Aktionen in Latvia... In Riga it proved possible, by means of appropriate suggestions to the Latvian auxiliary police, to get an anti-Jewish pogrom going [on July 4, 1941], in the course of which all the synagogues were destroyed and approximately 400 Jews killed. As the population on the whole quieted down very quickly in Riga, it was not possible to arrange further pogroms."[253] Indeed, during the short period between the Soviet retreat and the German advance, things stayed unbelievably calm in Latvia. There were almost no outbursts and political killings. Jukka Rislakki points out, "deliberate or spontaneous expressions of violence involving loss of human life were very rare, and even according to the worst possible calculations, the overall number of victims of politically motivated murders committed in the entire territory of Latvia did not exceed a few dozen... [There were] no pogroms, no mass executions."[254]

Events in Kaunas

In Kaunas, however, things went quite differently. On June 23, one day after the outbreak of the war, armed units of the LAF took control of the capital.[255] Lithuanians in the city were overjoyed. The day before, they had awakened to the sound of aerial German bombardments, which continued though the 22nd and 23rd. On the 23rd at 9:30 AM, Radio Kaunas played the Lithuanian national hymn and the newsreader started the broadcasting program with the words "Here speaks Radio Kaunas, here speaks free and independent Lithuania."[256] For most Lithuanians this was the day of liberation, the announcement that meant the end of the Soviet occupation. For many Jews, however, it was the worst message they could hear; it was the announcement that the Nazis were on their way and that their worst nightmares were about to become true. "Although crowds of Lithuanians greeted the Germans with flowers, it was no surprise that we closed our shutters, lowered our curtains, and locked ourselves up in our homes."[257] The atmosphere in the city had been whipped up further by a radio announcement by the Military Commandant of Kaunas, Jurgis Bobelis, reporting that arriving Germans had been shot at from Jewish homes and

253. Rislakki, Jukka: *The Case for Latvia*, p. 119
254. Rislakki, Jukka: *The Case for Latvia*, p. 112. Before the outbreak of the war, approximately 95,000 Jews lived in Latvia, of whom 45,000 lived in Riga.
255. Bubnys, Arūnas: *Lithuanian Police battalions and the Holocaust (1941-1943)*, p. 4
256. Tauber, Joachim, in *Holocaust in Litauen*, p. 41
257. Levin, Don, in *Hidden History of the Kovno Ghetto*, p. 222

from that day forward, as retribution, one hundred Jews would be executed for every German fired upon.[258]

One of the first and most notorious killings took place at Lietūkis Garage on Vytautas Boulevard. According to testimony by German officers who coincidentally passed by and watched the scene, several dozen Jews were herded together by Lithuanians with white bands around their arms. One of the Germans testified: "There was a large number of women in the crowd and they had lifted up their children or stood them on chairs or boxes so they could see better. At first I thought this must be a victory celebration or some type of sporting event because of the cheering, clapping and laughter that kept breaking out. However, when I inquired what was happening, I was told that the 'Death-dealer of Kovno' was at work and that this was where collaborators and traitors were finally meted out their rightful punishment."[259] Another German officer, Wilhelm Gunzilius, testified: "A young man (a Lithuanian) aged about sixteen, with rolled up sleeves was armed with an iron bar. From the group of men standing by, one man was led up to him at a time and with one or more blows on the nape of the neck he killed each one. In this way, in the course of an hour, he killed all forty-five to fifty. I took a number of photographs… (…) After he killed them all, the young men set the iron bar aside, fetched an accordion and clambered up above the corpses. Getting up on the 'hill,' he played the Lithuanian national anthem. I was familiar with the melody and people standing near me confirmed that this was their anthem. The conduct of the civilians, amongst whom were women and children, was unbelievable. After every blow of the iron bar, they applauded and when the murderer began to play the Lithuanian anthem, they began to sing it to the accompaniment of the accordion. In the front row of the crowd, there were women with children in their arms, watching all that was happening"[260]

The October 15 report of Franz Stahlecker describes what happened during the next days. "Klimaitis, who was the first to be recruited, succeeded in starting a pogrom on the basis of instructions he had been given by a small advance detachment that had been deployed in Kovno without any German orders or incitement being discernable. During the first pogrom, during the night of June 25-26, the Lithuanian partisans eliminated more than 1,500 [mostly religiously Orthodox] Jews, set fire

258. *The Persecution and Mass Murder of Lithuanian Jews*, p. 120
259. Klee, Ernst: *The Good Old Days*, p. 28
260. Faitelson, Alex: *The Truth and Nothing but the Truth*, p. 26. In Klee, Ernst: *The Good Old Days*, testimonies of three other German officers confirm this report. See pp. 28-35.

to five synagogues or destroyed them by other means, and burned down an area consisting of about sixty houses inhabited by Jews. During the nights that followed, 2,300 Jews were eliminated in the same way. In other parts of Lithuania, similar *Aktionen* followed the example set in Kovno, but on a smaller scale, and including some Communists who had been left behind. These self-cleansing *Aktionen* ran smoothly because the Wehrmacht authorities who had been informed showed understanding for this procedure."[261]

Attempts to stop the killing proved fruitless. Archbishop Juozas Skvireckas was approached by a Jewish delegation, begging him to tell Catholics not to participate in the mass killings. The archbishop answered he could do nothing but weep and pray. A week later, he personally welcomed *Generalkommissar* Adrian von Renteln to Kaunas. In an entry in his diary, Skvireckas made his position clear: "The thoughts of [Hitler's] *Mein Kampf* concerning the poisonous Bolshevik influence exercised by Jews on the nations of the world are worthy of note. The ideas are interesting indeed. They are true to life and present an insight into reality. Whether they belong to Hitler himself or to his associates is hard to say, but all this testifies to Hitler being not only an enemy of the Jews, but to the correctness of his thoughts as well."[262]

The Provisional Government also made no real effort to end the bloodshed. At the Cabinet meeting on June 26, Acting Prime Minister Juozas Ambrazevičius complained that "completely innocent persons are being arrested, their flats searched." However, it is not clear whether he was actually referring to Jews or ethnic Lithuanians. He expressed his worries about one of the main implementers of the pogroms, Algirdas Klimaitis: "Klimaitis" partisan unit is not working together with the headquarters of the Lithuanian Armed Forces. Meanwhile, the Lithuanian partisans are in contact with the LAF and the Provisional Government."[263] Yet only one member of the Provisional Government protested against the killings openly, during a Cabinet meeting the next day, on June 27. The minutes of the meeting read: "Minister [Landsbergis-] Žemkalnis reported on the extremely cruel torture of Jews in the Lietūkis garage in Kaunas. Decided: Notwithstanding all the measures which must be taken against the Jews because of their Communist activity and harm to the German Army, partisans and individuals should avoid *public* executions of Jews [my italics]. It has been learned that these actions have been committed by people who

261. Gitelman, Zvi: *Bitter Legacy*, p. 265 and Klee, Ernst: *The Good Old Days*, p. 27
262. Sutton, Kaunas: *The Massacre of the Hews of Lithuania*, p. 128
263. *The Persecution and Mass Murder of Lithuanian Jews*, p. 129

have no connection with the Activists' Staff, the Partisans' Staff, or the Lithuanian Provisional Government."[264]

Three days later, Kaunas Military Commander Bobelis informed the Provisional Government that a special concentration camp for Jews had been set up in the Seventh Fort. The Government decided to appoint Vice-Minister of Municipal Economy, V. Švipas, and Military Commander Bobelis responsible for the maintenance of the camp: "[The Provisional Government decides] to agree with the establishment of the Jewish concentration camp."[265] By doing so, the Provisional Government also took responsibility for what would happen there. The authors of The *Persecution and Mass Murder of Lithuanian Jews* leave no doubt about the role of the Provisional Government: "[It] failed in its responsibility to at least attempt to clearly state its opposition to the anti-Jewish violence beyond urging avoidance of 'public massacres' of Jews."[266] In fact, in doing so it did nothing more than the Nazi occupiers themselves, who also soon called for an ending to the bloodbaths in the streets of Kaunas.

The above-mentioned "Concentration Camp for Jews" soon turned into a killing field. Between June 25 and July 8, thousands of Jews were rounded up and taken to the Seventh Fort and killed by Lithuanian auxiliary forces in the most brutal manner possible. The massacres that started on June 30 were led by *SS Obersturmführer* Erich Ehrlinger, commander of *Einsatzkommando 1b*, and after a few days taken over by *SS Standartenführer* Karl Jäger.[267] Two Lithuanian police battalions (1st and 3rd) took part in the killings, with a squad led by Bronius Norkus being the most

264. *The Persecution and Mass Murder of Lithuanian Jews*, p. 135. The document is reprinted in the same book on pp. 235-236
265. *The Persecution and Mass Murder of Lithuanian Jews*, p. 137. Brandišiauskas, Valentinas in Holocaust in Litauen, p. 53
266. *The Persecution and Mass Murder of Lithuanian Jews*, p. 135
267. Jäger was born in Switzerland in 1888 and joined the Nazi party in 1923, the same year he joined the SS. In 1938, he became the head of the *Sicherheitsdienst* (SD) in Münster. During the invasion of the Netherlands on 10 May 1940, Jäger was named commander of *Einsatzkommando 3*, a unit of *Einsatzgruppe A*. From July 1941 until September 1943, Jäger was assigned commander of the SD *Einsatzkommando 3* in Kaunas. Reassigned back to Germany near the end of 1943, Jäger was appointed commander of the SD in Sudetenland. He escaped capture when the war ended, assumed a false identity and was able to stay in hiding until March 1959. Arrested and charged with his crimes, Jäger committed suicide in prison while he was awaiting trial in June 1959. A biography of Karl Jäger by Wolfram Wette can be found in *Holocaust in Litauen*, pp. 77-89

active of all.[268] During his interrogation in 1959, Karl Jäger described what he saw when he visited the Fort after the murders. It seemed to him that Norkus's men "had been shooting indiscriminately from outside into [the crowd]." He had been very much upset by what he saw, and also other Wehrmacht units were very much distressed, having seen the mountains of several thousands of corpses piled up.[269] Franz Stahlecker had to return to Kaunas to apologize to the Wehrmacht, saying that "nervous Lithuanians have simply overdone it."[270] In total, some 5,000 Jews were killed at the Seventh Fort.[271]

268. Bubnys, Arūnas: *Lithuanian Police Battalions and the Holocaust (1941-1943)*, p. 8-9 and Faitelson, Alex: *The Truth and Nothing but the Truth*, pp. 57-73. There are also disputed reports that also a Kaunas basketball team was invited to participate in the killings. In *The Persecution and Mass Murder of Lithuanian Jews*, Dieckmann and Suziedėlis conclude that there is no sufficient documentary evidence that this actually happened, which again others (e.g. Faitelson) contest. The main problem with the available evidence is that it is largely based on materials stemming from interrogations by the NKGB after the war, which cannot be regarded as a totally reliable source. This illustrates some of the difficulties one faces when trying to establish what happened in Lithuania under German occupation. German occupation was followed by Soviet occupation and their regime had a strong urge to make a political point rather than uncovering the full truth.

269. *The Persecution and Mass Murder of Lithuanian Jews*, p. 140. How double hearted Karl Jäger was can be seen from his report of December 1, 1941, in which he describes his visit to some prisons. "These people had been detained by partisans mainly on the basis of denunciations. Many personal scores had been settled in the process. Nobody cared what became of them. You had to visit the prisons and stop for just a moment in the overcrowded cells, which as far as hygiene was concerned defied description, to believe the conditions in there. In Jonava – and this is one example among many – sixteen men were kept in a dark room in a cellar 3 m long, 3 m wide and 1.65 m high for five weeks. They could all have been released since there were no charges against them. Girls aged between thirteen and sixteen were incarcerated because they had applied to join the Communist youth in order to get work. In such cases, we had to take quite radical measures to hammer the message home into the heads of the relevant Lithuanian authorities." See. *The Persecution and Mass Murder of Lithuanian Jews*, p. 231

270. *The Persecution and Mass Murder of Lithuanian Jews*, p. 140

271. *The Persecution and Mass Murder of Lithuanian Jews*, p. 139. Later 300 Soviet prisoners of war had to bury the decomposing corpses. However, the mass graves continued to pose a problem because of the scorching heat. Five weeks later, local residents still complained about the unbearable stench and swimming in the Neris and Nemunas rivers remained forbidden at least till the end of July because the water was "poisoned by the corpses." See: *The Persecution and Mass Murder of Lithuanian Jews*, p. 142

Also in the 4th Fort, Jews were killed *en masse*, and Lithuanian members of the 3rd Police Battalion participated. In total, some 2,500 Jews were killed. Later, the executions moved to the 9th Fort, beginning on October 4, 1941. During that day alone, 1,845 Jews were killed with the participation of almost all of the 3rd Lithuanian Police battalion, as well as some 20 Germans.[272] On October 29, the 9th Fort was the scene of the killing of 9,200 Jews (including more than 4,000 children). The 1st Police Battalion escorted the Jews from the Kaunas Ghetto to their execution, which was handled by the 3rd Police Battalion together with 20 Germans. Later, the Fort was also used for the killing of Jews from other countries, all with the participation of Lithuanian policemen. In total, some 26,000 Jews would be killed in the Kaunas Ninth Fort alone.[273]

It was not only in the Kaunas Forts that the Lithuanian police battalions excel in barbarity. The 12th Police Battalion headed by Antanas Impulevičius even caused the Germans to halt the killing of Jews temporarily.[274] The battalion was later involved in the killing of Jews in the town of Slutsk, which they did with so much enthusiasm that *Gebietskommissar* Carl issued a complaint to general commissioner Wilhelm Kube, in which he wrote that "I must point out to my deepest regret that the [execution of the action] bordered on sadism. They town itself offered a picture of horror during the action. With indescribable brutality on the part of the German police officers and particularly the Lithuanian partisans, the Jewish people, but also among them White Russians, were taken out of their dwellings and herded together… Everywhere in town shots were to be heard and

272. Bubnys, Arūnas: *Lithuanian Police battalions and the Holocaust (1941-1943)*, p. 10
273. Bubnys, Arūnas: *Lithuanian Police battalions and the Holocaust (1941-1943)*, p. 11. One of the German officers who participated in the killings, Helmut Rauca, managed to escape to Canada where he was granted Canadian nationality. He was arrested in Toronto in 1982, extradited to West Germany in April 1983 and died in prison awaiting trial in October 1983. See, among others, Littman, Sol: *Rauca of Kaunas; War Criminal on Trial* and Matas, David: *Justice Delayed*, pp. 96-97 and 132-133. Rauca was one of many war criminals who found refuge in Canada, which, by any means, had a faulty detection system. A report drawn up for an Investigative Committee in 1983, the Deschênes Commission, concluded that among the 620,000 immigrants to Canada between 1947 and 1967, there were "significant" numbers of war criminals from twelve European countries including Lithuania. The report also concluded that as late as 1983, war criminals were admitted to Canada. See Matas, David: *Justice Delayed*, p. 157
274. According to an order of October 16, 1941, the Lithuanian battalions were to be used primarily for the destruction of the Jews in the villages. See Martin Dean in Nikžentaitis, Alvydas: *The Vanished World of Lithuanian Jews*, p. 286

in different streets the corpses of Jews accumulated… Two fully armed Lithuanian policemen had to be arrested for looting and several more had to be forcibly thrown out of shops."[275] Of particular brutality, Carl noted the fact that some of the executed Jews had been able to crawl out of their graves after having been covered – in other words, they had been buried alive. "I beg you to grant me one request," Carl added. "In the future, keep this police battalion away from me by all means." The protest deeply angered Wilhelm Kube, who forwarded copies to his superiors and indicated that the fact that wounded people had been able to crawl out of their graves was "*eine so bodenlose Schweinerei*" (such an unbelievable scandal) that it had to be reported to Hitler and Göring.[276] Also in other cases German officers asked their superiors to end the "spontaneous cleaning operations" of the first days, because they were appalled by what they saw.[277]

Vilnius

Vilnius was, of course, a prize target for the Germans. The city had the largest Jewish community and, on top of that, was historically the base of many Jewish socialist and communist groups, and thus a "center of Judeo-Bolshevism." The city formally remained under Soviet control until June 24, 1941, when the city fell to the invading Germans. However, most Soviet troops left the city during the night of June 23.[278] The following days the city was almost continuously bombed,[279] but remained, in fact, somewhat unattended, as only a few Germans troops stayed behind while the rest continued their attack on the Soviet Union. As a result, the Germans had to rely to a large degree on local Lithuanian support and so the main forces in the city were Lithuanian partisans and remnants of the 29th Corps of the pre-Soviet Lithuanian Army that regrouped the moment the invasion had started.[280]

Vilnius resident Grigory Szur describes the atmosphere in the city vividly in his memoirs and reports that many killings took place during that intermediate period.[281] Schoschana Rabinovici writes in her memoirs that she saw the first German soldiers in the city on June 24 and that the moment the Soviets left, members of the pre-Soviet Lithuanian police appeared on the streets. "They patrolled the streets and helped the German Army to maintain 'order.' They lent special assistance in pursuing and fighting

275. Sutton, Karen: *The Massacre of Jews of Lithuania*, pp. 142-143
276. Sutton, Karen: *The Massacre of Jews of Lithuania*, p. 143
277. Sutton, Karen: *The Massacre of Jews of Lithuania*, p. 131
278. Kruk, Herman: *Last Days of the Jerusalem of Lithuania*, p. 46
279. Kruk, Herman: *Last Days of the Jerusalem of Lithuania*, pp. 46-47
280. Priemel, Kim in *Holocaust in Litauen*, p. 31
281. Shneidman, N.N.: *The Three Tragic Heroes of the Vilnius Ghetto*, p. 11

the Russian forces. With our own eyes [my step-sister] Dolka and I saw the Lithuanian police occupy the post office across the street."[282] Yet at the same time, the "Jewish issue" seems not to have been the main concern of the Lithuanians who took control of the city. An *Einsatzgruppen* report of July 9, 1941, stated that "the Lithuanian activists are trying in all possible ways to exploit the unclear situation and to give the city of Vilnius a purely Lithuanian character by decorating the city with eye-catching Lithuanian flags."[283] Stahlecker wrote in his report: "As far as the Lithuanian population in Vilnius is concerned, the Jewish problem is secondary to the Polish."[284]

Close on the heels of the German Wehrmacht came *Einsatzgruppe A* commanded by *SS-Standartenführer* Franz Walter Stahlecker. A *Sonderkommando* of *Einsatzkommando 9* (EK9) was set up at 12 Vilenska (Vilniaus gatvė), under the command of SS officers Horst Schweineberger and Martin Weiss. This *Sonderkommando* had a Lithuanian unit, the *Ypatingas būrys,* headed by the Lithuanian officer Juozas Sidlauskas, which functioned under the authority of Martin Weiss and consisted of a group of some one hundred young Lithuanians. Members of this *Ypatingas būrys*, often named "catchers" or "chappers," roamed the streets in search of young male Jews, who, after being found, were never seen again. As Noah Shneidman recalls: "I was startled and shocked to learn about the fate of those apprehended by the 'catchers,' the more so since among the 'catchers' were several young Lithuanians that I knew. They were former students of the local Lithuanian high school and members of a well-known basketball club. I was astonished to learn how little time it took to unleash the evil instinct in those who were previously regarded as decent young men. Given unlimited power they were now ready to murder just for the fun of it.[285] Also Schoschana Rabinovici remembers the "catchers" vividly: "The chappers were shock troops made up of Lithuanian youths and students, who had voluntarily signed up to fight against the Jews. These

282. Rabinovici, Schoschana: *Thanks to my Mother*, p. 10
283. Yitzhak Arad in Nikžentaitis, Alvydas: *The Vanished World of Lithuanian Jews*, p. 180
284. Yitzhak Arad in Nikžentaitis, Alvydas: *The Vanished World of Lithuanian Jews*, p. 180
285. Shneidman, Noah: *Jerusalem of Lithuania*, p. 48. Shneidman further writes: "Only twenty former members of the "*Ypatingas būrys*" were arrested, out on trial, and convicted by Soviet and Polish authorities. Most others moved to North America and Australia where they were accepted with dignity as courageous fighters against Communism and Soviet rule. In 1985, some twenty former 'catchers' were still alive."

troops were often dressed as civilians, but were mostly recognizable by their black-leather jackets."[286]

Initially the impression was that they had been taken away for forced labor. Only later did the Jewish community realize that they had been taken to the Paneriai forest outside the city and killed by Germans and Lithuanian auxiliary forces.[287]

Anti-Jewish measures followed soon after the arrival of the Germans. On July 8, 1941, an order was issued stating that all Jews must wear a special patch on their back and, subsequently, on their chest. The commandant of the town of Vilnius, *Oberstleutnant* (lieutenant colonel) Max Zehnpfennig, signed this order. But two days later another commander, *Oberst* Georg Neymann, ordered that the Jews should not display these patches but must, instead, wear the yellow Star of David.[288] In addition, Jews were forbidden to walk along the main streets of the city, and shops were ordered to sell them food only in limited amounts. Jewish people were fired from their

286. Rabinovici, Schoschana: *Thanks to my Mother*, p. 18

287. Shneidman, N.N.: *The Three Tragic Heroes of the Vilnius Ghetto*, p. 13. The Lithuanians involved in the shootings at Paneriai also belonged to the Ypatingas būrys. The combined German - Lithuanian force operating in Paneriai was composed of three separate sub-units: 1. a unit responsible for transporting victims to site from Lukiškės jail. This consisted of local Lithuanians working in cooperation with the Ypatingas būrys and a small group of German *Einsatzgruppe* members. When larger operations were carried out, soldiers of the Vilnius battalions assisted them in transporting victims to the site; 2. a unit responsible for guarding the site to prevent curious bystanders from accidentally straying into the killing area. This comprised mainly Germans who guarded the site perimeter against uninvited visitors, especially German soldiers and officers not involved in the killing activities; 3. a unit that carried out the murders composed almost entirely of Lithuanian members of the Ypatingas būrys. Very few Germans actually participated in the murders since there was no shortage of local Lithuanian volunteers. The most detailed and horrific account of the murders at Paneriai are the memoirs of Kazimierz Sakowicz, *Ponar Diary 1941-1943*

288. In other European countries, this obligation came at a much later date: in Holland this was imposed on April 29, 1942; in Belgium on June 3, 1942; in France on June 7, 1942; in Bulgaria in August 1942 and in Hungary on March 31, 1944. See Faitelson, Alex: *The Truth and Nothing but the Truth*, p. 12. The reason is undoubtedly that the ostracism and subsequent extermination of Jewry in the Soviet Union was on the top agenda of the Germans from the very first day of the war, while in Western Europe a much more gradual process was chosen and in countries like Hungary and Bulgaria, which belonged to the Axis-powers and therefore pro-German, the rules were adopted at a much later stage when the German troops occupied these countries.

jobs, deprived of the means of personal transportation and radios, forbidden to use public transport, and prohibited from public places.
The first organized shootings of Jews in Vilnius occurred on July 4, 1941 (or possibly even earlier), after the military administration was replaced by a civil administration. On the same date the Germans ordered the establishment of a *Judenrat* (Jewish Council) which was intended to control the Jewish ghetto police and various departments of work, health service, social welfare, food, housing, etc. Of special importance was the department of work. The *Judenrat* believed that as long as the Jewish workforce was of use to the Germans, the ghetto would not be liquidated. This was a kind of warranty, allowing Jews to retain some hope of continued existence and eventual survival. Almost all men and women of suitable age and fitness were employed in different factories and workshops, but were often also moved to forced labor.

According to Noah Shneidman, between the time of the German occupation of the city and the creation of the ghettos on September 6, 1941, 35,000 Jews either vanished or were killed outright.[289] By the end of 1941, the murdered Jews of Paneriai numbered at least 48,000, the majority of them from Vilnius.

Outside the two big cities

In the provinces, the killings started spontaneously, often locally organized, but fairly soon took on a systematic character and were organized with German *Gründlichkeit.* At first the Jewish elite was registered and killed. Subsequently, all Jews who were not productive – women, children, elderly – were annihilated, and last came those who had been members of the work force and could now be eliminated. A system developed by *Rollkommando* Hamann proved to be extraordinarily effective, thanks to the active and diligent support of local authorities. As a first step, Jews were subjected to expropriations, forced labor, harassments and forced to wear a clearly visible sign that they were Jews. "Thus within weeks Lithuania's Jews had been effectively identified and segregated, their harm to society enunciated to the public. The concentration stage was next – the Jews would have to be corralled."[290] To that effect, a system was set up by which Jews were rounded up in towns and villages, transported to so-called collection points and from there transported further to the designated execution sites. Local civil authorities collected all the necessary demographical data and transmitted the individuals to the higher officials at the request of

289. Shneidman, N.N.: *The Three Tragic Heroes of the Vilnius Ghetto*, p. 13
290. *The Persecution and Mass Murder of Lithuanian Jews*, p. 144

the police authorities in Kaunas.[291] "In the provinces, smaller temporary Jewish ghettos were established, for example, in Telšiai, Žagarė, Raseiniai, Skuodas, Jurbarkas, Kėdainiai and other towns. In fact, there were provisional ghettos and gathering points in each and every district. Sometimes these small ghettos existed but a few weeks, at times, for months (as in Telšiai). But as a rule, these 'ghettos' were, in fact, temporary holding areas for Jews awaiting their death and were eliminated during the operations organized by [*Einzatskommando*] 3 which gained momentum rapidly after mid-August 1941."[292]

All over Lithuania, local gangs or units formed by the *Lietuvių Aktyvistų Frontas* (LAF) took things into their own hands and organized local shootings. Also here the killings went on with extraordinary speed and vengeance and with active participation of local Lithuanians.[293] Jews were herded together, driven into the woods and shot. The Genkind family, who tried to flee the onslaught, was witness to one of those killings. "When I got closer to the bank, I looked up and stiffened. On the other side of the river, a group of naked people was standing in the water. ... Before them were standing members of the Riflemen's Union, Lithuanian nationalists, dressed in old Lithuanian uniforms, their guns in position. One of the men shouted 'Fire!' and they pulled the trigger."[294] In Jurbarkas, some thirty Lithuanians participated in the extermination of approximately 1,900 Jews, and in Alytus, a town 60 kilometers south of Kaunas with a population of just over 9,000 inhabitants, some 2,200 Jews were executed in August-September, the first execution being on August 13. By mid-September not one Jew was alive in the region around Alytus, which had a total population of 123,000 inhabitants.[295] These are just a few examples; elsewhere the picture was very much the same.[296] Everywhere, the killings started after mid-August and, with some exceptions, ended by October-November 1941.[297] The horror of these killing surpasses all imagination. Not only were the Jews murdered in the most brutal, systematic manner, they were literally erased from the face of the earth. Their possessions were stolen,

291. *The Persecution and Mass Murder of Lithuanian Jews*, p. 146
292. *The Persecution and Mass Murder of Lithuanian Jews*, p. 145
293. See: Puišytė, Rūta: *Holocaust in Jurbarkas.*
294. Quoted in Tauber, Joachim in *Holocaust in Litauen*, p. 43
295. See Dieckmann, Christoph: *Alytus 1941-1944; Massenmorde in einer Kleinstadt*, and Bubnys, Arūnas: *The Holocaust in the Lithuanian Province 1941.* Bubnys mentions a total population of 7,500 persons in Alytus in 1930, of whom 2,300 were Jews.
296. A detailed account of the killings in some of the provinces can be found in Bubnys, Arūnas: *The Holocaust in the Lithuanian Province 1941*
297. For instance, in Vilkaviškis the last mass killing too place on December 1, 1941.

their personal belongings divided among the killers or destroyed; everything reminiscent of their existence ceased to exist, and all this within a period of not more than four months. The Lithuanian rural landscape changed fundamentally; all that remained of five centuries of Jewish life were a few cemeteries and synagogues that escaped destruction and at least two hundred execution sites dotting the countryside.

Also in the Eastern part of Lithuania, anti-Communist partisans, who had been fighting the Soviet authorities, played a vicious role and participated actively in many of the future killings. In towns with hardly any Lithuanian community (the region had been part of Poland until 1939 and most of the inhabitants were Polish, Jewish and Byelorussians), Lithuanian anti-Communist partisans from elsewhere assumed a leading role in the mass murder of Jews. Most of the men had been members of the Riflemen's Union before 1940, and they were now out for revenge. For instance, in the region around Pabradė and Švenčionys, many thousands were rounded up, taken to pre-selected places in the forest and murdered. On September 1, all Jews in Pabradė were forced to move to a temporary ghetto. On September 27, approximately 300 of them were taken to the shooting range Polygon further west of the town, and brutally murdered. A larger group was kept in Army barracks for periods of ten days, living under terrible circumstances, and subsequently taken to the forest west of Svenčioneliai. There they were, together with almost eight thousand other Jews from the region, mowed down with machine guns and finished off by Lithuanian partisans, while the Germans stood by watching. The shootings continued for several days; the mountains of decomposing corpses covered with only a thin layer of sand made the earth move for more than a week.[298] The *Einsatzgruppe A* reported by October 15 that 71,105 Jews had been killed in Lithuania.[299] In total, according to Karen Sutton, 133,346 Jews had been killed by December 1941.[300] A map and listing made by Franz Walter Stahlecker, commander of *Einsatzgruppe* A, indicate that 136,421 Jews were murdered in Lithuania by the end of 1941.[301]

According to Arūnas Bubnys, the most important groups in the mass murders in the provinces were Hamann's *Rollkommando*, local self-defense units, local partisan groups and police officers. "Mass shootings were

298. Van Voren, Robert: *Lost History*, p. 203
299. Gitelman, Zvi: *Bitter Legacy*, p. 266
300. Sutton, Karen: *The Massacre of the Jews in Lithuania*, p. 6. The figure comes from a report of December 1, 1941, to the Commander of the SD, in which it is reported that a total of 137,346 Jews had been killed by then, of which 3,050 were in the Minsk area. See *The Persecution and Mass Murder of Lithuanian Jews*, pp. 221-229
301. Rubenstein, Joshua et.al.: *The Unknown Black Book*, p. xl1

often led by German Gestapo officers but there were many small towns where people were murdered without direct German involvement."[302] Bubnys concluded that the Third Company of the 1st Police Battalion was particularly active in the killing of Jews. In his calculations, he comes to no less than 11,598 Jews killed by this unit.[303] Usually, the Germans did the organizational part of the "job," and left the dirty work to the Lithuanians. "The so-called flying squad would leave for the operation only after all the preparatory work had been completed: the Jews condemned to death were pushed into one place, guarded by local police and 'partisans,' with a more abandoned place selected for their execution (mostly forests or distant fields), where a pit was dug. As a rule, the assigned soldiers or volunteers of the 3rd Company would go on such missions in the province. Several Gestapo officers would also come by motorcar to the planned place of massacre. The December 1, 1941, report by K[arl] Jäger specified a long list of places where allegedly Hamann's platoon jointly with Lithuanian 'partisans' performed executions. Archival documents allow ascertaining that participation of the soldiers of the 1st Police Battalion did not take place in all the places specified in K. Jäger's report (particularly those in the province). It can only be guessed that in quite a few places in Lithuania the Jewish were killed by the units of local police and 'partisans' without Hamann's flying squad [*Rollkommando*] taking part."[304] The last mass murders in the provinces took place in Lazdijai (November 3, 1941) and Vilkaviškis (November 15, 1941)

As the reports of *Einsatzgruppe A* testify, the rapid annihilation of the Jews of Lithuania was only made possible because of the eager participation of the local population. In some cases, sheer opportunism guided local officials. In Jurbarkas, for instance, the mayor of the town, Jurgis Gepneris, showed himself to be a perfect opportunist. While having been in charge of the local *stolovaya* [public kitchen] during the Soviet occupation and a supporter of the Communists, he then turned around and served the Germans faithfully, delivering his Jewish citizens into their hands. Of the 4,400 inhabitants of Jurbarkas, 1,900 were Jews and only a few individu-

302. Arūnas Bubnys in Nikžentaitis, Alvydas: *The Vanished World of Lithuanian Jews*, p. 213

303. According to his data, this company took part in the killings in Alytus, Ariogala, Babtai, Butrimonys, Garliava, Jieznas, Krakės, Lazdijai, Pasvalys, Petrašiūniai, Rumšiškės, Seirijai, Simnas, Vilkija. Possibly the same company was also involved in killings elsewhere in Lithuania. See Bubnys, Arūnas: *Lithuanian Police Battalions and the Holocaust (1941-1943)*, p. 13

304. Bubnys, Arūnas: *Lithuanian Police Battalions and the Holocaust (1941-1943)*, p. 13. Bubnys concludes that the 3rd Company of the 1st battalion was responsible for 35,000-60,000 Jewish deaths during the second half of 1941.

als would eventually survive the massacres. Gepneris' opportunism went so far that he later changed his name to Höpfner to look more German.[305]

The German invasion found the Russians militarily unprepared and the civilian population disoriented and demoralized. Exploiting the superstitious anti-Semitic prejudices of the local population, their hatred of the Soviets and, last but not least, the uncertainty and anxiety about their own future, the Germans masterfully utilized the Lithuanians' passive and active compliance and collaboration in their drive to round up and kill the Jews. Of the 23,000 Jews that tried to flee the country with the Soviets, 8,000 were killed along the way.[306] Many of them were, tragically enough, Jews that had been turned away at the border with the Soviet Union, as only people who could prove they were members of the Communist party were allowed to cross.[307] By the time the Soviets changed that policy, the country had already been occupied fully by the Germans.[308]

Karl Jäger, Commander of *Einzatskommando 3* in Vilnius, reported on December 3, 1941, that "the goal to clear Lithuania of Jews was rendered feasible because of a mobile unit under the command of SS *Obersturmbannführer* Joachim Hamann, who adopted my goal without reservation and successfully ensured the cooperation of Lithuanian partisans and civilian institutions concerning this matter…"[309]

As noted earlier, the activities of these Lithuanian auxiliaries were so in tune with German plans that by the end of July 1941, twenty local police battalions with an average membership of some 400 men were formed. Under the supervision of Franz Lechthaler, commander of the 11th Battalion of the German reserve police, about 8,400 Lithuanian volunteers

305. *The Persecution and Mass Murder of Lithuanian Jews*, p. 158
306. See also Szur, Grigori: *De Joden van Wilno*, p. 41. The data are somewhat conflicting. According to Rimantas Zizas, member of the International Commission for the Evaluation of the Crimes of the Nazi and Soviet Occupation Regimes in Lithuania, some 8,000 Jews succeeded in fleeing the country. Yitzhak Arad estimates are lower, 4-6,000, while the historian Dov Levin estimates some 15,000 managed to flee, which corresponds with the figures mentioned in the text. See *The Persecution and Mass Murder of Jews*, p. 104
307. One of such situations is described by Herman Kruk in his *The Last Days of the Jerusalem of Lithuania*, p. 59, when a group of 3,000 Jews was deceived by the NKVD and made to get off the train, which then suddenly continued in the direction of the Soviet Union with only Soviet Jews on board, leaving the whole group of 3,000 refugees stranded. Also Jews trying to flee Latvia who were not members of the Communist Party were turned back. See Rislakiki, Jukka: *The Case for Latvia*, p. 111
308. Sutton, Karen: *The Massacre of the Jews of Lithuania*, p. 121
309. Gitelman, Zvi: *Bitter Legacy*, p. 268

were charged with murdering the local Jews. As we saw, the 12th Police Battalion was involved in killings in the Minsk-Baranoviche area in October 1941, where they excelled in barbarity.[310] In the end of 1941, Lithuanian police battalions were reported to have participated in *Aktionen* in the Byelorussian towns of Slonim and Novogrodek.[311] According to a German document of July 1942, a total of nine Lithuanian Police Battalions were active outside of the country at that time, with a total strength of 4,500 persons. In the summer of 1942, the killings resumed in Byelorussia and, again, Lithuanians were involved, in, among others, Slonim, where the whole Jewish quarter was burnt down and some 12,000 Jews either perished in the fire or were shot when trying to escape the flames.[312] Later, Lithuanian battalions performed duties as guards in Ukraine at the building site of a road where Jews were used as forced laborers and in the concentration camp, Majdanek. One unit also took part in the destruction of the Warsaw Ghetto.[313]

Conflicts of conscience

However, not all of the Lithuanian police battalion members were ready to participate in the mass murder. According to Bubnys, "Before the mass killings started, the soldiers of the TDA Battalion had never taken part in operations of a similar kind. Being unable to confront the Nazis openly, a big part of them tried to secure dismissal from office or escape participation in the killings in other ways. Between July 5-11, 1941, 117 soldiers were dismissed from service in the battalion. (…) The Commander of the 1st Company of the TDA Battalion, Capt. Bronius Kirkila, did not withstand cruelties that he experienced [as a witness or perpetrator] and committed suicide on July 12, 1941."[314] Kazys Izdelevičius, a policeman who participated in the mass murder of Jewish men in the Rainiai forest, later testified: "During the killings, I was drunk (before the killings we

310. see pages 84-85, describing the killings in Slutsk
311. In Slonim, the first Aktion took place on July 17, 1941, and left 1,200 Jews dead. The second Aktion of November 13, 1941, saw the murder of 9,400 Jews. On June 29, 1942, a third Aktion resulted in 12,000 Jews killed. The fourth, killing the remaining 350, was on September 21, 1942.
312. See Van Voren, Robert: *Cold War in Psychiatry*, p. 25-26 and Martin Dean in Nikžentaitis, Alvydas: *The Vanished World of Lithuanian Jews*, p. 289
313. For instance, the 2nd Police Battalion from Kaunas participated in killings in Byelorussia together with the 11th German Reserve Police Battalion, during which some 17,000 Jews were murdered. Another Police Battalion was sent to Majdanek, where it guarded the camp. See Gitelman, Zvi: *Bitter Legacy*, p. 101
314. Bubnys, Arūnas: *Lithuanian Police Battalions and the Holocaust (1941-1943)*, p. 9

were always offered alcohol). That is why I was brave enough to commit that bloody crime. When the intoxication left me, usually after the murder of ten-twelve groups consisting of thirty-forty people each, I felt like I wanted to vomit. I had to leave the line of the killers. (...) I cannot give you a clear answer why I took part in the killings of the Jewish people. The Germans gave me an order and I shot them."[315]

Not only did Lithuanians have difficulty in completing their tasks; there were also German officers who could not bear the horrors they witnessed or were forced to commit. The same Izdelevičius testified: "There were some Germans among the perpetrators, all from the SS and lower ranking officers. A few were present through the shootings. Others would try to shoot and leave the site..."[316] A member of *Sonderkommando 6* wrote: "As a result of the considerable psychological pressures, there were numerous men who were no longer capable of conducting executions and who, thus, had to be replaced by other men. On the other hand, there were some who could not get enough of them and often reported to those executions voluntarily."[317] Dr. Klaus Hornig was a police officer who, in 1941, was added to police battalion 306 in Lublin, Poland and received orders to kill Jews and Party commissars of the Red Army. He refused the order, leading to his own arrest, and wrote a letter to the editor in 1979 stating: "My neighbors, police battalion 309, were for several weeks involved in the killing of Jewish families, even with unborn children; they were shot with machine guns like grain in a cornfield. The policemen were, after having returned from their *Aktion* to the barracks of Zamość, demoralized to such an extent that they could not be returned home in that state. Sensitive men were sitting in the barracks having crying outbursts, while less sensitive ones went into town, got drunk with vodka, had knife fights and abused Polish women and girls. As a result, the leader of the Order Police in Krakow, police General Winkler, ordered these men sent on a four week holiday in the spas of Krynica and Zakopane."[318] Another member of one of the *Einsatzgruppen* testified later: "When we were about to fire, a boy [of seven or eight years old] looked at me seeking help. At that moment, I felt as if I were to kill my own child. Confused as I was, I shot only some

315. Quoted in Nikžentaitis, Alvydas: *The Vanished World of Lithuanian Jews*, p. 236
316. Quoted in Nikžentaitis, Alvydas: *The Vanished World of Lithuanian Jews*, p. 236
317. Klee, Ernst: *The Good Old Days*, p. 60
318. Hornig, Klaus: *Man konnte auch nein sagen.* AZ Leserforum, March 16, 1979. Klaus Hornig refused to participate by referring to article 47 of the Military Penal Code, which stipulated that an order could be refused if it went against one's conscience. He was arrested on order of SS Chief Heinrich Himmler and eventually wound up in concentration camp Buchenwald.

time after we got the order to fire. The shot missed its target. Then I had a nervous breakdown and had to be relieved immediately from the execution command... As a result of the breakdown, I became grey within a couple of months."[319]

Even the infamous *Standartenführer* Karl Jäger, the author of the cold, businesslike "Jäger report" summing up the killings in Lithuania that led to the extermination of 137,000 persons, is reported to have suffered from nightmares. A colleague SS officer of Jäger, Heinz Jost, reported in 1959 that Jäger was an old simple guy who seemed hard on the outside but was soft within and that during an evening talk, Jäger had confided to him that "he could not go to sleep, that he only saw women and dying children, that he even had visions, and that he couldn't go home anymore because he himself had children and grandchildren. He was a lost man. He could not be helped by a visit to a sanatorium or a holiday because he could not longer find peace."[320] In another testimony, the same Jost reported that Jäger had said he couldn't sleep because of the executions in which he took part. He was constantly haunted by nightmares, couldn't face his wife with a clear conscience and would no longer be able to hold his grandchildren on his lap.[321] In the end, Jäger was arrested in 1959 and committed suicide during the pre-trail investigations; he was 73 years old.

Also *Reichsführer SS* Heinrich Himmler noted the difficulty of the task for the executioners. He himself had apparently been quite shaken when attending a mass execution in Minsk on August 15, 1941, together with General Erich von dem Bach-Zalewski. Himmler's condition deteriorated visibly as the executions went on. He apparently fainted when blood landed on his face during one execution.[322] Von dem Back told Himmler: "Look at the eyes of the men in this *Kommando*, how deeply shaken they are! These men are finished for the rest of their lives. What kind of followers are we training here? Either neurotics or savages!"[323]

319. Kühne, Thomas: *Belonging and Genocide*, p. 58
320. Wette, Wolfram in *Holocaust in Litauen*, p. 85
321. Wette, Wolfram in *Holocaust in Litauen*, p. 86
322. Earl, Hilary: *The Nuremburg SS-Einsatztgruppen Trial*, pp. 6-7. Other sources say he almost fainted, e.g. Höhne, Hans: *The Order of the Death's Head*, p. 336. Wolff, the head of his personal staff, commented: "Good for him to see what he expects people to do."
323. Kühne, Thomas: *Belonging and Genocide*, p. 84, and Christopher Browning in Cesarani, David: *The Final Solution*, p. 142. Bach-Zalewski himself could not stand the psychological stress and was eventually hospitalized. According to Hans Höhne, he spent the nights screaming because of hallucinations. His treating physicians told Himmler that "he is suffering particularly from hal-

The task to kill the enemies of the Reich who infected the purity of the German race, was, in the view of Himmler and his collaborators, a holy duty to Germany that had to be performed with toughness and determination. Yet at the same time, understanding the difficulty of shooting civilians *en masse*, particularly women and children, a fair degree of leniency was allowed towards those who either refused to participate or discontinued their involvement out of moral qualms or just couldn't stand facing the horrors. In a speech to his generals in October 1943, he explained that it needed to be done as a service to the country: "Most of you here know what it means when 100 corpses lie next to each other, when 500 lie there or 1,000 are lined up. To have endured this and, at the same time, to have remained a decent person – with exceptions due to human weaknesses – has made us hard. This is a page of honor in our history which has never been and never will be put in writing."[324] For Himmler, the emotional stress was one of the driving factors to find other and less "personal" means of extermination, which eventually led to the gas vans and, later, the gas chambers.

Ghettoization

It is estimated that 80% of the Lithuanian Jews were killed before the end of 1941, within six months after the German invasion. The surviving 43,000 Jews were concentrated in the Vilnius, Kaunas, Šiauliai and Švenčionys ghettos and forced to work for the benefit of German military industry.[325] Living conditions were miserable, with severe food shortages, outbreaks of disease, and overcrowding.

A great deal has been written about the Vilnius and Kaunas ghettos and there are several diaries that shed a very piercing light on the daily struggle to survive in both. Many of the stories are shocking, heart rendering and surpass all imagination. They are testimonies of persecution, arbitrariness, brutal and systematic murder, but also of indomitable spirits, human inventiveness and the desire to survive even the worst ordeals.[326]

lucinations connected with the shootings of Jews which he himself carried out..." See Höhne, Hans: *The Order of the Death's Head*, p. 334

324. Kühne, Thomas: *Belonging and Genocide*, p. 4

325. In Vilnius, about 20,000 Jews remained alive; in Kaunas, 17,500; in Šiauliai, 5,000-5,500; and in Švenčionys, 500. See Nikžentaitis, Alvydas: *The Vanished World of Lithuanian Jews*, p. 187

326. Among the best diaries are those of Herman Kruk: *The Last Days of the Jerusalem of Lithuania*, Yale University Press, 2002; Harry Gordon: *The Shadow of Death; The Holocaust in Lithuania*, University of Kentucky Press, 1992; Avraham Tory: *Surviving the Holocaust; The Kovno Ghetto Diary*. Harvard University Press, 1990; Noah Shneidman: *Jerusalem of Lithuania; The Rise and Fall of Jewish Vilnius*. Mosaic Press, 1998.

Kaunas

In Kaunas, the Germans concentrated some 29,000 Jews who survived the initial pogroms in a ghetto established in the district of Vilijampolė (Slabodka) between July and August 15, 1941. It was an area of small wooden and primitive houses with no running water, which had been cleared of its mainly Jewish population during the June pogroms by Lithuanian activists when thousands of Jews had been killed. "The center of Vilijampolė is dilapidated and dirty. The streets and yards are in an unsanitary condition, because there are no clinics, no bathing facilities, no disinfection institutions, and no disinfectants available there."[327] The ghetto had two parts, the "small" and "large" ghetto, separated by Paneriai Street and connected by a small wooden bridge over the street. Each ghetto was enclosed by barbed wire and closely guarded. Both ghettos were overcrowded, with each person allocated less than 1.5 square meters of living space. The Germans continually reduced the ghetto's size, forcing Jews to relocate several times. The small ghetto was destroyed on October 4, 1941, and almost all of its inhabitants were killed at the Ninth Fort. Later that same month, on October 29, 1941, the Germans staged the "*Grosse Action,*" during which they shot 9,200 Jews at the Ninth Fort in one single day.

The ghetto in Kaunas provided forced labor for the German military. Jews were employed primarily as forced laborers at various sites outside the ghetto, especially in the construction of a military airbase in Aleksotas. The *Ältestenrat* (Council of Elderly) or Jewish Council, headed by Dr. Elchanan Elkes, also created several workshops inside the ghetto for those women, children, and elderly who could not participate in the labor brigades.[328] Eventually, these workshops employed almost 6,500 people.

327. Tory, Avraham: *Surviving the Holocaust*, p. 30

328. Elchanan Elkes is considered one of most distinguished leaders of Jewish ghettos in Eastern Europe. Elchanan Elkes, the son of a rabbi, was born in 1879 in Kalvarija. In part self-educated, he also received an extensive traditional Jewish education. He completed his medical studies in Königsberg (now Kaliningrad) and received his medical degree in neurology and other specialties in 1903. For seven years, he practiced as a doctor in the village of Berezino in Byelorussia. During the First World War, Elkes served as a physician in the Russian Army and was awarded a number of decorations. From 1923, he was head of the department of internal medicine in the Bikkur Holim Jewish hospital in Kovno, as well as practicing privately. For eighteen years, he served as physician to the German embassy in Kovno, as well as being the personal physician to the German ambassador to Lithuania.

When on August 5 in the ghetto of Kaunas an "*Ältestenrat*" had to be formed, nobody wanted to accept the position, including Elkes. An impassioned appeal was made to him by Rabbi Yakov Moshe Shmukler: "The Jew-

The council hoped the Germans would not kill Jews who were producing for the army.

Especially during its first year of existence, the ghetto was subject to constant *razzias* and *Aktionen*. For instance, on September 26, 1941 shortly after Elchanan Elkes had taken office, he had a confrontation with Willy Koslovski, a member of the Gestapo. Koslovski, who lived opposite the ghetto, claimed that shots had been fired at his residence the night before. He demanded that 500 Jews be surrendered to him to be shot. Elkes replied that, among Jews, it was forbidden to deliver people for execution. Even if the entire community were threatened, they should all choose death rather than deliver even one of their congregation. If Elkes would not deliver 500 people, Koslovski threatened, he would take more than that number. Elkes replied: "It may cost [the lives of] all 45,000 Jews in the ghetto, but I shall not deliver any Jews to you to be shot." Half an hour later, the Germans cordoned off a section of the ghetto and 1,608 Jews were rounded up and shot at Fort IV in the so-called "*Koslovski Aktion.*"[329]

It was the beginning of almost daily harassments and murders that culminated in the *Grosse Aktion* on October 29, 1941. During this *Aktion* the whole Kaunas ghetto population was forced to gather on Demokratų Square in the ghetto in order to participate in a selection between those who still had the chance to live and those who were condemned to die. "The ghetto fence was surrounded by machine guns and a heavy detachment of heavy armed German policemen, commanded by Captain Tornbaum. He had also at his disposal battalions of armed Lithuanian

ish community of Kovno stands on the brink of destruction. Our daughters are being raped, and our sons executed. Fellow Jews! The German oppressor demands that we appoint an *Oberjude*, but what we need is a faithful community leader. In this historic hour, the most appropriate candidate among us is Dr Elkes. Therefore we appeal to you, Dr Elkes: In the eyes of the German criminals you will fill the position of Oberjude, but to us you will be community leader... And now we beg you: Assume, without fear, the position as our leader. With extreme reluctance and despite his failing health, Elkes agreed to become chairman, one of the few Judenrat leaders to be elected by his peers, rather than appointed by the Nazis. "If this be the situation and you think that it is my duty to accept the post, then I shall do so," he said. It was to be the final meeting of the Jewish community in Kovno.

On 8 July 1944, the ghetto was liquidated and Elkes himself was sent via Stettin to Landsberg, one of the Kaufering complexes of Dachau sub-camps. Although very ill himself, he was still dedicated to healing and was placed in charge of the Lazarett, the camp "hospital." He died there on October 17, 1944, after a hunger strike.

329. Tory, Avraham: *Surviving the Holocaust*, pp. 38-39

partisans. A crowd of curious Lithuanian spectators had gathered on the hills overlooking the ghetto. They followed the events taking place in the square with great interest, not devoid of delight, and did not leave for many hours. [330] In the end some 9,200 Jews were selected.[331] "The procession… proceeding from the small ghetto to the Ninth Fort, lasted from dawn until noon. Elderly people and those who were sick collapsed by the roadside and died. Warning shots were fired incessantly, all along the way, and around the large ghetto. Thousands of curious Lithuanians flocked to both sides of the road to watch the spectacle until the last victims were swallowed up by the Ninth Fort. In the Fort, the wretched people were immediately set upon by the Lithuanian killers who stripped them of all valuable articles – gold rings, earrings, bracelets. They forced them to strip naked, pushed them into pits, which had been prepared in advance, and fired into each pit with machine guns, which had been positioned there in advance. The murderers did not have time to shoot everybody in one batch before the next batch of Jews arrived. They were accorded the same treatment as those who had preceded them. They were pushed into the pit on top of the dead and dying, as well as those still alive from the previous group. So it continued, batch after batch, until the 10,000 men, women and children had been butchered. Villagers living in the vicinity of the fort told stories of the horrors they had seen from a distance and of the heart rendering cries that emanated from the fort and troubled their waking hours day and night."[332]

Life for children in the ghetto was particularly harsh and, as they were non-productive elements, they were in constant danger. When education was banned in 1942, an underground school was established in defiance of the ban. Almost all of the children, approximately 2,500, were removed and killed during the *"Kinder Aktion"* of March 27-28, 1944. From 1942, births were not permitted in the ghetto and pregnant women faced death. Still, a number of babies were successfully smuggled out of the ghetto to willing Lithuanian foster mothers and survived the war.

Vilnius

In Vilnius, the formation of the ghetto started with an event that later became known as "The Great Provocation." The goal was to have a pretext to clear the mostly poor inhabitants of the Jewish quarter in the Vilnius Old Town and by liquidating them make room for the rest of the - mostly afflu-

330. Tory, Avraham: *Surviving the Holocaust*, p. 50
331. Regularly the number of 10,000 victims is mentioned, but most reliable sources keep the number at 9,200 victims.
332. Tory, Avraham: *Surviving the Holocaust*, p. 58

ent - Jewish residents in the ghetto. On August 31, two Lithuanians, who had broken into an apartment belonging to Jews, shot at German soldiers in civilian clothes who were standing in front of a cinema on the corner of Stiklių and Didžioji streets. The Lithuanians fled the apartment, then returned with waiting German soldiers, seized two Jews, accused them of firing on the German soldiers, beat them and shot them on the spot. The local militia subsequently ransacked Stiklių and Mėsinių streets and Jews were beaten up. At night, in "retaliation," the Nazis drove all Jews out of the neighborhood. The next day the women and children on remaining streets were seized, as well as the men who were at work. All were first taken to Lukiškės Prison and from there sent to the Paneriai forest, where they were killed. During this "Great Provocation," up to 5,000 people were murdered, including ten members of the *Judenrat*.[333]

On September 6 and 7, 1941, the Nazis herded the remaining Jews into the parameters of two ghettos. Six thousand of them were taken to Lukiškės Prison and, from there, to Paneriai[334] for extermination. During this action, another 3,334 Jews were killed.[335] Converts, "half-Jews" and spouses of Jews were also forced into the ghetto. The move to the ghetto was carried out under the Lithuanian police guards and was extremely hurried and difficult, and Jews were not allowed to use transportation. They could take only what they were physically able to carry. The ghetto area was split into two with a non-ghetto corridor running down Vokiečiu Street. This made it easier for the Nazis to control what the victims knew of their fate beforehand, facilitating the Nazis' goal of total extermination.

Conditions in the ghetto were extremely poor. The area was crowded, with unsanitary conditions, leading to disease and daily death. The ghetto became well known because of its distinguished medical tradition that was maintained during the Ghetto years. The first director of the Jewish hospital was Jacob Gens, a former Lithuanian officer who, when appointed the Chief of the Ghetto, ran the hospital like a military operation. In particular, thanks to his extraordinary efforts the Vilnius Ghetto had no major epidemics and relatively few deaths due to disease.

By the end of October 1941, the Nazis had murdered all the 6,500-7,500 inhabitants of the smaller second ghetto north of Vokiečiu Street.[336] They declared that from that point on only 12,000 Jews would remain in the larger ghetto to serve the needs of the German military and economy. In

333. Arad, Yitzhak: *The Holocaust in the Soviet Union*, p. 145
334. Other names for the forest are Ponar, Ponary
335. Arad, Yitzhak: *The Holocaust in the Soviet Union*, p. 145
336. Arad, Yitzhak: *The Holocaust in the Soviet Union*, p. 146

reality, 20,000 remained in all. The Germans systematically carried out *Aktionen* to reduce the number of sick and elderly and to meet quotas on the total of the population allowed. These *Aktionen* were conducted on a regular basis until January 1942, after which the "quiet period" started.

The center of cultural life in the ghetto was the Mefitze Haskole Library, which was called the "House of Culture." It contained a library of 45,000 books, a reading hall, an archive, a statistical bureau, a room for scientific work, a museum, a book kiosk, a post office, and a sports ground. Groups, such as the Literary and Artistic Union and the *Brit Ivrit* Union, organized events commemorating Yiddish and Hebrew authors and put on plays in these languages. The popular Yiddish magazine, *Folksgezunt,* was continued in the ghetto and its essays were presented in public lectures.

The Vilna Ghetto was well known for its theatrical productions. Jacob Gens, as head of the ghetto, was given the responsibility for the starting this theatre. Performances included poetry by Jewish authors, dramatizations of short stories, and new work by the young ghetto people. The Ghetto Theatre was a great source of revenue and had a calming effect on the public. By mid-January 1943, a total of 111 performances had been given and a total of 34,804 tickets were sold. The theatre was renovated to accommodate a bigger audience and create a better-looking environment. The last theatrical production, *The Flood*, was produced by the Swedish dramatist Henning Berger and opened in the summer of 1943, in the last week of this Ghetto's existence. This play, set in an American saloon during a flood, featured a group of people who banded together during a time of danger and need.

Other cities

In Šiauliai, over 2000 Jews were killed before the remaining Jews were herded in two ghettos, one in the Kafkaz area of the city and the other in the Trakų neighborhood, about 500 meters away. About 5,500 Jews were forced to live in an area of about 8000 square meters of living space. The guards of the ghetto perimeter were Lithuanians. Immediately following the establishment of the ghetto, a series of new killings started. First 47 children of the Jewish orphanage as well as their teacher were killed, then 150 elderly and sick were taken away, then 50 members of the intelligentsia were shot, etc. etc. Most of them were driven to the prepared pits in the forest and killed there.

The majority of the Jews in the ghetto, about 750 people, were employed in the Frenkel Leather Factory. Jews also worked at the local airport widening the landing strips, like the Jews of the Kaunas ghetto (in Aleksotas), and others worked in various workshops founded by the Ghetto administration. Part of the income was used to establish the hospital in the Kafkaz Ghetto area.

Between January 1942 and September 1943, the Šiauliai ghetto when through a sort of "quiet period," just like the ghettos in Kaunas and Vilnius. There were occasional incidents that ended in murder but, under the circumstances, it was quiet and this was exploited by the residents for cultural and educational purposes.

The fourth main ghetto, in Švenčionys, together with smaller ghettos in Oshmiana, Mihalishki and Soly, held approximately 7,000 Jews.

Jewish resistance

Both the Vilnius and the Kaunas ghettos had armed resistance units. In Vilnius, the *Fareynikte Partizaner Organizatsye* (United Partisan Organization, FPO) was formed on January 20, 1942. The motto "We will not go like sheep to the slaughter" came from one of its leaders, Abba Kovner. It was one of the first resistance organizations established in the Nazi ghettos during World War II. The FPO represented the full spectrum of political persuasions and parties in Jewish life. It was led by Yitzhak Wittenberg, Josef Glazman, and Abba Kovner. The goals of the FPO were to establish a means of self-defense for the ghetto population, to sabotage German industrial and military activities and to join the partisan and Red Army's fight against the Nazis.

In the early summer of 1943, the Germans caught a member of the Communist underground who revealed some contacts under torture. The *Judenrat*, in response to German threats, tried to turn Yitzhak Wittenberg, the head of the FPO, over to the Gestapo. The FPO was able to rescue him after he was seized in the apartment of Jacob Gens in a fight with Jewish ghetto police. Gens faced a dilemma: if he didn't hand over Wittenberg, the ghetto faced German retaliation. On the other hand, handing over resistance leader to the Germans would not go down well in history. In the end, pragmatism reigned, and Gens managed to turn the majority of the population against the resistance members, claiming they were provoking the Nazis and asking rhetorically whether it was worth sacrificing tens of thousands for the sake of one man. Ghetto inhabitants assembled and demanded the FPO give Wittenberg up. Ultimately, Wittenberg himself made the decision to submit to the Nazi demands. He was taken to Gestapo headquarters in Vilnius and was reportedly found dead in his cell the next morning.[337] Most people believed he had committed suicide.

337. Sutton, Karen: *The Massacre of the Jews of Lithuania*, p. 181

Rumor had it that Gens slipped him a cyanide pill in their final meeting. In the end, however, Wittenberg's heroic decision gave the ghetto only little respite.

The FPO was thoroughly demoralized by the chain of events and began to pursue a policy of sending young people out to the forest to join the Jewish partisans. This was controversial as well because the Nazis attempted to kill all family members of people who had joined the partisans. In the Vilna ghetto, a "family" often included non-relations who registered as a member of a family in order to receive housing and a pitiful food ration. Ghetto chief Jacob Gens played a double role in this; on one hand, not intervening when young Jews left for the forest, yet, on the other hand, opposing it because in his view it would result in the immediate liquidation of the ghetto if the Germans found out. In total, some 1,600 Jews managed to escape to the forest. Some 850 joined Soviet-Lithuanian brigades (the largest contingents belonging to those of Vilnius – 400 Jews – and Kaunas – 200 Jews). However, in many cases joining the partisan movement proved to be a disappointment. Being nationalist-oriented, they were not trusted by the Communist movement and were forced to give up their Jewish orientation; the Lithuanian nationalist partisans were, on the whole, fiercely anti-Semitic and did not want to have Jews in their midst. Some stayed separate, living independently in the forest, yet when discovered by Lithuanians in the area, they were betrayed and killed, either by Germans or Lithuanian auxiliary forces.[338]

When the Nazis came to liquidate the Vilnius ghetto in 1943, ten weeks after Wittenberg had surrendered to the Germans, Jacob Gens again faced with an impossible dilemma, decided to take control of the liquidation in order to keep the Nazi forces out of the ghetto and away from a partisan ambush. The result was, however, that he helped fill the quota of Jews to be exterminated, which also included those who could have participated in a fight for survival but were not necessarily part of the resistance.

Also in Kaunas, several Jewish resistance groups existed. The resistance had secret training areas in the ghetto, and managed to establish contact with Soviet partisans in the forests around the city. In 1943, the General Jewish Fighting Organization (*Yidishe Algemeyne Kamfs Organizatsye*) was established, uniting the major resistance groups in the ghetto. Under this organization's direction, some 300 ghetto fighters escaped from the ghetto to join Jewish partisan groups. Some 70 of them died in action. The *Judenrat* actively supported the underground. Also a number of the ghetto's Jewish police participated in resistance activities and 34 members

338. Sutton, Karen: *The Massacre of the Jews of Lithuania*, pp. 182-183

were executed by the Germans for refusing to reveal specially constructed hiding places used by Jews in the ghetto.

Final liquidation

In the autumn of 1943, the SS assumed control of the Kaunas ghetto and converted it into *Konzentrationslager Kauen*, the Kovno concentration camp. The role of the *Judenrat* was drastically curtailed. The Nazis dispersed more than 3,500 Jews to sub-camps where strict discipline governed. On October 26, 1943, the SS deported more than 2,700 people from the main camp. The SS sent those deemed fit to work to Vaivara concentration camp in Estonia, and deported surviving children and the elderly to Auschwitz, where they were exterminated.

On July 8, 1944, the Germans evacuated *KZ Kauen*, deporting most of the remaining Jews to the Dachau concentration camp in Germany or to the Stutthof camp near Danzig (Gdansk) on the Baltic coast. Three weeks before the Soviet army arrived in Kaunas, the Germans razed the ghetto to the ground with grenades and dynamite. Some 2,000 survivors burned to death or were shot while trying to escape the burning ghetto. The Red Army occupied Kaunas on August 1, 1944. Of Kaunas' few Jewish survivors, 500 had survived in forests or in a single bunker that had escaped detection during the final liquidation.

The secret archives organized by the ghetto inhabitants documenting what happened also survived. This had been one of Elkes' first acts as chairman: to institute the creation of an archive. Over the next three years, a wealth of material was secretly accumulated, including artist's illustrations, photographs, minutes of meetings, diaries, poems, historical records of the entire ghetto as well as individual departments, and much more. A great deal of the archive was destroyed with the liquidation of the ghetto, but what remains provides an extraordinary record of the gradual extinction of what had been a vital Jewish spiritual and cultural center.

At the end of the summer of 1943, also in Vilnius, the "quiet period" came to an end. Between August 6 and September 5, over 7,000 Jews were deported to Estonia by order of Heinrich Himmler. Under the supervision of *Oberscharführer* Bruno Kittel, the ghetto was "liquidated" between September 23rd and 24th, 1943, and the majority of the Jewish population were sent to the Vaivara concentration camp in Estonia, killed in the forest of Paneriai, or sent to the death camps in German-occupied Poland.

A small remnant of Jews remained after the liquidation of the Vilnius Ghetto, primarily at the Kailis slave labor camp and at the HKP (*Heeres-*

kraftpark, an outfit involved in repairing German military automobiles) slave labor camp. The HKP camp was commanded by Wehrmacht Major Karl Plagge, who, with the help of some of his men, managed to shield many of his workers from being sent to Paneriai for extermination. One of the worst events here was the so-called *Kinder Aktion* carried out by the SS on March 27, 1944, during which virtually all 250 the children were hauled away and murdered. Only several of them, including the later well-known artist Samuel Bak, survived by hiding in *malinas*, hideouts that had been prepared in advance.[339] On July 1, 1944, Major Plagge informed the camp inmates that an "evacuation" was being planned. The message was understood and, knowing that the evacuation meant their extermination, many people tried to escape or hide in the *malinas.*[340] In the end, some two hundred and fifty Jews at HKP survived the war. They represent the single largest group of Jewish survivors of the Holocaust in Vilnius.

In September 1943, analogue with the Kaunas ghetto, the Šiauliai ghetto became a concentration camp. The Kafkaz ghetto was liquidated, five external camps were erected and the inmates were dispersed among the various camps. In November 1943, 574 children, 191 older people, 26 invalids and 4 women were taken away and killed. A similar action took place in the outlying camps with the same results.

At the beginning of July 1944, all of the Jews were returned from the outlying camps to the ghetto and were not allowed to work anymore. On July 25, 1944, the Ghetto inmates were transported to the concentration camp in Stutthof and, from there, to other camps in Poland and Western Germany. Their fate was similar to the fate of the Jews of Kaunas.

Finally, the 7,000 Jews from the Švenčionys ghetto and the smaller ghettos in Oshmiana, Mihalishki and Soly were murdered in what later became known as the "*Kaunas train Aktion.*" The impression was created that all would be transferred to the ghettos in Kaunas and Vilnius. Initially, 1,250 selected Jews were sent to Vilnius and arrived without problems. A further 1,500 were sent from the Oshmiana ghetto to labor camps in the Vilnius region. Hence, it seemed logical that the further transports would also reach their destination. However, it was a trap: the trains bypassed Vilnius and went straight to Paneriai, where the 4,000 passengers were killed by the 1st Lithuanian Police Battalion led by Captain Juozas Truskauskas.[341]

339. See Bak, Samuel: *Painted in Words*. Indiana University Press, 2001
340. See *The HKP Jewish Labor Camp*, p. 25
341. Arad, Yitzhak: *The Holocaust in the Soviet Union*, pp. 315-317

Lithuanian support to Jews

Of course, there were also Lithuanians who sided with the Jews, and who endangered their own lives trying to save them from extermination. A relatively large number of Lithuanians (approximately 800) was honored with the title of "Righteous Among Nations" by Yad Vashem in Israel. This fact is often used as an argument to show that many Lithuanians did not participate in the Holocaust and, instead, tried to save their compatriots. Indeed, between the stories of horror and betrayal, there are stories of extraordinary courage in helping Jews stay out of the hands of the Germans and their Lithuanian collaborators and some of these Lithuanians were killed as punishment. In Jurbarkas, about a dozen people actively helped Jews, and at least one of them paid for this with his life.[342]

In total, according to the Jewish museum in Vilnius, some 3,000 Lithuanians helped the Jews in one way or another.[343] Some of the stories are published in the book "*Whoever Saved One Life...*", published in 2002 by the Genocide and Resistance Research Center of Lithuania. The book also contains the names of all the Lithuanian "Righteous among Nations" that were known at the time of the publication. The book contains interesting information yet, at the same time, it is written in the same defensive style of many Lithuanian publications and statements on the matter, clearly focused on trying to diminish Lithuanian collaboration and compliance by evoking the image of a multitude of brave Lithuanians saving Jews from their fate.[344] This defensive, self-righteous attitude is unfortunate, because it blurs the true picture of what happened and also makes an "objective" analysis of the events as they unfolded in the country impossible. All data show that these Jew-rescuers were the exception (like in many if not most other countries in Europe, one might add) and that the overwhelming majority of the population excelled in silence and indifference.

In fact, there is also virtually no evidence of any public protest on the part of the Lithuanians against the killings of the Jews.[345] And there is also no

342. See: Puišytė, Rūta: *Holocaust in Jurbarkas*
343. Dieckmann, Christoph in *Holocaust in Litauen*, p. 73
344. Kuodytė, Dalia and Stankevičius: *Whoever Saves One Life; The Efforts to Save Jews in Lithuania between 1941 and 1944.* Garnelis, Vilnius, 2002
345. Only a few cases have been recorded. For instance the priest of Varėna, Jonas Gylys, openly expressed his protest against the killings. On the eve of the massacre in that town, he asked the Chief of Varėna Police to let him visit the Jews that had been herded together in the synagogue. Although the Chief of Police refused, he still came to the synagogue and comforted and consoled the condemned. He was driven away by police. After the execution of the Jews, Gylys strongly condemned the killing from the pulpit on September 14,

evidence that Lithuanians tried to help the Jews in an organized fashion. In Poland, a country with rampant anti-Semitism, some attempts were made by the Polish resistance to help the Jews. The Main Welfare Council (*Naczelna Rada Opiekuncza*) tried to save as many children as possible and ŽEGOTA, the Council for Aid to Jews (*Rada Pomocy Żydom)*, provided thousands of Jews with forged documents, places to hide, food, money, etc..[346] No such organization existed in Lithuania. To the contrary, the Lithuanian anti-Soviet and anti-Nazi resistance remained strongly nationalistic and anti-Semitic throughout the war and, thus, the Jews had little chance of getting any help and support form them.[347]

In conclusion, it is clear that without Lithuanian collaboration, many of Lithuania's Jews would have perished during the war. However, one should not forget that the argument that resistance against the German was not possible goes limp if one considers the extremely effective way in which the Lithuanians sabotaged the German efforts to set up a Lithuanian SS-division or to recruit Lithuanians for work in Germany, as we will see in the next chapter. Sadly, one can only conclude that the Lithuanians were very effective in fighting for their own cause, but that the overwhelming majority looked the other way when it came to Jews. They were just not considered to be Lithuanians, or Lithuanians worth of fighting for.

1941: "The innocent people were beaten by the Lithuanians in uniforms who also pushed old people and pregnant women, they also shed innocent blood in Varėna forest. The victims suffered as Christ suffered from the Jews. And they looted their property without waiting for the blood to dry." See Bubnys, Arūnas: *The Holocaust in the Lithuanian Provinces 1941*

346. The Council to Aid Jews (Žegota) operated under the auspices of the Polish Government in Exile through the Government Delegation for Poland, in Warsaw. Žegota's express purpose was to aid the country's Jews and find places of safety for them in occupied Poland. The organization had around one hundred (100) cells, operating mostly in Warsaw where it distributed relief funds to about 3,000 Jews. The second-largest branch was in Krakow and there seem to have been smaller branches in Vilnius and Lviv. In all, 4,000 Jews received funds from Žegota directly, 5,600 from the Jewish National Committee and 2,000 from the Bund (because of overlaps, the total number of Jews helped by all three organizations in Warsaw was about 8,500). This aid reached about one-third of the Jews in hiding in Warsaw, but mostly not until late 1943 or 1944.

347. Sutton, Karen, *The Massacre of the Jews of Lithuania*, p. 122

Chapter 5 – Issues of Compliance and Collaboration

If there is anything that the Second World War showed, it is the old truth that mankind, except a few heroes and saints, is neither good nor bad, not black or white but grey. He struggles along in a confusing twilight zone and suddenly, unexpectedly, finds himself in a landscape with only one color left. It is virtually impossible to escape from there.

J.C.H. Blom[348]

The Dutch nation abandoned the Jews.

Dr. C. Hilbrink[349]

As we noted earlier, the Soviet occupation of 1940-1941 greatly increased the already present anti-Semitism in the country, particularly when German and LAF propaganda incited many to view the "Jew-Communists" as traitors of the Lithuanian nation who had supported the Soviet takeover of the country. Many people still believe that this is one of the main reasons why so many Lithuanians either turned against their Jewish neighbors stood by and watched, or later claimed that the Jews were punished because of their own participation in crimes committed by the Soviet occupying regime.

I will come back to this issue later, but whether true or not, it is only a partial explanation. Also in countries that were not subjected to a Soviet occupation prior to the Nazi-German invasion, the population stood by and watched, and scores of people actively participated in the killings or deportations. This touches upon a much more general issue, that of compliance and collaboration, and before returning to the Holocaust in Lithuania, it is important first to address these complex issues.

There are few countries in Europe where the population refused by and large to participate in the Nazi extermination machinery or to allow them to implement their plans unobstructedly. Denmark is one of those exceptions and, as a result, only 0.76% of the Jewish population did

348. Blom, J.C.H.: *In de Ban van Goed en Fout*, p. 65
349. Hilbrink, Dr. C.: *In het Belang van het Nederlandse Volk*, p. 13

not survive the war.[350] However, on the other hand the Danes actually never resisted the German occupation itself. In fact, earlier in the late nineteenth century, the political and military elite of the country had come to the conclusion that resisting German occupation was useless and, in April 1940 when Germany invited Denmark to accept its protection against a British and French attack, it was accepted. The majority of the population agreed with the decision and, as the resistance leader, Aage Bertelsen, later wrote: "We were all in favor of a policy of collaboration, also my wife."[351] Thus, Denmark remained a sovereign state where King, government and Parliament remained in charge until mid-1943. Equally, the Norwegians were initially not against some sort of arrangement with the Germans. Only when the latter insisted on appointing the Norwegian fascist leader Quisling as Prime Minister did the negotiations fail.[352]

As far as their collaboration in the implementation of the Final Solution is concerned, Italy and Bulgaria also stand out. In Bulgaria, the government successfully resisted the deportation of some 50,000 Jews (although at the same time 11,343 Jews were deported from Macedonia and Thrace, territories occupied by Bulgaria) and Italy managed to avoid deportations until September 1943, when Germany took effective control of the coun-

350. Van der Heijden, Chris: *Grijs Verleden*, p. 232. One of the reasons of this extraordinarily low percentage is probably not only the refusal of the Danes to participate but also because the Danish governmental structure remained intact until August 28, 1943, when the government resigned rather than yield to new German demands that German military courts try future saboteurs. The following night, martial law was declared and German authorities took direct control over the Danish military and police forces. Until then, Germans were not allowed to carry out arrests, deportations or executions without going through the official Danish power structures. See Lammers, C.J.: *Vreemde Overheersing*, p. 134
351. Rings, Werner: *Leven met de Vijand*, p. 75, 77
352. Lammers, C.J.: *Vreemde Overheersing*, pp. 121-122. Of the governments of the Western European countries that were occupied, all but three decided to move to London and continue to fight German occupation. The Belgian King chose for imprisonment in Belgium, while it took the Belgian government three months to finally arrive in London. The French government of Pétain capitulated and continued to rule the "free" part of France from Vichy. "*Vichy-France*" collaborated extensively with the German Third Reich. And the Danish government and King remained in place, as a third exception. See Rings, Werner, *Leven met de Vijand*, p. 60

try after the Badoglio Armistice,[353] even then many Italians helped Jews stay out of the hands of the Germans.[354]

Interestingly, Lithuania does not present a uniform picture. On one hand, Lithuanians very actively and even enthusiastically participated in the murder of their Jewish fellow countrymen, fueled by a deep vengeance towards this easy scapegoat for their misfortune. They were also motivated by the desire to please the German occupying forces maximally in the hope they would achieve their ultimate goal of independence. When that dream did not materialize, they stubbornly resisted all attempts by the Germans to be used for their war effort thereby unwittingly showing that their involvement in the extermination of the Jews was not so much the result of having no choice but rather of a willingness to comply and collaborate.

When looking at all the acts of defiance by the Lithuanians, one can only admire their steadfastness and stubbornness in their resistance against the foreign ruler. The archbishop of Kaunas, Juozas Skvireckas, who in the early days of the German occupation had refused to intervene on behalf of the Jews and had characterized Hitler's ideas as being not only interesting but also correct, now told the head of *Einzatskommando 3,* Karl Jäger, that he was not welcome. Attempts to form a Lithuanian SS unit faltered completely and also the formation of Lithuanian building battalions failed. With the war progressing, German attempts to compromise proved to be completely ineffective. Promises that Lithuanian units would only be deployed in Lithuania itself were not believed and fear that they would be sent to the front kept most Lithuanians from joining. Threats, razzias, etc., all proved surprisingly ineffective. Only in February 1944, with the Red Army already on Lithuania's doorstep, the formation of a Lithuanian military force under the leadership of General Plechavičius proved to be very successful. Now the Soviets were closing in and Lithuanians joined in order to try to fend off a second Soviet occupation.

However, the formation of the unit turned out to be far too successful for the German's liking. By March 5, 1944, some 30,000 Lithuanians had applied to join the unit's ranks and were awaiting mobilization, of which approximately 4,000 served earlier in the Lithuanian Army during the years of independence. Seeing how big the force was turning out to be,

353. The Badoglio Armistice was an armistice signed on September 3, 1943 between Italy and the Allied armed forces, who were then occupying the southern end of the country, entailing the capitulation of Italy. Following the armistice, Germany invaded the north and started the implementation of the *Endlösung* (Final Solution) on Italian soil.

354. See Sutton, Karen: *The Massacre of the Jews in Lithuania*, p. 8

the Germans got cold feet and started imposing restrictions. For instance, insufficient weaponry was allotted, trying to keep the force rather ineffective. When, in May, rumors spread that the unit was to be deployed to Latvia and Estonia in order to release German troops for front duty, a mass desertion started. On May 15, 1944, Plechavičius and 100 of his officers were arrested, of which 20 were shot. Of the 13,000 troops that were to be demobilized, only some 3,500 did so. Most of the others fled to the forest with their arms and many of these formed the core of the partisan forces fighting the Soviets until well into the 1950s.[355] The tragedy is that among those who bravely fought against the Soviet oppressor, were those who also actively participated in the killing of Jews.

Compliance: the Dutch example

Dutch society before the Second World War had a specific character that very much influenced the turn of events during the German occupation. The country was divided into a number of "pillars," or *zuilen,* which strongly separated certain dominations in Dutch society. This compartimentalization was originally caused by the fact that in the sixteenth century, after the 80 year war against the Spaniards, the Protestant northern part of the country gained control over the predominantly Catholic south. In the nineteenth and early twentieth century, this division became stronger when mass movements started to be formed and, as a result, the country became divided between Protestant, Catholic and Social Democratic "pillars," with the neutral or non-aligned part of the country forming a fourth, the liberal one. Being part of one of these "pillars" meant that a Dutch citizen would spend his or her life almost exclusively within his/her own environment. All aspects of life – churches, political parties, trade unions, newspapers, radio broadcasting corporations, etc., were aligned to a specific "pillar," each having its own culture, beliefs, values and ways of life.

As none of the "pillars" had a majority of the population as its constituency and a permanent coalition of two or three "pillars" was not feasible, a compromise culture developed in which the elite of each of these "pillars" would meet with the other elites and together, behind closed doors, they would decide what was best for the country. "By presenting the compromises as being technical in nature and based on the principle of equal sharing, since a concession did not affect ideology as such, the elites could maintain the trust of their constituency, which was kept together by their common convictions and beliefs."[356] At the same time, the Jewish part of the population did not really belong to any "pillar" nor did they have one

355. See Sutton, Karen, *The Massacre of the Jews of Lithuania*, pp. 199-201
356. Blom, J.C.H: *In de Ban van Goed en Kwaad*, p. 33

of their own. The Jewish workers usually belonged to the social democratic pillar and the bourgeoisie to the liberal one.[357] In that sense, the Jewish population in The Netherlands concentrated mostly in Amsterdam (where 10% of the population was Jewish), was much more a part of general society than the Jewish part of Lithuanian society, which, in fact, functioned more or less as a Dutch-style "pillar" within Lithuania.

After the German army occupied The Netherlands in May 1940, the overwhelming majority of Dutch citizens tried to continue their previous life as much as possible and saw the resistance as an irritating obstacle, because every resistance act led to a severe German response and measures that curbed their daily liberties. Only when the outcome of the war became clear and the German defeat was inevitable did this attitude change.[358] This compliance with the existing political "reality" was much more extensive in The Netherlands than acknowledged for many years after the war, and much more extensive than in many of the other countries of Western Europe. The fact that a Jew had far more chances of surviving the war in Germany than The Netherlands is certainly no exaggeration.[359] Interestingly, internationally the Dutch are still considered to have been brave resisters of German oppressor, an example for others, but it is a false image that many Dutch continue to maintain abroad, undoubtedly as the result of their own ignorance of the real state of affairs.

The Dutch government which, together with the complete Royal family, fled to London on the fourth day of the war, was hardly capable of governing the country from across the North Sea. On top of that it was weak, disorganized and, for a long time, totally unaware of what was happening in their country.[360] While the French very quickly developed an intelligence

357. Blom, J.C.H: *In de Ban van Goed en Kwaad*, p. 34
358. For a detailed and balanced view on the attitude and behavior of the Dutch population during the Second World War, see *Grijs Verleden* (Grey Past) by Chris van der Heijden. Olympus, 2009, in particular pp. 130-168.
359. According to statistics, of the 566,000 Jews in Germany, 24% percent perished, while 71% of the 140,000 Dutch Jews did not survive the war. In comparison, in Belgium, 44% of the Jews perished; in France, 22%; and in a country like Denmark, which is well known for its resistance to German policies, only 0.76% of the 7800 Jews did not survive the war. According to the same statistics, 83% of the Lithuanian Jews were killed; however, that number does not include the Jews that fled to Lithuania from Poland in 1939 or were deported by the Germans, so the percentage is higher and close to the Polish figure, where 89% of the 3.3 million Jews perished. See Van der Heijden, Chris: *Grijs Verleden*, p. 232
360. The peculiar behavior and attitude of the Dutch Government in Exile was later commented upon by the British newspaper, *The New Statesman and Nation*, which wrote: "The weakness of the Dutch Government is best illustrated

network that kept them abreast of what happened at home, the Dutch remained ignorant for a long time to come. As a result, much of the governing depended, in fact, on the Dutch civil service that remained behind and, following instructions as worded in the *Landoorlogreglement* (Land War Decree), remained on duty to "serve the interests of the Dutch people." According to an addition to this decree, the so-called *Aanwijzingen* (Instructions), civil servants had to remain on duty because this was in the interest of the population. The fact that they would be serving the interest of the occupier was, in general, considered less of a disadvantage than it would be for the general population if the civil administration would stop working. Most of the civil servants were not aware of these *Aanwijzingen* until the war started when they were disseminated among them and some had the instructions in their drawer in an unopened envelope, [361]

The Supreme Commander of the Dutch Forces, General Winkelman, in whom the Dutch government had entrusted the highest authority, also confirmed that civil servants should stay on duty in the interest of the nation and that the Secretary-Generals of the various ministries had the authority to come to an agreement with the newly appointed German *Reichskommissar für die besetzten niederländische Gebiete* Arthur Seyss Inquart.[362]

by its failure to resist the impact of Big Business, which is not – as it was in Holland – restricted or counterbalanced by public opinion in Parliament and press. (...) Many who, for the sake of unity, have been reticent about what was going on in and around their Government, began to see outlines of a scheme to replace German Fascism by a brand of new Dutch "managerial" Fascism. They saw with alarm the encirclement of the Government and the occupation of important posts by the new management." *The New Statesman and Nation*, August 12, 1944

361. See Rings, Werner: *Leven met de Vijand*, p. 99. In the summer of 1943, a Commentary on the Instructions was published by the illegal press, which restricted the levels of collaboration with the Germans for Dutch civil servants. Earlier, in February 1943, Prime Minister in Exile, Sjoerd Gerbrandy, had announced on the London-based Dutch radio, Orange, that civil servants should not participate in measures that were focused on feeding the German war machinery with Dutch goods or Dutch citizens. In October 143, the Commentary on the Instructions was officially authorized by the Government in exile. However, in some cases, the Commentary made things even worse for the civil servant. While in the Instructions he was allowed leave his position in case he would have a conflict of conscience, this was no longer allowed in the Commentary on the Instructions and the person concerned had to refuse orders and wait until he was dismissed. See Lammers, C.J.: *Vreemde Overheersing*, p. 105
362. Arthur Seyss-Inquart (1892-1946), originally born as Artur Zajtich as son of a Czech school principal, was a lawyer by profession. He was instrumental in arranging the Austrian Anschluss to Germany in 1938. Following the invasion

Winkelman was arrested by the Germans on July 2 and sent as prisoner of war to Germany, after which the highest Dutch administrative authority remained in the hands of the Secretary-Generals. On the German side, the highest authority became *Reichskommissar* Arthur Seyss Inquart, with directly under him four General Commissioners, including the chief of the SS and Police Hanns Albin Rauter being in charge of security and thereby also responsible for the deportation of Jews.[363] Seyss Inquart explicitly provided the Secretary-Generals with certain quasi-legislative powers and even a salary raise to the level of that of ministers.[364]

Already in September 1940 the cleaning of the Dutch civil service started. An order was issued that Jewish civil servants were no longer to be promoted or appointed to new positions. Shortly after, Dutch civil servants were asked to sign a "declaration of being Aryan." Virtually all agreed and signed and, thus, they separated themselves from their Jewish colleagues and, by doing so, made the purge of Jews from the civil service a very easy task for the German occupier. It was a Dutch senior civil servant, Jacob Lentz, who created the internal passport for the Dutch that was so difficult to falsify; thus, pleasing the Germans so much that they took him to Berlin to meet Hitler and be honored. This internal passport became a crucial tool in separating the Jews from the Dutch and in laying the groundwork for their deportation to Auschwitz, Sobibor and other extermination camps.[365] "... Dutch civil servants have declared themselves *en masse* "Aryan" when asked to do so. It took a long time for many to reach impassable moral barriers because of their 'healthy' egoism and the urge to save one's own skin (and power) caused. In the case of even more

of Poland, Seyss-Inquart became administrative chief for Southern Poland and, in May 1940, *Reichskommissar* of The Netherlands. At the Nürnberg Trials, he was found guilty of crimes against humanity and later executed by hanging. He was the last to mount the scaffold and his last words were, "I hope that this execution is the last act of the tragedy of the Second World War and that the lesson taken from this world war will be that peace and understanding should exist between peoples. I believe in Germany."

363. The four *Generalkommissare* (General Commissioners) were: Hans Fischböck, *Generalkommissar für Finanz und Wirtschaft* (finance and economy); Hanns Albin Rauter, *Generalkommissar für das Sicherheitswesen* (safety), who also had the function of *Höhere SS- und Polizeiführer* (chief of SS and Police) and was thus responsible for the deportation of Jews. He was directly subordinate to *Reichsführer-SS* Heinrich Himmler; Fritz Schmidt, *Generalkommissar zur besonderen Verwendung* (special tasks) who, after his suicide in June 1943, was succeeded by Willi Ritterbusch; Friedrich Wimmer, *Generalkommissar für Verwaltung und Justiz* (government and justice).
364. Lammers. C.J.: *Vreemde Overheersing*, p. 79
365. Van Voren, Robert: *Op Zoek naar Robert van Voren*, p. 49 and Hilbrink, Dr. C.: *In het Belang van het Nederlandse Volk*, p. 77

Dutchmen, these barriers never came in sight. The resistance and those surrounding it were only a very small minority. But they were the ones who showed their contemporaries and also us, that it was possible to do something."[366] Of course, Dutch civil servants were not the only ones who diligently continued the work they had been hired for and followed the instructions of their superiors to the letter. As Donald Bloxham points out in his book *The Final Solution – a Genocide*, "many German bureaucrats worked effectively in their posts from Weimar through the Third Reich to the later Federal Republic – from democracy to genocidal dictatorship to democracy."[367]

Shortly after, on November 21, 1940, all Jewish civil servants were dismissed from their jobs and Jewish professors fired from their positions. When the Universities of Leyden and Delft protested, they were immediately closed down by the Germans. They would reopen only in April of the next year. At that time, restrictive measures followed one after the other. Parks, cinemas, concert halls, museums and other public places became forbidden for Jews. In early 1941, the civil administration received the instruction to register all citizens of Jewish descent and to mark their identity papers with the letter "J." The instructions were again followed meticulously. Even the Jews collaborated without resistance, seemingly proud of their heritage and going at lengths to prove that they were of real Jewish descent. However, gradually they were removed from public life and on July 15, 1942, the first train with deported Jews left Amsterdam for *Durchgangslager* Westerbork in the Eastern part of the country.[368] It was a transit point on way to Poland, a first stop on their way to their death.

Not only did civil servants adapt themselves to the new reality in The Netherlands, the same counted for the Dutch police. Following the defeat in May 1940, they had been instructed by their superior, Secretary General of the Ministry of the Interior Tenkink, to assist the Germans in arresting inhabitants of "enemy planes."[369] Dutch historian Chris van der Heijden summarizes: "Civil servants did their job, police officers earned themselves some extra money, and citizens shrugged their shoulders

366. Hilbrink, Dr. C.: *In het Belang van het Nederlandse Volk*, p. 13
367. Bloxham, Donald: *The Final Solution*, p. 270
368. Westerbork had been built in 1939 to house Jewish refugees from Germany. It cost one million Dutch guilders and was fully funded by the Dutch Jewish community. Also all living expenses were paid for by the Jewish community. A second camp was supposed to be built, but the location was turned down because the Dutch Queen torpedoed the plan: the location was too close to her palace Het Loo, some twelve kilometers. See Citroen, Michal: *U wordt door Niemand Verwacht*, p. 65, 86-87
369. Hilbrink, Dr. C.: *In het Belang van het Nederlandse Volk*, p. 78

impotently."[370] Indeed, Dutch police continued to do their job and assisted the Germans in rounding up Jews for deportation. As one Utrecht policeman said after the war, defending his complicity: "It was quite worthwhile to take on extra duty hours [to round up Jews]. Not only because of the money, but when returning to the station in Utrecht you would get a bag with well-decked sandwiches. And that at a time when you could well use something extra."[371] Later one of the members of the resistance commented on the police calling them "blockheads who fought to be able to earn 2 ½ guilders more by bringing a transport of [arrested] good Dutchmen for the Gestapo to Middelburg, because it was further away than Nijmegen or Utrecht, cities that could be reached within one working day."[372]

In Amsterdam, the police was gradually molded into compliance, but not without a hurdle. Several confrontations with the Germans forced the police force to give up its resistance against anti-Jewish measures, with a crucial factor in its active participation in the deportation of Jews being the role of the pro-German Chief Constable Sybren Tulp, a former lieutenant colonel of the Royal Dutch East Indian Army (KNIL). His military background and 26 years of service in the colonies made Tulp a perfect candidate for the imposition of measures focused on one particular ethnic group. When, in September 1942, nightly police *razzias* started in order to speed up the deportation process, Tulp personally supervised the actions. A month later, he fell ill and, because his successor clearly lacked the authority to implement the deportation campaign, the regular Amsterdam police was taken off the job; the *razzias* were continued by the Order Police and later by a volunteer service.[373] Tulp passed away on October 22, 1942, coincidentally three days after his half-brother Haring Tulp, a member of the resistance, died in concentration camp Buchenwald.

As Guus Meershoek concludes in *The Amsterdam Police and the Persecution of the Jews*, the success of the deportation process in The Netherlands was very much the result of Dutch compliance, and "the German contribution… can easily be overrated. Most German authorities were not in a position to deal with the Dutch administration effectively. Often, their brusque interventions did not immediately produce the desired result. (…) For a long time the Dutch authorities adopted a conciliatory attitude with the aim of preventing the occupying forces from imposing their demands

370. Van der Heijden, Chris: *Grijs Verleden*, p. 223
371. Vernooij, Arnold: *Grenzen aan Gehoorzaamheid; Houding en Gedrag van de Utrechtse Politie tijdens de Duitse Bezetting.*, p. 67
372. Hilbrink, Dr. C.: *In het Belang van het Nederlandse Volk*, p. 203
373. For a detailed report on the Amsterdam police see Meershoek, Guus: *The Amsterdam Police and the Persecution of the Jews, in Berenbaum, Michael: The Holocaust and History*, pp. 284-300

by force. The Dutch administration wanted to retain control, apparently at any price."[374] At the same time, while Dutch civil servants complied diligently with the orders issued by the Germans, the population stood by and watched, or tried very hard not to see what was happening to their fellow countrymen. Otto Bene, working with the German Foreign Ministry, wrote in June 1943 in one of his reports: "The Dutch population is completely again the transports, but in general it shows outwardly a lack of interest."[375] Even the *Joodsche Raad* (Jewish Council) that had been set up by the Germans as a liaison between them and the Jewish community they intended to exterminate, tried to collaborate as correctly and diligently as possible. A Jew from Utrecht commented during the war: "It is our common fault and the Jewish Council is no exception that our enemies possess a perfect administration of Jews."[376] I will come back to the issue of the *Judenrat*, as the Germans called it, later.

That attitude of going with the flow and accommodating the German occupiers also pertained, for instance, to Dutch libraries. Books that could be considered offensive to the Germans were removed. For instance, the director of the library in Haarlem reported in September 1940 that he had removed 400 books "such as immigrant literature and everything in connection with the Jewish question that could be considered offensive." Several years before, he had praised the library as a bulwark of democracy, but in July 1940 he urged his colleagues to keep the new reality into account.[377] A list of 30,000 forbidden titles was assembled, approximately 1% of the total holdings of Dutch libraries, and librarians were urged to throw away a book too many than one too few.[378]

As Dr. C. Hilbrink pointed out in his study, Dutch firms worked extensively for the German occupational forces. And that work not only concerned the production of neutral or innocent products, but also the removal of buildings to clear the way for German artillery, repairing bombed airport tarmacs, and even direct contributions to the war industry itself. "So how could [the Dutch citizens] respond negatively to German requests to help in defending the country against the advancing allied forces? Pillboxes were not specifically mentioned in the Land War Decree [that regulated what was allowed], but one could hardly refuse to participate in their construction, as long as they only served to protect against allied attacks from sea? And thus Dutch firms were given permission by Dutch authori-

374. Meershoek, Guus: *The Amsterdam Police and the Persecution of the Jews*, in Berenbaum, Michael: *The Holocaust and History*, p. 296
375. Van der Heijden, Chris: *Grijs Verleden*, p. 223
376. Van der Heijden, Chris: *Grijs Verleden*, p. 219
377. Van der Heijden, Chris: *Grijs Verleden*, p. 161
378. Van der Heijden, Chris: *Grijs Verleden*, p. 162

ties to build airports, hangars and storages. They could also be used for civil purposes, couldn't they, and one could hardly ask the Germans what the ultimate purpose would be."[379] According to reliable data, the Dutch fulfilled 84% of the production quota established by the Germans, while the Belgians and French fulfilled only 76% and 70% respectively. In particular, the contribution by the Dutch marine and airplane industry was praised extensively by the Germans.[380]

Dutch railways

One of the most shocking cases of collaboration with the Germans by the Dutch industry is that of the Dutch railways (*Nederlandse Spoorwegen*). Until the railway strike of September 1944, the Dutch railways worked without a hitch, transporting German troops and their war machinery, even in the immediate weeks following the occupation of Holland when troops and materials had to be transported to Belgium and France where the war was still going on in full glory. This, in spite of the fact that the Instructions of the *Landoorlogreglement* (Land War Decree) very clearly stated that railway personnel "must stubbornly refuse to transport troops, ammunition or war machinery of the enemy."[381] However, the management of the Dutch railways never showed these instructions to their personnel, as it was not considered necessary. Thus they continued to do their jobs and later, in 1943, the same Dutch Railways transported the Dutch military prisoners of war sent to Germany.[382] In addition, some 410,000 Dutch forced laborers were transported, without a problem, as well as the 112,000 Dutch Jews sent to their deaths in the extermination camps in Poland.

In September 1944, when the Allied troops reached the south of The Netherlands and it seemed evident that the war would be over within days or weeks, an all-encompassing railway strike finally ended this extensive collaboration.[383] The railways remained out of order until the final lib-

379. Hilbrink, Dr. C.: *In het Belang van het Nederlandse Volk*, p. 43
380. Lammers, C.J.: *Vreemde Overheersing*, p. 61
381. Hilbrink, Dr. C.: *In het Belang van het Nederlandse Volk*, p. 51
382. Initially, after the occupation of The Netherlands, Dutch military prisoners of war had been sent home as a sign of goodwill on the part of the Germans. However, in 1943, they were considered a security risk and hence were recalled.
383. However, the employees of the Dutch railways did not plan to suffer personally from the strike, and demanded full payment of their salaries, overtime and Christmas benefits. In total, 37 million Dutch Guilders were paid to them by the Dutch government in exile. See Rings, Werner: *Leven met de Vijand*, p. 107

eration of the country in May 1945. After the war, the strike came at the latest hour when victory was certain even though eventually postponed until the next springand was presented by the management as one of the most important acts of resistance in The Netherlands: "We, as a business, had set ourselves the goal to fulfill its important task for the prosperity of the Dutch people to the best of our ability and by doing so to contribute to maintaining the morale of our people at an acceptable level, necessary to persevere in the resistance against the German occupation. (...) On September 18 [1944] our business, the largest business in The Netherlands, where the pulse of our economy was beating the strongest, went completely dead, as a result of which the German war machinery was rid of an important weapon, an act of resistance, which by its size, its strict discipline in its implementation, was incomparable to anything else and was an honor to the whole of the Dutch people."

After the war, the top managers of the Dutch Railways were interviewed by a Parliamentary Investigative Commission and, when reading their responses, one can only shiver at the emptiness of their explanations, the absence of an understanding of what they had contributed to, and the lightness with which they tried to justify their collaboration. They even explained that they tried to send the Jews to Poland as in passenger trains as long as possible to make the trip more pleasant and, when that was no longer possible and the Germans insisted that boxcars were to be used, this was actually better because the Jews had a lot of luggage and that could be transported much easier like this.[384] "The Dutch railways allowed its subsidiary Spoorbouw NV to construct a special railway line between the town of Hooghalen and *Durchgangslager* Westerbork to be used for the deportation of Jews. Money was not an issue, as it was paid from the stolen Jewish property. Also there were sufficient work forces: 'Many Jews worked outside the camp, for instance, on the railway line from Hooghalen to Westerbork. They [the Jews] had to build it themselves. Also experts of the Dutch Railways must have been there, who commanded the Jewish forced laborers'."[385]

However, the attitude of the management of the Dutch Railways was not much different than that of the leadership of the Dutch civil service. The highest authorities among them, the Secretary-Generals at the various Ministries, remained at their posts and continued their work as undisturbed as possible. Even undisturbed to such an extent, that on October 28, 1941, the Secretary-Generals of Justice, Internal Affairs and Trade and Industry ordered the Dutch population not to be involved in acts of sabotage and not to hide allied pilots from planes that had been shot down: "... not

384. Hilbrink, Dr. C.: *In het Belang van het Nederlandse Volk*, pp. 14-21
385. Hilbrink, Dr. C.: *In het Belang van het Nederlandse Volk*, p. 43

to sabotage, as was established in the case of distribution rules and the falsification of documents. (...) These things... are pernicious and directed against the Dutch people. Try to understand what time we are in. Understand that the German government will not allow this wrong attitude. It can endanger the life of many. Assist, in order to make sure that our people are not harmed by acts of irresponsible and criminal elements."[386] A few months later, in February 1942, Secretary General for Education, Science and Protection of Culture Jan Dam sent out an instruction to all schools that requests to post posters of the SS or the national socialist youth movement *Nationale Jeugdstorm* should be met. Only after several incidents in which school directors refused to follow this order and wound up in police precincts for questioning, did he soften the tone of his instruction.[387] Jan Dam was a former Germanist and, although not a fascist, considered to be *Deutschfreundlich.*

One of the most compliant Secretary-Generals was that of Internal Affairs, Karel Johannes Frederiks, who was responsible for the Dutch police and was one of the authors of the above-mentioned circular letter and who later expressed the feeling that he had considered the resistance to have been a bother, "who attacked us in their petty publications... and by doing so decreased our authority vis-à-vis the Germans."[388] After the war, Frederiks would voice the opinion that, of course the occupation had been "lousy," but that he at the same time had enjoyed now being "Queen, Minister and Parliament united in one person."[389] He agreed to "organize for the Jews whatever could be arranged" but that at the same time he felt "it went a bit too far" to "abandon the rest of the Dutch" for that purpose. Of course, they had discussed what to do with regard to the deportation of Jews, but every time "the problem popped up as to what would happen if they refused. Of course it was possible for the Germans to do it themselves But one never knew what would be unleashed if one had said 'no'."[390]

So instead of trying to save the hundred and forty thousand Dutch Jews, Frederiks put together a list of Jews who should be saved from deportation. He was joined by the earlier mentioned Secretary General for Education, Science and Protection of Culture, Jan van Dam, who also started collecting names. Later the leader of the Dutch fascist movement NSB, Anton Mussert, also provided names of people he would like to see saved.

386. Hilbrink, Dr. C.: *In het Belang van het Nederlandse Volk*, p. 47, 80
387. Hilbrink, Dr. C.: *In het Belang van het Nederlandse Volk*, pp. 61-62
388. Quotes from the records of the Parliamentary Investigative Commission, quoted in: Hilbrink, Dr. C.: *In het Belang van het Nederlandse Volk*, p. 80
389. Lammers, C.J.: *Vreemde Overheersing*, p. 79
390. Quotes from the records of the Parliamentary Investigative Commission, quoted in: Hilbrink, Dr. C.: *In het Belang van het Nederlandse Volk*, p. 78

Initially the lists contained names of some Jewish friends of the compilers, but when they were approached by many desperate Jews, they developed criteria to be put on the list: Jews who had a special contribution to the development of the German *Reich*, such as having been an important artist, member of the German Wehrmacht during the First World War, or membership of the Dutch fascist movement NSB. However, Frederiks and Van Dam were not free of nepotism and corruption and so also other Jews managed to get their names on the list. In the end, the Germans agreed to the plan, with the understanding that this might facilitate the execution of their larger deportation plans and some 670 Jews were marked for "special treatment" this way. They were not deported to Poland but kept in three "Reservation camps" in Holland and eventually transported to the model concentration camp Theresienstadt. Most of them survived the war.[391]

As Dr. C. Hilbrink points out, one should not forget, however, the context in which the management of the Dutch Railways functioned and made their decisions. "The complete availability of the administrations at municipalities and other institutions of public administration, the almost unhitched involvement of the Dutch police, the signing of the declarations of being "Aryan" *en masse* and other forms of massive collaboration, enabling the occupier to implement the *Endlösing* in occupied Netherlands as *reibungslos* [flawlessly] as possible, show us that the Dutch Railways were in this… completely in line with the national tendency."[392]

However, for many lower placed civil servants, including railway workers, things were much more difficult, as they often saw the consequences of their compliance. It was they who had to be around when the trains were loaded with Jews, it was they who saw the desperation. One railway employee remembered: "In the Jew trains, *Sonderzüge*, were only Jews. They rode during the night and day. They were to depart immediately. On the stations these trains were guarded and the train itself had a wagon with guards, *Grüne Polizei*. At the stations people threw things into the train, while the Jews threw notes outside. The Jews were mostly in boxcars…"[393] Another added: "It was not done to discuss about what was transported. Many of us wondered about the Jews: why did you surrender yourself? We knew nothing about [what would happen in] Poland, often the Jews themselves didn't know neither. They were going, we thought, to work camps."[394] Many of the railway employees Hilbrink interviewed

391. Hilbrink, Dr. C.: *In het Belang van het Nederlandse Volk*, p. 78. See also www.villabouchina.nl
392. Hilbrink, Dr. C.: *In het Belang van het Nederlandse Volk*, p. 111
393. Memories of a former railways employee, quoted in Hilbrink, Dr. C.: *In het Belang van het Nederlandse Volk*, p. 115
394. Hilbrink, Dr. C.: *In het Belang van het Nederlandse Volk*, p. 115

for his book, fifty years after the war, showed how painful it had been to be involved in a vital element in the deportation and destruction of the Jews. Often they still avoided talking about it. There were very few cases of sabotage or resistance[395] and those who refused to be involved in the transportations went into hiding, as refusal to work was not accepted by the compliant management and could result in arrest and worse. In that sense, it was more difficult for railway employees than for other civil servants, as it was carefully registered who had been where doing what, while in municipal administrations, things could be altered or removed without leaving a trace.

(Absence of) resistance

If one compares the numbers of resistance fighters in The Netherlands with those in Belgium and France, the difference is quite shocking. During the first two years of the war, The Netherlands had only several hundred resistance fighters but after the summer of 1942, the number grew. This is not so strange, as the fortunes of war were turning against the Germans. They had lost the first battle of El Alamein in the summer of 1942 and, thus, their advance in North Africa had been halted; also on the Eastern front, their advance had been stalled. The battle for Stalingrad, which would be the turn of the war, had started. In 1943 there were, according to various reliable sources, several thousand members of the resistance and, in the summer of 1944 (that is, after the invasion in Normandy), that number had grown to 25,000. By the end of the war, the number was 45,000. In comparison, Belgium counted some 70,000 resistance fighters, and France, 400,000 (approximately 1 percent of the population, against 0.25% in The Netherlands). In comparison, the Dutch Fascist Party had approximately 27,000 members in 1940. At the end of that year, another 23,000 had joined (as they seem to have joined for purely opportunistic reasons, they were called "*meikevers*" (may bugs, because they joined after the May 1940 occupation of the country) and in July 1942, Party leader Anton Mussert decided that to avoid having too many of these opportunists among their ranks, a trial period had to be introduced. By the end of 1941, the Party reached its maximum membership of 70-80,000, far more than the number of people who joined the resistance.[396]

As far as the occupational forces are concerned, their numbers were actually quite limited. In total, not more than 650-700 people filled the ranks of the *Sicherheitspolizei* (Sipo) and *Sicherheitsdienst* (SD), including typists, drivers, etc. The *Ordnungspolizei* (Order Police) were about 3,000

395. Several cases are highlighted by Dr. C. Hilbrink in his book, see pp. 115-118
396. Hofman, J.: *De Collaborateur*, p. 46

in number and the occupational military forces, approximately 20,000. Keeping the country under control depended, therefore, very heavily on the active collaboration of local forces, including the Dutch police.[397]

In addition, the acts of resistance in The Netherlands were much smaller in numbers than in Belgium and France. The first member of the Dutch fascist movement NSB was killed only on February 5, 1943, while at that time already some 50 collaborators had been killed in Belgium. In total, several dozen collaborators and Germans were killed in The Netherlands, whereas Belgian resistance killed several hundred of them, and French resistance, 5,000. The difference in numbers of acts of sabotage is no less striking: In France in October 1941 alone, 162 acts of sabotage, in Belgium in September 1941, a total of 124 and in The Netherlands between August and October 1941, a total of sixty times.[398]

The compliant attitude of the Dutch population did not go unnoticed by the underground press in the country and quite a few made disparaging remarks in their publications. The underground newspaper, *Trouw,* wrote in June 1943: "The overwhelming majority is not ready to sacrifice. The weak and egocentric attitude does a lot of damage." *De Vonk* wrote several months later: "In our own country, the whole industry is working harder than ever before, but for the enemy." and *Het Parool* added in February 1944: "People are queuing up to hand over their radio sets."[399] *Trouw* also commented on the compliant attitude of the Dutch civil service and wrote in January 1944: "Under the supreme supervision of the enemy, the whole of The Netherlands has become one big business working for the enemy. Under the supreme supervision of the enemy, it is the Dutch, Dutch civil servants, who are in charge of that business and try to make it function as well as possible on behalf of the German war machinery.... That all is bad, but the worst is that we see how Dutch civil servants, the Dutch governmental administration – in general terms and without denying the positive exceptions – collaborate in implementing measures that are meant to betray or sell those Dutch to the Germans who are not willing to collaborate with the enemy..."[400]

And at the same time, interestingly, very little attention was paid in underground publications to the plight of the Jewish population. Not only newspapers reported very little about what was happening to their fellow countrymen, but also in literature, the fate of the Jews was mentioned

397. Lammers, C.J.: *Vreemde Overheersing*, pp. 45-46
398. Van der Heijden, Chris: *Grijs Verleden*, pp. 280-282
399. Van der Heijden, Chris: *Grijs Verleden*, p. 286
400. Hilbrink, Dr. C.: *In het Belang van het Nederlandse Volk*, p. 209

only sporadically. In *Vrij Nederlands Liedboek*, a collection of 130 poems written and published during the war, Jews are mentioned only nine times, and then only in connection with the good relationship that existed between Jews and Dutch, which the Germans had disturbed. Their fate is only mentioned once.[401]

Explanatory factors

There are several factors that help to explain this behavior. In analyzing the difference between the size of the resistance in The Netherlands and Belgium, Van der Heijden points out that Belgium had already been occupied before, in 1914-1918, and, thus, the Dutch population was less experienced and rather naïve as to what was awaiting them. In addition, the occupation had resulted in relatively few deaths both among Dutch military and civilians (with the bombardment of Rotterdam, when more than 800 citizens died, being an exception). Dutch prisoners of war were released quite soon after the end of hostilities, contrary to those in Belgium and France and, thus, the atmosphere was a more relaxed one. The Germans considered the Dutch as being of Germanic race and, thus, they approached the Dutch with a soft hand, hoping to win them over. As a result, the urge to resist was much smaller and it would take a long time before things got really worse and people were triggered into resistance.

Another factor that Van der Heijden mentions is the fact that Dutch are, by nature, very obedient. Indeed, the dominant religion in The Netherlands was Protestant, of which one of the main churches, *the Gereformeerde Kerk* (Reformed Church), believed that all authority was given by God and, therefore, one must accept.[402] Pastor J.H. Rietberg in the town of Maassluis worded this as follows: "God's Word also has to lead us in relation to our attitude towards the new rulers. We have to submit ourselves obediently to the government that has been given the authority over us. Jesus taught the same to the Jews. He recognized Roman dominance."[403] Former Prime-Minister Colijn also held that position. On August 10, 1940,

401. Van der Heijden, Chris: *Grijs Verleden*, p. 289
402. See Van der Heijden, Chris: *Grijs Verleden*, p. 159, and Van Voren, Robert: *Op Zoek naar Robert van Voren*, p. 114
403. Van Kaam, Ben: *Opstand der Gezagsgetrouwen*, p. 75. The same obedience to authority is mentioned by Auschwitz commandant Rudolf Hoess as one of the main elements in his own upbringing: "I can still clearly remember how my father who, on account of his fervent Catholicism, was a determined opponent of the Reich government and its policy, never ceased to remind his friends that, however strong one's opposition might be, the laws and decrees of the State had to be obeyed unconditionally." Hoess, Rudolf: *Commandant of Auschwitz*, p. 32

he concluded that: "However the war ends, one can actually see no other outcome than that the German supremacy on the European continent needs to be accepted."[404] In a booklet titled "On the border between two worlds," he expressed the view that a national Front should work with the Germans to accept the current reality. Johan Brouwer, a Dutch expert in Hispanics, wrote: "As the things stand internationally at this moment, the supremacy of the Germans on the continent is guaranteed for many years to come. In the mental uncertainty that many of us have with regard to the task and place of our country in the future, reality should be the starting point and lead to a new orientation and set of values." [405]

However, these may be explanatory factors of value to Dutch society in those days, yet they do not explain why collaboration with the Nazis was so extensive throughout Europe, also in other countries. Of course, Fascism and National Socialism were fairly broadly accepted political ideologies, much broader than often thought of today. For instance, in 1933, the Dutch crown princess Juliana married the German Bernhard von Lippe-Biesterveld, the latter being the commander of Dutch forces that helped liberate The Netherlands. At one of the parties he organized, Bernhard insisted that the favorite Nazi song "*Horst Wessellied*" be played, prompting the Jewish members of the orchestra to leave the hall in protest. In 1995, it was revealed that Bernhard had been a member of the NSDAP; he had also been a member of the Reiter SS and the SA, both military arms of the Nazi party.[406] But Bernhard was not alone in this respect; also some members of the British royal family – including Edward VIII, who was King for only 235 days - was not free from Nazi sympathies.[407]

404. Hilbrink, Dr. C.: *In het Belang van het Nederlandse Volk*, p. 176
405. Van der Heijden, Chris: *Grijs Verleden*, p. 134
406. For a detailed biography of Prince Bernhard see Van Zijl, Annejet: *Bernhard; een verborgen geschiedenis.* Querido, 2010.
407. In October 1937, the Duke and Duchess visited Nazi Germany, against the advice of the British government, and met Adolf Hitler at his Obersalzberg retreat. The visit was much publicized by the German media. During the visit, the Duke gave full Nazi salutes. The former Austrian ambassador, Count Albert von Mensdorff-Pouilly-Dietrichstein, who was also a second cousin once removed and friend of George V, believed that Edward favored German fascism as a bulwark against communism, and even that he initially favored an alliance with Germany. Hitler considered Edward to be friendly towards Nazi Germany and thought that Anglo-German relations could have been improved through Edward if it were not for the abdication. On the outbreak of the Second World War in September 1939, they were brought back to Britain by Lord Mountbatten on board HMS Kelly, and the Duke, although an honorary field marshal, was gazetted a major-general attached to the British Military Mission in France. In February 1940, the German Minister in The Hague, Count Julius von Zech-Burkersroda, claimed that the Duke had leaked the Allied war plans for the

In 1979 the German scholar, Werner Rings, published a book titled "*Living with the Enemy*."[408] The book caused a shockwave through Europe because, for the first time in a well-documented and organized fashion, a scholar pointed out to what extent collaboration had been a widely accepted practice in occupied Europe. The book pointed out that the contribution of occupied countries to the German economy amounted to more than 100 billion German marks, of which 60 million marks went straight into the German war machinery. The contribution was often much more than the German occupational authorities demanded. It showed how much people were trying to benefit. And not only did occupied countries contribute, but also countries such as Sweden and Switzerland very nicely profited from the German war industry.[409] The remarks by the Dutch underground press about the Dutch industry working harder than ever before must be seen in this light.

Yet also among collaborators you had many varieties. Chris van der Heijden puts it: "There were bastards among them, as well as good ones. There were men – and also women – who truly believed in the correctness of national socialism but had not been able to join due to circumstances such as the fact that they had been a civil servant or owned a shop. There were fellow travelers, weaklings, doubters, there were people who collaborated out of love for another human being and there were those who had been raised in collaboration. Each story is different and every attempt to summarize these stories in one format, as was attempted several times and explicitly after the war, says more about the author of the scheme than of the character of those who fit into the scheme."[410]

All in all, it is clear that the Holocaust would never have been possible with only active participation of the 100,000-500,000 persons who were actively involved in perpetrating these crimes.[411] In order to commit mass murder, there had to be a silent majority, not only one that complied with

defense of Belgium. When Germany invaded the north of France in May 1940, the Windsors fled south. A "defeatist" interview with the Duke that was widely distributed may have served as the last straw for the British government: Prime Minister Winston Churchill threatened the Duke with a court-martial if he did not return to British soil. In August 1940, a British warship dispatched the pair to the Bahamas, where, in the view of Churchill, the Duke could do the least damage to the British war effort.

408. Rings, Werner: *Leben mit dem Feind. Anpassung und Widerstand in Hitler's Europa 1939-1945.* The quotes in this book are from the Dutch edition, *Leven met de Vijand*, Becht, 1979.

409. Rings, p. 368-369

410. Van der Heijden, Chris: *Grijs Verleden*, p. 190

411. Waller, James: *Becoming Evil*, p. 16

the instructions from the occupational forces but also one that looked the other way, that preferred not to see, that concentrated on its own survival.

As James Waller writes in his book, *Becoming Evil*, "it could be argued that this indifference also allowed many ordinary Germans to become part of the destruction process. Perhaps it was not the hateful, rabid, revengeful eliminationist anti-Semitism that spurred the atrocities. Rather, perhaps it was because of the indifference to Jews – motivated, in part, by a 'moderate anti-Semitism' – ran so deep that many ordinary Germans could kill them just as easily as not. So rather than a deep, preceding ideological hatred, perhaps it was a *lack* of emotional connection that neutralized whatever aversion Germans might otherwise have felt for the Nazis and made such atrocities possible."[412] Of course, in the place of German, one could as easily put "Dutch" or "Lithuanian." And maybe even more easily, as Jews in Germany were much more assimilated and integrated into society than in, for instance, Lithuania.

For Thomas Kühne, Professor of History at Clark University, the issue of belonging to a community was a factor of central importance in the successful implementation of the Holocaust. In his view, the fact that participation made people part of a community, of a *Volksgemeinschaft* (people's community), helped them to commit mass murder or stand by, watch, and be complacent. This concept of *Volksgemeinschaft* was a central element in Nazi policy and was an issue that both the Left and Right strived for in post-World War I Germany. Already at the end of the nineteenth century, Heinrich von Treitschke taught his students that "it is only through war that a nation becomes a real nation. Only acting together makes a people really stick together."[413] The Germans had gone to war in 1914 enthusiastically, yet the First World War had destroyed the honor of Germany fundamentally and left the country divided, devastated, fractured. In order to regain the sense of unity, a new approach was needed, one in which *comraderie*, comradeship, became a central element, in which individual needs and emotions were suppressed and replaced with the needs of the community as a holy element to strive for and defend. As Stebastian Haffner wrote in 1939: "Widely praised harmless male comradeship completely destroys the sense of responsibility for oneself."[414]

Part of this concept of *Volksgemeinschaft* was the cleansing of the nation of its internal dangers, its undesirable elements, the parts that threatened its

412. Waller, James: *Becoming Evil*, p. 47
413. Kühne, Thomas: *Belonging and Genocide*, p. 165
414. Quoted in Kühne, Thomas: *Belonging and Genocide*, p. 32

purity and, thus, its survival. Jews (and not only Jews but also the mentally ill and mentally handicapped, Sinti, Roma, homosexuals, etc.) formed this mortal danger and thus had to be disposed of. And by doing so, the Nazi's reached two goals: "When Germans carried out genocidal war against the Jews and other 'undesirables' in order to realize the utopia of a purified nation, they did more than destroy what they considered to be dirty and dangerous. They experienced togetherness, cohesion, and belonging, and they deluded themselves into believing they would attain a homogenous and harmonious social body, cleansed of pollution, conflict, and inner enemies."[415] Thus, men, and also women, strived to be diligent and even perfect members of the social group, and thus they "competed in performing the Nazi's revolutionary morality that invalidated individual responsibility, human compassion, and human rights."[416] According to Kühne, it is exactly this sense of belonging, of comradeship, that kept the nation together after 1942 when it became clear that the Germans were losing the war.

Compliance in Lithuania

Interestingly, if one takes this concept of a nation purifying itself by exterminating the "foreign element" that endangers its national purity and togetherness, this image also fits Lithuanian society in the late 1930s and beginning of the 1940s. Lithuania was a young nation, created after several centuries of foreign domination and a Germany wanting to create a buffer zone against Russia with satellite countries. Lithuania was stimulated to separate itself from the Russian Empire, causing its fragile national pride to be hurt deeply on several occasions, not in the least by its forced acceptance of Polish domination over Vilnius and Vilnius region. The country was also hurt by its loss of Klaipėda and the Klaipėda region, its acceptance of Soviet troops on its territory and, in the end, its inability to protest, let alone resist, Soviet occupation in June 1940. To recover this pride, to recreate a national unity, a national togetherness, the nation had to be cleansed of a foreign element within itself, being the Jews. Whether many or only a few were pro-Communist was of no significance – Jews were, because of their isolation, a foreign element and thus victimizing them became the tool to recreate Lithuania's national pride. Also Kühne thinks that this factor played an important role in the active participation of local collaborators: "Eastern European nationalists did not differ much from the Nazis… The obsession with racial and ethnic homogeneity fueled mass violence throughout the twentieth century. Jewish Commu-

415. Kühne, Thomas: *Belonging and Genocide*, p. 4
416. Kühne, Thomas: *Belonging and Genocide*, p. 6

nists had polluted the community before the Germans arrived, according to these views."[417]

As we have seen, a considerable number of Lithuanians participated in the extermination of their Jewish compatriots yet, in absolute figures, it is only a very small minority of the population. However, the largest contribution to the massacre was again, as in The Netherlands, an indifferent population and, most importantly, a compliant bureaucracy. From the Provisional Government in Kaunas all the way down to local mayors and police officers, all looked the other way, fulfilled orders and did what they were asked to do: register all Jews, expropriate and humiliate them, herd them into buildings or temporary ghettos and, in the end, send them to their deaths.

At best, local officials remained indifferent to the fate of their Jewish compatriots, sometimes not referring to them as Jews but as people of Jewish nationality or citizens of Jewish nationality.[418] However, there are only sporadic reports that use denigrating references or anti-Semitic language – this being all the more frightening, as it indicates that rounding of Jews was just another job, nothing to get excited about. In no way can it be that the officials did not know what happened with their prey. As the authors of *The Persecution and Mass Murder of Lithuanian Jews,* Christoph Dieckmann and Salius Sužiedėlis, write: "Any ignorance of fact was fleeting; as the process unfolded, denial very quickly required purposeful evasion. Certainly, as August 1941 came to a close, even the thickest police head must have grasped that the Jews of the provinces were being corralled not for 'deportations,' but to their deaths."[419] Some of the documents show an Orwellian cynicism, such as a report by Šiakiai Director Chief V. Karalius who, in his report to the Director of the Police Department, refers to Jews having been "dispositioned" and "disposed of."[420] Christoph Dieckmann and Saulius Sužiedėlis conclude: "The fact that, ultimately, no Lithuanian political or police institution could have prevented the mass murder of the Jews in no way mitigates their responsibility. (…) In fact, even the most Nazified collaborators were to later admit their shame in the involvement of Lithuanians as butchers and henchmen: if the Germans insist on a *Judenfrei* Baltic, some implied, let them do it, at best a cynical attitude of indifferent passivity which further incriminates those who actively participated in the enterprise."[421]

417.Kühne, Thomas: *Belonging and Genocide*, p. 81
418. *The Persecution and Mass Murder of Lithuanian Jews*, p. 152
419. *The Persecution and Mass Murder of Lithuanian Jews*, p. 153
420. *The Persecution and Mass Murder of Lithuanian Jews*, pp. 155-156
421. *The Persecution and Mass Murder of Lithuanian Jews*, p. 156

Did the Lithuanians have a choice? Yes, conclude Dieckmann and Sužiedėlis. "There was room for individual choice both among the German and Lithuanian actors. The chief of the Tilsit (Telšiai) German police did not permit his units to take part in the massacres, even though his adjutant had pressed him strongly on the matter. The chief of the Lithuanian police in Jurbarkas resigned his office after the first shootings."[422]

Victim and perpetrator? The *Judenräte*

Special attention should be given to the position of the so-called *Judenrat* (Jewish Council), which the Germans set up in virtually all of the ghettos. The basic idea of the *Judenrat* was that the Jews would bear responsibility for the daily life in their own ghetto, yet, at the same time it was a perverted system of making Jews accomplices in the biggest crime: the extermination of Jewish presence on European soil. After the war, the role of the *Judenrat* was discussed extensively and, depending on the time of the discussion and the ability of the discussant to look at its role from a distance, it was at times condemned and, at other times, condoned. In particular, the fact that some of the *Judenräte* were involved in preparing lists of people to be deported has often been considered to be scandalous collaboration with the Nazis.

For instance, Hannah Arendt,[423] author of some of the fundamental works on totalitarianism and, herself, a former German of Jewish descent who managed to escape in time to the United States, is very clear with regard to her position *vis-à-vis* the *Judenräte*. She felt that they bore partial responsibility for the extermination of the Jews in Europe because wherever Jews lived, there were recognized Jewish leaders and this leadership, al-

422. *The Persecution and Mass Murder of Lithuanian Jews*, p. 164

423. Hannah Arendt (1906-1975) was born into a family of secular German Jews near Hannover and grew up in Königsberg (now Kaliningrad) and Berlin. She studied philosophy in Marburg and wrote her dissertation in Heidelberg on the concept of love in the thought of Saint Augustine, under the existentialist philosopher-psychologist Karl Jaspers. The dissertation was published the same year, but Arendt was prevented from habilitating, a prerequisite for teaching in German universities, because she was Jewish. She worked for some time researching anti-Semitism before being interrogated by the Gestapo and thereupon fled Germany for Paris. In 1941, Arendt escaped with her husband and her mother to the United States. Arendt became active in the German-Jewish community in New York. After World War II, she returned to Germany and worked for Youth Aliyah, an organization that had saved thousands of children from the Holocaust. In 1950, she became a naturalized citizen of the United States.Arendt served as a visiting scholar at the University of California, Berkeley, Princeton University and Northwestern University. She died at age 69 in 1975.

most without exception, cooperated in one way or another for one reason or another with the Nazis. "The whole truth was," according to Arendt, "that if the Jewish people had really been disorganized and leaderless, there would have been chaos and plenty of misery but the total number of victims would hardly have been between four and half and six million people.'"[424] Of course, Hannah Arendt wrote these words in the early 1960s, fifteen years after the end of the war, and is very much reflecting the mood at that time. How had it been possible that so many people had been killed, with seeming active participation of its leaders and without a wave of revolts and strong resistance? How was it possible that the Jews first dug their own graves before being shot?

In general, however, the discussion touches upon a very complex yet central issue: what to do when a victim becomes perpetrator at the same time? For Lithuania, this discussion is of importance, as the country fell victim to repeated occupations, yet saw a considerable number of its citizens participate in atrocities, giving it also the "status" of perpetrator. Some of those who became involved, willingly or unwillingly, could not bear the responsibility, and ended their lives. As we saw earlier, one of the Lithuanian TDA battalions, Capt. Bronius Kirkila, did not withstand cruelties that he experienced [as a witness or perpetrator] and committed suicide on 12 July 1941.'"[425] Also Adam Czerniakow, who had been chairman of the Warsaw *Judenrat*, killed himself on July 23, 1942, unable to master the unbearable burden of being the interface between a murderous force and a nation that had no chance to escape being murdered.[426]

In Amsterdam, the ghettoization started at a moment when the majority of Jews in Lithuania already had met their end in the killing fields. On January 10, 1942, the first deportation of Amsterdam Jews began and a week later, the concentration of Amsterdam Jews in a ghetto started. Initially, the Jews themselves established a "coordination committee" in order to form a sort of unified front against the Germans and to have a mechanism through which negotiations would be possible. However, the Germans set up their own *Judenrat* and gradually the "coordination committee" dissolved itself into this structure.

424. See for instance Arendt, Hannah: *Eichmann in Jerusalem; A Report on the Banality of Evil*. New York, 1965

425. Bubnys, Arūnas: *Lithuanian Police Battalions and the Holocaust (1941-1943)*, p. 9

426. Adam Czerniakow's diary was published after the war and is one of the most impressive and heart rendering monuments to the fate of Jewry on the European continent. See: Hilberg, Raul (et.al.): *The Warsaw Diary of Adam Czerniakow*. Elephant paperbacks, 1999

In general, the *Joodsche Raad* [Jewish Council] as it was called in Amsterdam, was seen as an instrument of the Germans and, in fact, that is exactly what it was. Many feared the *Joodsche Raad* because in a way it had powers over life and death, it could decide who was allowed to stay and who would be transported, to meet an inevitable death. There is a joke that a Jewish woman opens the door and is shaken when two unknown men are standing in front of her. They introduce themselves as members of the German police, the *Grüne Polizei*. "Oh, thank God," she says, "I thought you were from the *Joodsche Raad*."[427]

The Amsterdam *Judenrat* was led by two prominent Amsterdam Jews, Abraham Asscher and David Cohen. Abraham Asscher belonged to one of the wealthiest diamond producers in the city,[428] while David Cohen was an Egyptologist and Professor of History at the University of Amsterdam. Both survived the war, by coincidence, as the only members of the Amsterdam *Judenrat* and, until their deaths, they were surrounded by endless debates concerning their collaboration with the Germans. They helped prepare lists of those who would be deported and, worse of all, they avoided being killed themselves because of their positions.[429] In 1965, the

427. Van der Heijden, Chris: *Grijs Verleden*, p. 217

428. The Asscher Diamond Company was founded in 1854 and given its international fame by Abraham Asscher and his brother Joseph. In 1907, the brothers opened a new factory in Amsterdam and soon they received a request from King Edward VII of Great Britain to cleave the legendary Cullinan Diamond, the largest rough gem-quality diamond ever found

429. In September 1943, most of the remaining staff of the *Joodse Raad*, including Asscher were deported and Cohen. Asscher survived his imprisonment at Bergen-Belsen and returned to Amsterdam after the conclusion of the war. Professor David Cohen survived Theresienstadt concentration camp, but all other members of the Jewish Council perished, including the Chief Rabbi of Amsterdam L.H. Sarlouis. The Dutch government instituted investigations against Asscher and his colleague David Cohen into charges of collaboration. A *Joodsche Eereraad* (Jewish Council of Honor) was also established to investigate wartime collaboration charges on behalf of the Jewish community. It was particularly concerned with activity after August 15, 1942; a point from which, according to the accuser's post-war perspective, it was considered obvious that the *Joodse Raad* was assisting in a mass-murder of Dutch Jews in occupied Poland's extermination camps. However, as a simple matter of fact this was not obvious to either Jews or non-Jews in Holland at the time, as all testimonies confirm, in fact it was kept strictly secret by the Nazi occupiers, and certainly was not made known to the Jewish Council in Amsterdam.

By the time (in 1947) the Council of Honor ruled to exclude Asscher and Cohen from ever holding public office in the Dutch Jewish Community, Asscher, deeply wounded by the unjust charges, as he saw them, were leveled against him, had left the Community. When Asscher died in 1950 and in accordance with his wishes, he was not buried in a Jewish cemetery. However, prominent Jewish-Dutch historian Jacques Presser, himself a survivor of the Holocaust, wrote in his book "*De Ondergang*" (The Demise): "The historian establishes the fact that on the list of 7,000 [of people who should be deported to Poland], two names did not appear: those of Asscher and Cohen. He only establishes the fact, nothing more."[430] But it was clear what Presser thought: the two should have sent themselves to the extermination camps.

A much more balanced view of the two men appeared in the 1980s, when the black and white picture of the 1960s and 1970s was gradually replaced by shades of grey, to which I will return later. However, it is important to note that the behavior of David Cohen, in fact, very much fit into the picture of that time. As I wrote earlier, Dutch society was divided into *zuilen*, "pillars," and among the leadership of these "pillars," the implementation of a policy of reason and compromise was almost a holy credo. David Cohen belonged to the Dutch elite and, as a member of many committees and societies, had been one of the leading Jews in the country. He did nothing else but continue the policy after the Germans had occupied the country: agree to compromises, follow a course of reason and, by doing so, try to gain time in the hope that the consequences for the Jewish population could at least be postponed, if not averted.[431] David Cohen himself tried to explain this position after the war in a testimonial tiled *Pro Domo* but, at that time, his arguments were considered a weak defense of unacceptable behavior.[432] In a review of a biography of David Cohen, in which this testimonial was published for the first time, Dutch historian J.C.H. Blom compared Cohen's behavior with that of most mayors of Dutch towns: try to postpone, win time, and compromise where necessary.[433]

In the ghetto in Vilnius, the behavior of the *Judenrat* was not much different, as one can judge by the detailed dairy of Herman Kruk and other testimonials and diaries. Also here, the Jewish Council and later the Ghetto Chief Jacob Gens tried to mediate, to appease the Germans and to limit

in the same year, due to constant protests and appeals, the Jewish community tribunal after reconsidering the charges reversed and annulled its decree to exclude both Asscher and Cohen from official posts in the Jewish community, exonerating them completely. The Dutch government, taking its cue from the Jewish community, dropped all charges of its own the year following. However, in the 1960s the debate resumed, among others because of the publication of Presser's book.

430. Presser, Jacques: *De Ondergang*, p. 526
431. See Blom, J.C.H: *In de Ban van Goed en Kwaad*, pp. 52-53
432. See Blom, J.C.H: *In de Ban van Goed en Kwaad*, pp. 53
433. In Dutch: "pappen en nathouden," best translated as "go with the flow." See Blom, J.C.H: *In de Ban van Goed en Kwaad*, pp. 54

the damage. Gens strongly believed that the only survival for the Jews was to make themselves indispensable as a workforce. Gens put it himself: "I, Gens, lead you to your death; and I, Gens, want to save Jews from death. I, Gens, order hideouts to be blown up; and I, Gens, do all in my power to create work certificates, employment, and anything else that serves the ghetto. I calculate the amount of Jewish blood and not the price of Jewish honor. If I am asked for 1,000 Jews, I deliver them. For if we, Jews, do not deliver them, the Germans will come and take them by force and then it will not be a question of 1,000 but of thousands and the entire ghetto will perish. By delivering hundreds, I save thousands and by delivering 1,000 I save 10,000."[434] In the end, however, almost nobody survived, and Gens was executed by the Germans the moment he was no longer needed.

This idea of Gens that being indispensable would prevent a total annihilation now might seem outlandish, but, in fact, it was not at the time. The extermination of Jews in Lithuania was halted in the end of 1941 because the Germans understood that they were a vital element in the economy. In Šiauliai, for example, the *Gebietskommissar* Hans Gewecke protested against the killing of all Jews by Hamann's *Rollkommando* because they were needed in the economy: "It is impossible to carry on work without the Jews. This is especially the case in the leather tanning industry. Every single artisan in this industry is Jewish."[435] Hamann responded that he didn't care, but was ordered by his superiors to back off. Already in early October 1941, a meeting was held in Kaunas to discuss the issue, and the outcome was a request to *Reichskommissar* Lohse to suspend the killing of Jews. It took, however, until December 1, 1941, for Lohse to order the suspension of the execution of irreplaceable Jewish workers. As a result, the total extermination of Jews on Lithuanian territory before the end of 1941 was only prevented because they were of economic significance.

Jacob Gens

Jacob Gens was an interesting character. Having been an officer in the Lithuanian Army and also a member of the Riflemen Union, he was, in a way, both a Jewish and a Lithuanian nationalist who believed he had to serve both. As Noah Shneidman points out, "Gens combined his Lithuanian patriotism with a right-wing Jewish nationalism. (…) He identified himself completely with the Lithuanian state."[436] To present Gens as a

434. Shneidman, N.N.: *The Three Tragic Heroes of the Ghetto*, pp. 120-121
435. Sutton, Karen, *The Massacre of the Jews of Lithuania*, p. 142
436. Shneidman, N.N.: *The Three Tragic Heroes of the Vilnius Ghetto*, p. 106. Under Soviet occupation, Gens joined the anti-Communist underground and, after a period of persecution by the Soviet authorities and unemployment, he

willful collaborator with the Germans is a very crude simplification of reality. Yes, he tried to gain time and agreed to hand over a smaller part of his community in the hope he could save a larger part, yet at the same time he also offered hope to the community. And that counted actually for many of the *Judenräte*: they created the conditions for the Jewish community to continue its daily life and maintain its spirit. Instead of becoming totally disenchanted and both morally and physically degenerated, most of the ghettos became centers of hope, of an indomitable spirit, of a sustained humanity against all odds. Gens proved to be very effective in that respect.

While serving as director of the Jewish hospital in the ghetto, he hid some leading Jewish figures and helped them stay out of German hands. Later, in many instances, Gens covered up for activities of the Jewish underground and, at least, some of the arms they received came to them via Gens. "On one hand, Gens showed some support to the resistance movement, while, on the other, he wanted to muzzle and control it because he feared it could endanger the existence of the whole ghetto."[437] This was the eternal dilemma of a man who had entered a cat-and-mouse game with the Germans, trying to save as many Jews as possible and, at the same time, knowing that in order to do so, he had to sacrifice others.

This double attitude also existed in relationship to young ghetto inhabitants who escaped to the forest to fight the Germans in partisan brigades. Gens did not stop them from escaping yet, at the same time, he considered their escape to be a danger to the ghetto. In June 1943, he said at a meeting of the ghetto police: "We are faced with the problem of escape to the forests. Here is my position: getting to the forest is easier for me than for any of you.[438] (…) But I don't want to go…. Because now there is a question: one or 20,000? … Supposing 500 persons left. When I think of that, I put myself in [Gestapo head] Neugebauer's place. If I were in his shoes, I would liquidate the whole ghetto in one go, because one has to be an idiot to let the ghetto become a reserve force for partisans. But Neugebauer is

managed to secure a job through the help of an old Lithuanian comrade-in-arms. However, when a week before the German invasion many members of the bourgeoisie, intelligentsia and former Lithuania military were rounded up for deportation to Siberia, Gens had to go into hiding again. A week later, German troops rolled into Lithuania; yet Gens, being a Jew fully aware of the risks, refused to flee to the USSR and was appointed by the same Lithuanian friend to the position of Director of the Jewish Hospital.

437. Shneidman, N.N., *The Three Tragic Heroes of the Vilnius Ghetto*, p. 123

438. Jacob Gens was not obligated to wear a Jewish yellow star on his clothes, could leave the ghetto whenever he wanted and even had a bicycle to get around the city.

no idiot. He is smarter than all of us… We can certainly say that the forest is working for the benefit of the ghetto, working to bring liberation. Quite right. But my task is to protect the loyal ghetto so long as it exists. No one ought to be able to reproach me.'"[439]

Jacob Gens full well understood that his role was a dubious one, one that would later be judged: "…If I, Jacob Gens, survive, I shall come out soiled and with blood dripping from my hands. And yet I shall present myself willingly to be judged. To be judged by Jews. I will say: 'I did everything in my power to save as many Jews as possible from the ghetto and lead them to freedom. And in order that at least a remnant of Jews should survive, I personally had to lead Jews to their deaths; and so that some people should be able to leave the ghetto with clean consciences, I had to wallow in filth and act without conscience.'"[440]

In the end, a week before the liquidation of the Ghetto, Gens reported himself to the Gestapo, in spite of a warning from Gestapo officer Martin Weiss that he would be killed. He refused to escape, however, and was shot by Gestapo Chief Rolf Neugebauer personally.[441]

439. Shneidman, N.N., *The Three Tragic Heroes of the Vilnius Ghetto*, pp. 123-124
440. Shneidman, N.N., *The Three Tragic Heroes of the Vilnius Ghetto*, p. 121
441. Shneidman, N.N., *The Three Tragic Heroes of the Vilnius Ghetto*, p. 130

Chapter 6 – The Human Dimension

The person who, with inner conviction, loathes stealing, killing, and assault may find himself performing these acts with relative ease when commanded by authority. Behavior that is unthinkable in an individual who is acting on his own may be executed without hesitation when carried out under orders.

S. Milgram[442]

Explaining is not excusing; understanding is not forgiving. Not trying to understand the perpetrators in human terms would make impossible not only this study but any history of Holocaust perpetrators that sought to go beyond one-dimensional caricature.

Christopher Browning[443]

How is it possible that human beings become active participants in a mass murder? How can one explain that seemingly ordinary, decent citizens turn into the most brutal murderers one could imagine?

Over the past decades, more and more studies have focused on this issue, partially because the passing of time has allowed people to take some distance from the terrible realities of the Second World War, but undoubtedly also because the end of the Second World War has not led to an end to mass killings and genocide. The disasters of the Pol Pot regime in Cambodia in 1975-1979, the mass murder of Tutsis in Rwanda in 1994 and the terror inflicted on the population of Southern Sudan by the northern regime that resulted in more than two million dead- all are ample proof that mass killing is not a matter of the past. Even on the European continent, exactly that happened, what people after the war said should never happen again: in the former Yugoslavia people were uprooted, killed *en masse* for religious and ethnic reasons and the name Srebrenica is irrevocably connected to the mass murder of more than 6,000 Muslim men by the army of the Bosnian Serb, Ratko Mladic.

In fact, the Holocaust was only part of the multifaceted genocide that the Nazis inflicted on Europe, reason for Donald Bloxham to call Germany

442. As quoted in Hofman, J.: *De Collaborateur*, p. 276
443. Browning, Christopher, *Ordinary Men*, p. xx

in 1933-1945 a "genocidal dictatorship." Apart from exterminating much of the Jewish presence on European soil, the Germans also killed most of its mentally handicapped and mentally ill in the so-called T4 operation,[444] (in the course of it, experimenting with gas vans that were later used for Jews as well and preceded the more "effective" gas chambers in the extermination camps). They also killed some two million ethnic Poles as well as more than three million Soviet prisoners of war, in both cases because they were seen as inferior species and considered "useless mouths" that could not be fed.[445] In devising their grandiose "*Generalplan Ost,*" which would have altered the racial composition of the lands between Germany and the Urals fundamentally, the Nazis expected some 30 million urban Soviet citizens to die of starvation.[446] Also, one should not forget that the Second World War was in fact only the "third and most violent period of transnational and interethnic conflict in recent European history in which matters were violently brought to a head," as Donald Bloxham writes. "The second was the period 1912-1922, from the Balkan wars before the First World War to the Greco-Turkish war after it. Earlier still was the 'eastern crisis' of 1875-8, as new Balkan states emerged with the decline of the Ottoman Empire, which also lost territory to Russia in the Caucasus."[447] In these cases, the genocidal target was multifaceted, not focusing on one single nationality or race alone. For instance, while the Armenian and Assyrian Christians were massacred, there was massive ethnic cleansing of Muslims in the Balkans and the period ended with ethnic cleansing between Greece and Turkey. However, of all these genocides, the Holocaust is probably the best documented one.

This issue is important in the context of analyzing the Holocaust in Lithuania since Lithuanians often tend to feel unjustifiably singled out and that was not only in Lithuania that the overwhelming majority of the

444. The Aktion T4 was the name used for the Euthanasia Program in Nazi Germany starting in October 1939 and officially lasting until August 1941 (but continued unofficially until the end of the war). The name T4 was an abbreviation of the address Tiergartenstrasse 4 in Berlin, which was the headquarters of the operation. During this operation, thousands of people with mental illness or mental handicap were killed. According to official Nazi files, during the official stage 70,273 people were killed. The Nuremberg Trials found evidence that German and Austrian physicians continued the extermination of patients after October 1941 and that, in fact, about 275,000 people were killed. More recent research based on files that were recovered after 1990 gives a figure of at least 200,000 physically or mentally handicapped people who were killed by medication, starvation, or in the gas chambers between 1939 and 1945.
445. Bloxham, Donald: *The Final Solution*, p. 10
446. Bloxham, Donald: *The Final Solution*, pp. 180-182
447. Bloxham, Donald: *The Final Solution*, p. 3

Jewish population was murdered. They point to the active participation of Latvian and Ukrainian auxiliary police battalions, who also helped kill Jews in Lithuania to Poland where, before the Second World War, 3.3 million Jews lived, of whom 90% were killed. In general, Lithuanians are quite reluctant to fully accept their own contributions to the Holocaust and point to their suffering at the hands of the Soviet occupational regime, thereby preferring to present themselves as victims of history, rather than perpetrators. For ethnic Lithuanians, the Soviet occupation had, indeed, far greater consequences than the Nazi occupation, during which actually relatively few ethnic Lithuanians died. The question is whether one could be victim and perpetrator at the same time.

In his book "*Becoming Evil: How Ordinary People Commit Genocide and Mass Killing,*" James Waller tries to analyze why people did the terrible things that happened in the 20th century and, undoubtedly, will continue to happen in this century as well. For instance, Waller discusses the concept of the "Mad Nazi," an idea that was very popular during the first years after the war and attempted to explain the Nazi murder machine by viewing it as the result of a mental disorder or aberration.[448] Some used this theory to explain the question of why so many people participated actively in the mass liquidation of nations and groups. As Waller points out, this concept is not only wrong and many of the perpetrators were, in fact, ordinary citizens with families leading a very ordinary decent life before they went on killing sprees. But also many of the leading Nazis on trial in Nürnberg were actually highly intelligent, up to the level of "genius," and showed no signs of a mental disorder at all. One psychiatrist exclaimed, after examining some of the leading Nazis, that they were very normal, more normal than he himself was after he had examined them…[449]

Waller concludes that there are several stages that "help" a person to become a mass murderer, or to stand by and not interfere, or even to turn the other way and pretend it does not concern you. He divides them into *us-them thinking, moral disengagement* and *blaming the victims*.[450]

448. See for instance the case of Otto Ohlendorf, commander of Einsatzgruppe D, later in this chapter.
449. See also Van der Heijden, Chris: *Grijs Verleden*, p. 171. The IQ of Nazi leaders were, for instance, Hjalmar Schacht 143, Artur Seyss Inquart 141, Karl Dönitz 138, Hermann Göring 138, Alfred Rosenberg 127, Rudolf Hess 120. The lowest IQ level had Julius Streicher, the editor of the anti-Semitic propaganda journal *Der Stürmer*. His IQ was 106. The next in line was Ernst Kaltenbrunner, with an IQ of 113. For a complete list, see Hofman, J.: *De Collaborateur*, p. 65
450. Waller, James: *Becoming Evil*, p. 198

A key factor that helps a potential killer overcome the barrier between not participating and participating is that of *us-them thinking*. In fact, it is in many respects a prerequisite, as killing of "one of our own" is biologically, socially and morally unjustifiable, yet when the future victim has already become "one of the other," it opens the door to justification of the evil act. In the case of the Jews, physical death was preceded by social death, by excluding them from daily life. Parks, cinemas, theaters, cafes and restaurants: all public places became inaccessible. They were not allowed to walk on the sidewalks, were ostensibly marked as different with the obligatory yellow Star of David on their clothes and with the fat black stamp of "J" (*Jude*) in their identification cards. They were like trees in a forest that are marked before being cut – they were still there, but already selected for "production"; it is only a matter of time until they were reduced to shadows in a society that continued to function without them.

In the case of *moral disengagement*, the future victims are also *morally* put outside the boundaries of the group (or society) and moral values and rules no longer apply to them. Important elements in facilitating this disconnection are moral justification, in the course of which the future perpetrator finds sufficient reasons and justifications why killing is allowed or even becomes a necessary step (for instance to guarantee racial purity); dehumanization of the victims, by which they loose their human face and become mere "objects" to be discarded; and, finally, through euphemistic labeling of evil actions, by rewording "killing" into more acceptable vocabulary such as "disposing," "collateral damage" or – a Nazi favorite – giving the victims "special treatment. As Haig Bosmajian said, "The distance between the linguistic dehumanization of a people and their actual suppression and extermination is not great,"[451] and thus by "giving special treatment" to "goods," the perpetrator finds a way to deal with the terrible evil in which he is engaged.

An extreme example of this is a note written in June 1942 with regard to the gas vans in the extermination camp in Chelmo. In the note, improvements to the van structure are being proposed in order to increase the efficacy: "...the following technical changes are needed. The van's normal load is usually nine per square yard. In Sauer vehicles, which are very spacious, maximum use of space is impossible, not because of any potential overload, but because loading to full capacity would affect the vehicle's stability. So reduction of the load space seems necessary. It must be reduced by a yard absolutely, instead of trying to solve the problem, as hitherto, by reducing the number of pieces loaded. Besides, this extends the operating

451. Bosmajian, Haig: *The Language of Oppression*. University Press of America, 1983, p. 29

time, as the empty void must also be filled with carbon monoxide. On the other hand, if load space is reduced, and the vehicle is packed solid, the operating time can be considerably shortened. The manufacturers told us during a discussion that reducing the size of the van's rear would throw it badly off balance. The front axle, they claim, would be overloaded. In fact, the balance is automatically restored, because the merchandise aboard displays during the operation a natural tendency to rush to the rear doors, and is mainly found lying there at the end of the operation."[452] The document continues to explain that fixing lamps inside the van is necessary as "the load naturally rushes towards the light when darkness sets in, which makes closing the doors difficult. Also because of the alarming nature of darkness, screaming always occurs when the doors are closed." It takes a while for the reader to fully realize that the "merchandise" is, in fact, live human beings who are about to be gassed in "the operation." It's a gruesome example of total dehumanization.

At the same time we should not forget, as Thomas Kühne asserts, that degradation has a specific meaning for the perpetrator: it is constructive. "It binds the perpetrators to a collectivity and reinforces their solidarity. By destroying the symbols, the bonds, and the identities of their victims, the perpetrators strengthen their ethics of hardness and thus their own social identity."[453] And this solidarity, this sense of belonging is, in the view of Kühne, an essential factor in enabling people to become mass murderers. While reflecting on photos of the mass killings, he writes: "On the one hand we see a triumphant group of perpetrators, enjoying themselves committing or watching cruelty. They stick together, they act together, and they feel together. They experience belonging, the epitome of 'humanity' – a special notion of 'humanity' to be sure. On the other hand, there are the isolated, humiliated, naked victims – frightened and freezing, robbed of the signs of their personal identity, all looking alike, no longer retaining any identity."[454]

Finally, *blaming the victim* is a very easy way of transferring the guilt onto the victim. The American philosopher Berel Lang writes in *The Evil in Genocide* that "the perpetrator's justification for genocide often cites the responsibility of the targeted group, claiming that its decisions or actions have caused harm or represent a danger to others."[455] Of course, throughout the Holocaust literature, we find references to the danger that

452. Quoted in Bloxham, Donald: *The Final Solution*, pp. 27-28
453. Kühne, Thomas: *Belonging and Genocide*, p. 78
454. Kühne, Thomas: *Belonging and Genocide*, p. 78
455. Lang, Berel: *The Evil in Genocide*, in Roth, John K.: *Genocide and Human Rights: A Philosophical Guide*, New York, 2005, p. 12

Jews were said to cause to society, civilization and racial purity, and there are also many examples of people, both perpetrators and bystanders, who lamented why the Jews allowed themselves so easily to be led to their killing, as if it would have made any difference if their own behavior had been different. People completely tend to forget the fact that the Jews suddenly found themselves in a totally hostile environment, that their very neighbors turned out to be not only indifferent to their fate but sometimes even joined the perpetrators. They were stunned and resisting seemed to be utterly useless. As Alexander Donat wrote in his memoir, "They fought against hunger and starvation, against disease, against a deadly Nazi economic blockade. They fought against murderers and against traitors within their own ranks, and they were utterly alone in their fight. They were forsaken by God and by man, surrounded by hatred and indifference."[456] Yet in reality, with historical research progressing, it becomes increasingly clear that there were, in fact, still many acts of resistance,[457] and that one has to conclude that Jews were no different than their fellow countrymen: the majority of the population complied, followed orders, tried to survive by going along, and only a relatively small portion resisted actively. Why should it have been different for Jews?

Franz Stangl, the former commander of extermination camp Treblinka where, in a period of 15 months between 0.8 and 1.2 million Jews were gassed, added another aspect to this ability to commit the worst possible crime and still live with it: through *compartimentalization* of the brain: "What I had to do... was to limit my own actions to what I – in my own conscience – could answer for. At police training school, they taught us ... that the definition of a crime must meet four requirements: there has to be a subject, and object, an action and an intent. If any of these four elements are missing, then we are not dealing with a punishable offence. (...) The only way I could live was by compartmentalizing my thinking. By doing this I *could* apply it to my own situation; if the 'subject' was the government, the 'object' the Jews, and the 'action' the gassings, then I could tell myself that, for me, the fourth element, 'intent' (he called it 'free will')... was missing."[458]

And Stangl continued this compartimentalization all the way until he was faced with life-long imprisonment and a British journalist that did not let

456. Donat, Alexander: *The Holocaust Kingdom*, p. 7
457. In the Soviet Red Army, at least 500,000 Jews saw active service; more than 200,000 died in the course of the war. In spite of the fact that they comprised of only 2% of the population, 161,000 Jews received war decorations, which put them as the fourth ranking nationality. See Klier, John: *The Holocaust and the Soviet Union*, in Stone, Dan: *The Historiography of the Holocaust*, p. 279
458. Sereny, Gitta: *Into that Darkness*, p. 164

him off the hook. In fact, a unique factor made him *decompartmentalize* – namely the fact that Gitta Sereny became a friend, almost a priest to which he was finally allowed to confess. And during the last interview session, Stangl came to what can be considered the closest to admittance of his guilt. "He paused and waited, but the room remained silent. I have never intentionally hurt anyone… myself," he said, with a different, less incisive emphasis, and waited again – for a long time…. For the first time, in all these many days, I had given him no help. There was no more time. He gripped the table with both hands as if he was holding on to it. "'But I was there,' he said then, in a curiously dry and tired tone of resignation. These few sentences had taken almost half an hour to pronounce. 'So yes' he said finally, very quickly, 'in reality I share the guilt… Because my guilt… my guilt… only now in these talks…. Now that I have talked about it for the first time….' He stopped. He had pronounced the words 'my guilt': but more than the words, the finality of it was the sagging of his body and on his face. After more than a minute he started again, a half-hearted attempt, in a dull voice. 'My guilt,' he said, 'is that I am still here, that is my guilt. (…) I should have died. That was my guilt'."[459]

Who participated?

One of the main defendants in the 1947 Einsatzgruppen trial in Nürnberg was *SS-Brigadeführer* Otto Ohlendorf, former commander of *Einsatzgruppe D.* After his arrest Ohlendorf was extensively interrogated by the Americans at a moment when very little was yet known about the activities of the *Einsatzgruppen* in the East. The American interrogators were astonished: "The acts that Ohlendorf described were so uniquely and utterly horrifying that skeptical U.S. Intelligence officers often had difficulty believing their prisoner was in full possession of his sanity."[460] Psychologists had great difficulty understanding how a man could be so intelligent yet, at the same time, a mass murderer. As Hilary Earl writes, "Ohlendorf seemed perfectly comfortable with his horrific actions, discussing them within a framework of rational thought, as if they were simply the duties of a professional man who had carried on with his daily work schedule."[461]

459. Sereny, Gitta: *Into That Darkness*, p.364. Rudolf Hoess had much less difficulty expressing his guilt (Hoess, Rudolf: *Commandant of Auschwitz*, p. 80) yet, at the same time, when reading his autobiography, one wonders how much of that guilt feeling actually goes deep. In other words, he may know the word, but not the meaning.
460. Earl, Hilary: *The Nuremberg Einsatzgruppen Trial*, p. 55
461. Earl, Hilary: *The Nuremberg Einsatzgruppen Trial*, p. 58

In 1969, the German journalist, Heinz Höhne, analyzed who the members were of the *Einsatzkommandos* that orchestrated and carried out the killings in the East as the German troops invaded. His conclusion was that people were not selected because of being sadists or brutes. "In fact," he writes, "the Jew-liquidators were a curious collection – highly qualified academics, ministerial officials, lawyers and even a Protestant priest and an opera singer. (...) Even among the rank and file, enthusiasm for [SS Chief] Heydrich's duty in the East was so small that he had to comb all the Gestapo, *Kripo* (criminal police), and SD offices to obtain the necessary personnel. He was even compelled to scratch men out from the *Ordnungspolizei*[462] [Order Police] and *Waffen SS*; a Berlin Police battalion was disbanded and distributed by platoons to the individual *Einsatzgruppen*."[463] To the contrary, the candidates that were selected were selected exactly because they were "sane" and "ordinary" and not sadists and brutes. The leadership feared that those who would derive pleasure from the killings would not be trustworthy enough. Höhne writes: "The system and rhythm of mass extermination were directed not by sadists... [but by] worthy family men brought up in the belief that anti-Semitism was a form of pest control, harnessed into an impersonal mechanical system working with the precision of militarized industry and relieving the individual of any sense of personal responsibility." They were hardened men, "a determined army of death" as Höhne calls it. "Wholly dedicated to achievement, 'hardness' and camaraderie, they reached a degree of insensibility surpassed only by those soulless automata, the concentration-camp guards." Yet, he continues, "When faced individually with the thousand-fold murders they themselves had committed, all their façade of neo-German heroism collapsed. The Germanic knights shrank back into what they had always been – inflated mediocrities, carrying out their bestial handiwork with typical German self-pity, all the while thinking, with sentimental tears in their eyes, of their wives and children at home."[464]

Equally important is the fact that any person who became part of the German administrative system was, in principle, liable to become part of the killing machine. "Any member of the Order Police could become a guard at a ghetto or on a train," Raul Hilberg writes. "Every lawyer in the Reich Security Main Office was presumed to be suitable for leadership in the mobile killing units; every finance expert to the Economic-Administrative Main Office was considered a natural choice for service in a death camp.

462. The *Ordnungspolizei* consisted of men who were too old or unfit for regular military service and these units were used for policing duties in occupied territories, guarding trains with people heading for the extermination camps and guarding ghettos and mass execution sites.
463. Höhne, Hans: *The Order of the Death's Head*, p. 328-329.
464. Höhne, Hans: *The Order of the Death's Head*, p. 334-335

(...). However one may wish to draw the line of active participation, the machinery of destruction was a remarkable cross-section of the German population."[465] In other words, becoming part of the system was a sort of slippery slope, a path down the mountain with hardly a chance of escape unless one deliberately made a choice to do so (like police officer Klaus Hornig did, who refused to participate in the killings as a member of the *Einsatzkommando* and as a result wound up in Buchenwald himself. See later in this chapter). Instead, the overwhelming majority of men became part of the machinery of destruction, and not only because of peer pressure, but also because of so-called "pluralistic ignorance," a situation in which their seeming acceptance of what is "normal" is caused by the reluctance of all members of the group to speak up. As a result of this collective silence, individual members of the group convince themselves that what is happening is indeed normal, even though under usual circumstances, the person concerned would never have considered it normal at all.

But being on this slippery slope was far from enough to cope with the murderous task ahead. The members of the Einsatzkommandos were, therefore, well prepared in advance, as they were to implement the "heaviest task," as *Reichsführer SS* Heinrich Himmler called it. "The gradual process of what I term *Erziehung zum Mord* (rehearsing for murder) was facilitated by exercises aimed at strengthening group bonds and ensuring conformity to Nazi ideology, particularly anti-Semitism," writes German historian Konrad Kwiet. "In all police and SS units, special emphasis was placed on ideological indoctrination by means of regular political instruction. Within this training program, there was a comprehensive exposure to anti-Semitic literature, incendiary speeches and anti-Jewish films often screened on the eve of *Judenaktionen*."[466] Also, special attention was paid to the emotional well-being of the executioners. At the killing sites, alcohol and cigarette rations were distributed, troops were feted at dinner parties that quickly turned into evenings of binge drinking, and, after Aktionen, they were taken on excursions or even holidays.

On top of that the executioners were sort of "introduced" into the killings: the first rounds focused mainly on able-bodied men (who could be purveyed as potential enemy fighters), next came women and children who were seen as "useless eaters" and thus had to go as well. By the time women and children were murdered *en masse*, the killing had become routine and the members of the *Einsatzgruppen* had become dehumanized enough to carry out any orders. "After the first experiences with kill-

465. Hilberg, Raul: *The Destruction of European Jews*, p. 1011
466. Kwiet, Konrad: *Hitler's Willing Executioners and Ordinary Germans; Some Comments on Goldhagen's Ideas*

ing, 'ordinary men' displayed sentiments and modes of behavior which excluded any feeling of sympathy for the victims and were symptomatic for the destruction of all moral and human values."[467] And finally, the killings took place in what Donald Bloxham calls "zones of exception," meaning ghettos, mass execution sites, the anti-partisan "free fire zones" and the extermination camps: "The zones of exception conditioned behavior as much as did attitudes to specific groups," writes Bloxham. "This is true of any environment in which the rules are just different and it helps explain why, when soldiers and policemen returned from the places of exception to a land of 'normality' (Germany) at war's end, they reintegrated relatively easily."[468] Yet in the course of the war, in particular when the Germans started losing and their armies were retreating rapidly in face of the Allied forces, the difference between "zones of exception" and the "land of normality" gradually faded away.

Those who participated in the killings could, according to Konrad Kwiet, be divided into three groups: The hardened killers or *Dauerschützen* (permanent shooters), who excelled in brutality and zeal and formed the core of the Einsatzgruppen. Next came the largest group, the grey mass, who felt uneasy about their participation, needed time to get adjusted to it but, in the end, participated actively and sometimes even seemingly enthusiastically, because to them it was important how they were perceived by the group and that they were not seen as weak and without courage. The third group, by far the smallest, consisted of those who dared to resist and they had to pay a price. According to Christopher Browning, some 20% of those called to duty in the execution squads dared to resist. A former SD officer estimated in 1967: "Absolute executors about 30 percent, the anti-group about 20 percent and then a group in between, which stuck to the methods of the hell raisers."[469]

By coincidence, during my youth, I had skiing holidays together with my parents in a hotel in Austria that was also frequented by a middle-aged German. My father went to talk with him and it turned out that his life story was anything but usual. Having been an officer in the criminal police in Frankfurt, Klaus Hornig was inducted into a police battalion at the onset of the German invasion of the Soviet Union.[470] His police bat-

467. Kwiet, Konrad: *Hitler's Willing Executioners and Ordinary Germans; Some Comments on Goldhagen's Ideas*
468. Bloxham, Donald: *The Final Solution*, p. 285
469. Kühne, Thomas: *Belonging and Genocide*, p. 87
470. According to the data I have, Klaus Hornig was born in 1907 in Silesia as the son of a dentist. He had four sisters. He studied law in Wroclaw/Breslau and Königsberg (now Kaliningrad), and joined the Prussian police in 1930. In 1935, he became lieutenant in the national police *(Landespolizei)* based in

talion 306 was stationed in Lublin and, in November, they were ordered to participate in the execution of political commissars from the Soviet Army as well as Jews. Hornig refused, referring to article 47 of the Military Criminal Code that stipulated that a soldier could refuse an order if it was in conflict with his conscience. At the personal order of Heinrich Himmler, he was arrested and eventually delivered to concentration camp Buchenwald. In March 1945, he was sentenced to 5 years and 7 months for refusing to obey orders.[471] Liberated by the Americans in April 1945, he was arrested again because of his having been a member of a police battalion. Until 1947, he remained in custody, working in Nürnberg at the War Crimes Tribunal as a witness and an interpreter. Eventually, in 1986, he was given the *Bundesverdienstkreuz* (West German Order of Merit) for his bravery. We corresponded in 1986 and met that winter, but my plans to publish his memoirs faltered. They are still in my possession and are an unusual record of an exceptional man who did say no. Hornig was not the only officer who refused on basis of article 47, as we can see, for instance, from the book *Belonging and Genocide* by Thomas Kühne. However, he might have been an exception in having been arrested because of his refusal.

In a sociological-psychological study of the medical files and histories of 52 convicted Dutch war criminals, the Dutch psychiatrist Jacob Hofman tried to analyze the reasons why these men and women had collaborated with the German occupational forces and had been involved in crimes for which they were later convicted. After a careful analysis, he concluded that most of them had one or more of the following character traits: resentment or a hurt narcissism leading to vengeance, an overcompensated feeling of inferiority, (frustrated) self-assertiveness, sadism and destructive tendencies, a desire for power or prestige, strong urge to submit to

Frankfurt/Main. Later the *Landespolizei* was integrated into the Army and Hornig was promoted to the position of First Lieutenant. In October 1941, he was sent to Lublin to report for duty in the police battalion 306. Because of his constant criticism of operational matters and the brutality with which people were killed en masse, Hornig was discharged and sent back to Frankfurt/Main. In May 1942, he was arrested and via several prisons transported to Konzentrationslager Buchenwald.

471. Thomas Kühne incorrectly asserts in his book *Belonging and Genocide* that "no police officer, no SS man, no soldier in Nazi Germany ever suffered serious punishment for refusing to participate in the murder of Jews or other civilians." See Kühne, Thomas: *Belonging and Genocide*, p. 76. One explanation might be that Klaus Hornig refused to participate on ethical grounds and openly protested against the killing of innocent civilians. In most cases, those who refused claimed personal weakness as an excuse. See Boxham, Donald: *The Final Solution*, p. 263

authority and the desire to belong to a structured and disciplined unit. However, Hofman adds, not only the German oppressor offered the possibility to fulfill these desires, but also the resistance could provide an answer and, thus, some wound up on the German side and others on the side of the resistance. As Hofman's book points out, sometimes one child from a family would join the Germans, while the other would become part of the resistance.[472] It was often the circumstance that made one child go to one side, and the other to the other. In addition, "Joining the national-socialist movement did not necessarily lead to a form of collaboration, even if alone, because the price of treason was considered a high one for a political conviction. On the other hand, certainly not all collaborators were national socialists, and also not automatically criminals..."[473]

Also the Dutch scholar Dick de Wildt investigated the reasons why people became participants in the Nazi repressive machinery. He concluded that, in most cases, they were people whose behavior was caused by much more banal motives than idealistic ones. Often their recruitment happened rather coincidentally or friends, acquaintances and family introduced them. Their willingness to participate in the "bureaucracy of genocide" stemmed largely from pragmatic reasons. In other words, they were led purely by their self-interests. Concretely this usually meant the desire to survive, improvement of position (job, status, income), or avoiding having to go to the front. If one would have to summarize their profile in one word, it would be "opportunism" and not "idealism."[474]

Jacob Hofman concluded in his study about Dutch collaborators that it is impossible to maintain that the collaborators whose cases he examined were a bunch of sadists, bastards without a conscious or Machiavellians hungry for power.[475] In fact, half of the persons whose medical files were examined came from families that could be regarded as disharmonious or conflicting. Also, it was hard to establish exactly how many of the subjects of examination had been members of fascist or pro-German organizations before the war. However, only five had been members of the Dutch fascist party NSB. Most of them were found to be fearsome, emotionally immature persons with a normal intelligence yet with little internal harmony and stability.

In general terms, according to Hofman, most of the collaborators examined started out performing rather innocent jobs such as interpreting or

472. Hofman, J.: *De Collaborateur*, p. 268
473. Hofman, J.: *De Collaborateur*, p. 138
474. See Blom, J. C. H. *In de Ban van Goed en Fout*, p. 113
475. Hofman, J.: *De Collaborateur*, p. 274

being a censor, and gradually slid into more serious forms of collaboration. In their behavior, they fit into the increasingly strong confrontation within Dutch society between "good" and "evil," in particular during the last year of the war. From the moment they agreed to join the oppressor, they slid into isolation and became dependent on a system of coercion from which it was very difficult if not impossible to escape. As Hofman points out, one could see two group dynamic processes: on one hand, conforming to the group to which one belonged and on which one was dependent; on the other hand a decreasing sense of being responsible personally for acts perpetrated because they were demanded by the group and no dissent was accepted.[476]

Of all the persons examined, 29 had been charged with physical abuse or murder, but only among four of them was evidence found of sadism, in two cases, related to sexual desires. In none of the cases, however, was sadism, in any form, part of the motive for their deeds.[477] He concluded further: "One has to assume that the majority of those examined acted out of an elementary urge for self-preservation and prestige. Fear of German superiors, fear of the opponents and, in some cases, fear of being seen as fearful and soft of heart seem to have played major roles. One of the persons under investigation who had been involved in maltreatment of Jews explained his behavior as follows: 'You should not see the acts I performed as sadistic pleasure, because if that had been the case, then it would have been no difference for me whether one would hurt a Jew or a Christian. Why I did it? I will try to explain by using an example: you need to compare my behavior with that of one of the boys who are teasing a kitten. The one who joins later finds it a rather horrid spectacle, but to make an impression and above all not to be seen as less, he participates and hits even harder than the others, although deep in his heart he knows he is doing something wrong'."[478]

When discussing Latvian participation in the Holocaust, Jukka Rislakki also examined who the Latvians were that became involved in mass killings. Here the picture is the same: they were not rabid fascists and anti-Semitic activists, but rather socially marginalized and rather uneducated Latvians who were turned into willing tools of the mass murder machinery: "...Very few in the Commando's ranks were members of the extreme right Thundercross or of student fraternities. Rudite Viksne, who has investigated the backgrounds of all known Commando members, relates that typically they were poorly paid young laborers with an incomplete

476. Hofman, J.: *De Collaborateur*, p. 260
477. Hofman, J.: *De Collaborateur*, p. 272-274
478. Hofman, J.: *De Collaborateur*, pp. 270-271

secondary education or former policemen or soldiers, coming from "socially and morally marginalized groups" and driven by selfish motives, not by a lust for revenge or a hatred of Jews... Only one of them mentioned later in court that his motive was hatred of Jews.'"[479]

In the case of the Polish town of Jedwabne, all but seven of the 1600 Jews in town were killed on July 10, 1941. New York Professor Jan Gross carefully investigated the massacre and published a book in 2001 titled "*Neighbors*" in which he wrote: "...what the Jews saw, to their horror and, I dare say, incomprehension, were familiar faces. Not anonymous men in uniform, cogs in a war machine, agents carrying out orders, but their own neighbors, who chose to kill and were engaged in a bloody pogrom – willing executioners.'"[480] As Gross points out, the local population in Eastern Poland had various reasons to participate actively in the murder of the Jews in the summer of 1941, after the Germans had started their war against the Soviet Union and formerly Soviet occupied territories were now occupied by the Nazis. First of all, active participation helped them to "endear themselves to the new rulers.'"[481] This particularly counted for Poles who had collaborated with the Soviets and were hence prone to be arrested or fall victim to violence themselves. "It is not difficult to imagine that among the most active participants in the Jedwabne pogrom were several ... secret collaborators of the NKVD..."[482] Other factors were, according to Gross, the possibility to enrich themselves by stealing the property of the murdered Jews, the traditional animosity against the Jews (based on the conviction that Jews used fresh blood of innocent Christian children in the preparation of matzoh[483]) and, of course, the fact that the local population was whipped up by the arriving Nazi forces. An additional factor was the fact that Jews were said to have been particularly active in the Communist regime, and thus had to pay the price for their collaboration with the Soviets. As we have seen, this was also a major factor in Lithuania, and was very successfully used by the Germans to jumpstart the local population into action. In fact, the Germans had stimulated this "private initiative" by first stirring up anti-Semitism with their propaganda before the outbreak of the war, and by issuing a special directive by *SS Reichskommissar* Reinhardt Heydrich stipulating that pogroms by locals were permitted.[484] As Gross adds to his summing up: "Who could resist such a potent, devilish mixture?'"[485]

479. Rislakki, Jukka: *The Case for Latvia*, p. 118
480. Gross, Jan: *Neighbors*, p. 78
481. *Neighbors*, p. 109
482. *Neighbors*, p. 109
483. *Neighbors*, p. 80
484. Breitman, Richard: *The Architect of Genocide – Himmler and the Final Solution*. New York, 1991, pp. 171-173.
485. *Neighbors*, p. 109

Who were the Lithuanian collaborators?

In The Netherlands, the five years of German occupation were followed by a reinstitution of democratic rule. Collaborators and war criminals were, when possible, convicted and served at least part of their sentence, even though the post-war attitude of forgetting the past and building the future often led to sentences being cut short and people being back on the streets surprisingly quickly. In the years that followed, especially in the 1960s and beyond, much research was carried out to understand who collaborated with the Germans and why and psychiatric reports of those who had undergone psychiatric examinations during their pre-trial detention proved to be extremely interesting and enlightening materials.[486]

However, in Lithuania, German occupational rule was followed by Soviet occupational rule and after a few years, Soviet anti-Semitism resulted in the closing of Jewish organizations, Jewish museums, and the "de-Jewification" of memorials to the victims of the Holocaust. Even during trials against former Lithuanian collaborators in the mass killings, the interest in that part of their story was minimal.[487] As a result, the issue was frozen, as it were, and apart from some politically correct publications published in Soviet Lithuania, it remained so until the country recovered its independence. By then, however, many of those involved – both victims and perpetrators – had already died and much vital historical research material was lost.

And also after independence, the issue remained a disputed one. Lithuania was recovering its national pride, getting to terms with its complex Soviet past, and additional complexities were not needed. Lithuania was the first of the newly independent post-Soviet states to legislate the protection and marking of Holocaust-related sites. When Algirdas Brazauskas, President of Lithuania, addressed the Israeli Knesset in 2001, he offered a public apology to the Jewish people for the Lithuanian participation in the Holocaust. And on September 20, 2001, marking the 60th anniversary of the Holocaust in Lithuania, the Seimas (Lithuanian parliament) held a session during which historian Alfonsas Eidintas delivered an address accounting for the annihilation of Lithuania's Jews. However, at the same time, the country has been very slow in acknowledging the active collaboration with the German extermination machinery and many people have difficulty accepting the fact that some heroes of the anti-Soviet partisans were,

486. See, for instance, Hofman, J.: *De Collaborateur. Een Sociaal-Psychologisch Onderzoek naar Misdadig Gedrag in dienst van de Duitse Bezetter. 1981*
487. See, for instance, Puišytė, Rūta: *Holocaust in Jurbarkas*

at the same time, persons who committed crimes against humanity when participating in the killing of Jews.

Indeed, the composition of Lithuania's Jew-killers is a complex one and, unfortunately, many records available for study in The Netherlands are non-existent in Lithuania. The partisans who escaped Soviet arrest and managed to escape to the free West were received as national heroes and there was never any attempt to figure out whether their whole "partisan career" had been so admirable. Most died in freedom and took their histories with them to the grave. Others were less lucky and some were even extradited to Lithuania to be tried for war crimes, yet none of them ever served even one day in jail. As a result, it is impossible to carry out thorough studies the way Hofman managed to analyze the psychiatric reports of collaborators in pre-trial detention, and both Daniel Goldhagen and Christopher Browning managed to analyze the membership of Reserve Police Battalion 101 from Hamburg.

Still, one may assume that also the Lithuanian "Jew-liquidators" were no different than their "colleagues" in other countries. Many of the members of the TDA Police Battalions that worked alongside the *Einsatzkommandos* had been officers in the Lithuanian Army during the *interbellum* and were, thus, used to having discipline and carrying out orders. Others had been policemen so they, too, could hardly be considered irregulars. Among the partisans who were active in mass killings in the provinces, again many had been officers in the Lithuanian Army. They were, however, locally assisted by ordinary citizens, who either did not dare to resist or were guided by their hope that they would gain in one way or another – at least by being able to steal goods from the murdered Jews, which happened on a massive scale. As James Waller points out, this also was the main driving force for the hundreds of thousands of Hutus who participated in the killing of Tutsis in Rwanda in 1994: "[Their] major motivation for killing was to steal their victim's property – land, furniture, radios, or what little cash they carried. At the other end of the social spectrum were numbers of intellectuals and professionals – doctors, teachers, journalists, and even priests – who participated in the massacres. As New York Times correspondent Raymond Bonner wrote, 'It was not just a few young toughs and uneducated peasants who killed. The guilty cut across the social and economic strata'."[488] And then, again, the killings became possible because of the silent majority, those who preferred to look the other way, either because of indifference towards the fate of the Jews or because of a simple basic human character trait that all of us have, in one form or another: fear.

488. Waller, James: *Becoming Evil*, p. 73

In conclusion, maybe the terrible reality is that in principle we all are able to be not just compliant but also active, active as (mass) murderer. As Aleksandr Solzhenitsyn wrote: "The line that separates good and evil does not go through classes or groups, but right through every human heart. (...) A bridgehead of good will remain even in a heart occupied by evil and, likewise, even in the most merciful heart, there will be an impregnable hiding place for evil."[489] In his introduction to Rudolf Hoess' memoirs as Commander of Auschwitz, which he wrote before his execution in 1947, the well-known author Primo Levi writes "This book is filled with evil... it has no literary quality and reading it is agony... The author comes across as what he is: a coarse, stupid, arrogant, long-winded scoundrel, who sometimes blatantly lies."[490] Of course, considering the fact that Primo Levi survived Auschwitz, one cannot expect him to judge otherwise. However, when one reads Hoess' memoirs as detachedly as possible (which in itself is quite a task), one has to conclude something else: Hoess is just a typical not-too-intelligent human being, with all his fears and hopes and complexities ("Yet who is able to foresee the intricate course of man's destiny? What is right? And what is wrong?"[491]), and yet became one of the biggest mass killers in human history. That is, in fact, much more worrying than Hoess being a "coarse, stupid, arrogant, long-winded scoundrel." That means that ordinary human beings can become the worst criminals; there is no reprieve.

After the war

Alas this is not all: the story becomes even more complicated when one looks at the aftermath of the war and its disastrous consequences. Because even when the war ended, along with the need to fear German reprisals, the surviving Jews were welcomed back with suspicion: in The Netherlands, in Poland, and also in Lithuania. When Maria Orwid, who survived the Holocaust in Poland, entered the Jagiellonian University in Kraków in Poland and applied for membership in the students' union, the chairman of the selection committee asked her in front of everybody: "How did it happen that you live, colleague?"[492] People hadn't expected Jews to survive and see them back and the reaction was often a mixture of continued anti-Semitic feelings combined with both suspicion and guilt. Guilt, because people had either stood by and watched, had actively participated, or had stolen Jewish property as soon as their neighbors were taken away. Now

489. Aleksandr Solzhenitsyn, in the 1999 Holocaust Lecture by Prof. Philip Zimbardo, Holocaust Studies Center, Sonoma State University
490. Hoess, Rudolf: *Commandant of Auschwitz*, p. 21
491. Hoess, Rudolf: *Commandant of Auschwitz*, p. 64
492. Bomba, Jacek: *Overcoming Impossible*, p. 62

the witnesses were back and people were afraid of what that would mean: would they have to hand back the stolen property? Would these living witnesses of the atrocities mean that criminal court proceedings would become a possibility? Many returning Jews could not deal with this hostile attitude and emigrated, either to North America or to Palestine.

In The Netherlands, some 5,500 Jews returned from the camps, out of a total of 112,000 Jews deported. While fellow countrymen immediately picked up French, Belgian and Scandinavian survivors to transport them home, the Dutch often had to wait in the camps for weeks and even months.[493] And when finally arriving home, an unpleasant surprise awaited them. The prevailing attitude was that the returning Jews should not complain. One survivor remembered that when she arrived at Amsterdam Central Station "I heard people say that we should be glad that we had not been here. They said they had suffered such a terrible hunger. As if I had been in San Moritz."[494] A survivor from the camp in Theresienstadt was first transferred to Switzerland, where he went to school, received new clothes and his parents tried to get their lives back in shape. Two years later, back in Holland, they received an astronomical bill: the Dutch civil administration had kept an exact record of all the costs incurred and expected the Jewish survivors to pay back to the last penny.[495]

Sometimes upon their return to The Netherlands, Jewish survivors were even interned in the same camps as collaborators, sometimes even in the same dormitories, sleeping side by side. That happened, in particular, to the German Jews who fled to The Netherlands after Hitler ascended to power. They had lost their German nationality and were declared "stateless" by the Nazis, but after the war the Dutch gave back their German nationality and, thus, they were treated like any other German in The Netherlands, namely as citizens of a hostile nation.[496] In order to prevent being cursed upon as "dirty Nazis," they sewed back on the Yellow Stars that they just recently had been able remove from their clothes, as a means of identification. One survivor of the concentration camp Bergen Belsen, Joseph Weiss, was treated scandalously in camp Vilt in Southern Limburg, where the commander told him that he was definitely not a friend of the Jews and that Weiss would find that to be true. Weiss was livid: "We are stateless Jews who have been sent back to The Netherlands by Russian and American authorities, because everybody had to return to the country from which he was deported by the Germans. There were people in our

493. Citroen, Michal: *U Wordt door Niemand Verwacht*, p. 42
494. Citroen, Michal: *U Wordt door Niemand Verwacht*, p. 55
495. Citroen, Michal: *U Wordt door Niemand Verwacht*, p. 57
496. Citroen, Michal: *U Wordt door Niemand Verwacht*, p. 87

transport who didn't want to go to The Netherlands, but they were forced to."[497] Another returnee, Ina Rosenthal, remembers of the same camp in Vilt: "We were brought to a school building in Vilt, where members of the NSB and the SS were being held. In a classroom, there were army beds and we had to sleep between those SS men and NSB members. It was terrible. Around the playground, they had put barbed wire and we were treated like prisoners. The whole day they were shouting at you."[498] Also in Westerbork some 900 Jews were forced to live together with the new arrivals, members of the Dutch Fascist NSB. By the end of June, a remaining 300 Jews shared the camp with 10,000 NSB members.[499]

A camp commander in Limburg, Southern Netherlands, where returning Jews were interned, bitterly remarked that the Jews should stop complaining. Everybody had a difficult time during the war, but that didn't give them the right to complain. "That was the most often heard complaint: Jews were seen as noisy people, trying to attract attention, theatrical and not missing any possibility to put themselves in the front row. And then that whole business with the camps came in very handy indeed."[500] All of the survivors bitterly remember how different the reception had been in other countries; and by the time they entered the Netherlands, it was like a cold shower.

People were even surprised that Jews reclaimed their own possessions and even their pre-war positions. Famous is the remark by a Dutch woman who, with her husband, inhabited an apartment previously owned by a Jewish family, and suddenly finds the Jew on her doorstep to reclaim his possessions: "Why do we always have bad luck?! Why is it exactly *our* Jew who comes back?!"[501] Even the former underground newspaper, *Het Parool*, even though proudly referring to its resistance past, published an angry article on July 24, 1945 about the fact that former civil servant E. Polak wanted his pre-war position as member of the provincial parliament of Northern Holland back. "This report resulted in surprise in many circles... Mr. Polak left his position during the German invasion of our country without having any urgent reasons to do so."[502] Another former underground publication, *De Patriot*, wrote in the same month: "The resurfaced Jews should thank God for the assistance provided and make themselves small. Maybe much better people have perished. And that is something all 'resurfacers' should remember: there is a lot to repair. Many are the people who wound up in

497. Citroen, Michal: *U Wordt door Niemand Verwacht*, p. 88
498. Citroen, Michal: *U Wordt door Niemand Verwacht*, p. 88
499. Citroen, Michal: *U Wordt door Niemand Verwacht*, p. 89
500. Van der Heijden, Chris: *Grijs Verleden*, p. 357
501. Citroen, Michal: *U Wordt door Niemand Verwacht*, p. 115
502. Quoted in Van der Heijden, Chris: *Grijs Verleden*, p. 358

trouble while providing aid to Jews. At this time, Jews should refrain from excesses and should always keep in mind that they ought to be grateful."[503]

And hence, in the Dutch press, hardly any attention was paid to the extermination of the Jews. "Information on the extermination of Jews was limited to a few small reports," writes Michal Citroen. "Eyewitnesses of the conditions in the camps were not reported. Lists of missing or murdered Jews were not published, even if alone because of the length of the lists. But there was room for a discussion among non-Jews about anti-Semitism and 'the Jewish question.' Many articles and commentaries on these issues were published before May 1945 [in the Southern part of The Netherlands, liberated in September 1944]. Various authors made use of the opportunity to express their concern about the privileged position that Jews would retake after the war. Their writings show a hardly covered up anti-Semitism…"[504]

However, the hostility not only focused on the Jews themselves, but often also on those who had helped them survive. As Gross describes in "*Neighbors,*" members of the Wyrzykowski family that had saved seven of Jedwabne's 1,500 Jews were eventually forced to leave town for good and one of the family members even emigrated to the United States in order to escape the stigma.[505] Gross also recalls the story of a Polish woman who lived in a small town near Krakow who hid two Jewish children in her house. Neighbors incessantly demanded that she kill them and, in the end, she escaped this terrible fate for the children by pretending that she had drowned them in a nearby lake. "And we are left with the frightening realization that the population … sighed with relief only after its inhabitants were persuaded that one of their neighbors had murdered two small Jewish children."[506]

503. Van der Heijden, Chris: *Grijs Verleden*, p. 358. The same attitude was prevailing in other countries as well. Michal Citroen refers in his book, U Wordt Door Niemand Verwacht, to a Jew who survived the war and went to his home in Katowice to check and was told that he was not welcome. "When he said that the house and everything in it belonged to him, he was told that the past was not the same as the present. That he should be glad that he was still alive because that stupid Hitler had not even burned all the Jews. And if he would not leave quickly they would finish Hitler's job." See Citroen, Michal: *U Wordt door Niemand Verwacht*, p. 32

504. Citroen, Michal: *U Wordt door Niemand Verwacht*, p. 95

505. *Neighbors*, p. 85

506. *Neighbors*, p. 108

In light of this it, is not so strange that in 1946 a pogrom in the Polish town Kielce, which had a Jewish community of 25,000 before the war of which only 200 survived, resulted in the death of 46 Jewish survivors. In fact, when the pogroms were denounced in the local newspaper, mass strikes erupted throughout town and later in other cities as well, with demonstrating workers demanding a correction in the press and the release of the perpetrators, shouting "Down with the Jews!"[507] Also in Rzeszów and Kraków, violent anti-Jewish riots took place in July and August 1945. In total, between 1,000 and 2,000 Jews are said to have been killed during pogroms in Poland after the war.[508] Jews were, in a way, blamed not just for having caused their own liquidation (e.g. by supporting the Communist occupational forces and collaborating with the Soviets) but by having been mass murdered, they had brought shame on the Polish nation. The same reaction was felt in Germany, where the population reacted to the news of the mass killings by saying "poor Germany" instead of "poor Jews" – now the world will hate us for what the Nazis had done. In other words, the perpetrators took on the role of victims and the victims became the perpetrators of the shame brought upon the nation. Anti-Semitic outbursts were also seen in Slovakia where, in the village of Svinná, fifteen Jews who survived in a nearby concentration camp were killed several days after their liberation. A few months later, in September 1945, an outright pogrom took place in the Slovak town of Vel'ké Topol'cany. Also in Hungary and Romania, anti-Semitic outbursts were reported.[509]

Also in The Netherlands, the level of anti-Semitism was higher after the war than before. Even in books written shortly after the war, in which the resistance was praised sky high and a rather romantic upbeat image of the opposition to the Nazis was provided, the Jews were painted in a very negative and anti-Semitic image. For instance, K. Norel wrote in his book, *De Tirannie Verdrijven* (Expelling Tyranny), which, for many years, was obligatory reading for children and adolescents:[510] "The Jews did not pose any resistance to these pogroms…. The absence of resistance is not so strange. Jews might not be heroes, but they are definitely shrewd. Only when the Nazis stretched their claws out to their wealth and possessions did they wake up. And then they woke up completely. And with an enormous slyness, they kept away countless millions [of Dutch guilders] from the enemy."[511]

507. *Neighbors*, pp.98-99
508. Gerrits, André: *The Myth of Jewish Communism*, p. 136
509. Gerrits, André: *The Myth of Jewish Communism*, pp. 136-137
510. I was born in 1959, went to primary school in 1965 and I read this book many times during my youth
511. Van der Heijden, Chris: *Grijs Verleden*, p. 399

In Lithuania, the situation was very much complicated by the fact that one totalitarian regime was immediately replaced by the other. Many Jews who survived the war, particularly those who found themselves in the Western allied zones, did not return to Lithuania, shocked by the fact that their fellow countrymen had so actively participated in their extermination. Those who came back from the Soviet Union, some 12,000 in total, found a country in ruins and a regime that quickly reinstated its totalitarian order. Jewish nationalism was not allowed and, soon, anti-Semitism became a regular part of Soviet policy, and the threat of arrest, exile or execution soon returned, stimulating the urge to lie low and not rock the boat. On the other side, and in particular in the provinces, the partisans actively opposed the Soviet regime, even though there were also a considerable number of former "Jew-killers" among them. Thus the danger came from two sides and Lithuanians who actively helped Jews survive or who knew what had happened during those fateful months of June-December 1941 when 80% of their Jewish fellow countrymen were killed, followed the same line. They preferred to keep silent out of fear of being killed by Forest Brothers (partisans fighting the Soviet regime) as witnesses or "Jew-sympathizers." Although the Jewish population in, for instance, Vilnius reached the level of more than 20,000 at the end of the 1950s, the majority were not Lithuanian Jews, but "immigrants" from Georgia and Moldova, who had been attracted by the possibility of finding easy housing in the almost empty city. In short, the totalitarian atmosphere in the country ended the chance of coming to terms with the past. As Cypriot-American psychoanalyst Vamik Volkan writes in his book *Bloodlines*, "Living under a totalitarian regime does not allow the expression of ethnic sentiments that can lead to political instability. Achieving peaceful coexistence between ethnic groups through oppression by a central power is only a pseudo-solution to the problem, and… the price paid for it is too high."[512]

512. Volkan, Vamik: *Bloodlines*, p. 226

Chapter 7 – Why Did it Happen?

> *I, as a Lithuanian, am obliged to speak about the guilt of Lithuanians. Sadism and robbery, scorn and shameful indifference to people cannot be justified. Worse than that, they cannot be explained, they exist in such dark corners of individual and national consciousness that to seek rational reasons for them is a fruitless exercise.*
>
> Tomas Venclova[513]

> *There are two means to unite a people – common ideals and common crime.*
>
> Adolf Hitler (1923)[514]

The fundamental change on nation building during the first half of the twentieth century created an environment that very much stimulated the extermination of large ethnic groups and the development of a policy of ethnic cleansing. The major states in Central Europe at the end of the nineteenth century had been multi-ethnic states, in which nations lived side by side and people usually did not have a one-dimensional understanding of their own ethnic background. An inhabitant of the Austro-Hungarian Empire could be Hungarian, or Czech, or a combination of the two (or of more nationalities) but was, first of all, an Austrian-Hungarian. This perception started to change especially after the disintegration of the Ottoman Empire and the First World War, and the idea that one ethnic group had the right to its own state – and thus exclude other ethnicities from equal rights within that state – became a dominant factor in European politics. In particular, the totalitarian Soviet and Nazi regimes strengthened the concept of "nationality" (even though the Soviets claimed to be internationalists and that nationality as such was to be a secondary factor). During the ethnic cleaning programs in the Second World War and afterwards, Soviet or Nazi internal passports often determined one's fate.[515]

In the case of Lithuania, the situation was further complicated by the fact that the joint Polish-Lithuanian past resulted not only in many frustra-

513. From an article of Tomas Venclova, published in 1976 in the Moscow Jewish samizdat journal *Evrei v SSSR*, issue 12.
514. Quoted in Kühne, Thomas: *Belonging and Genocide*, p. iv
515. For a full, enlightening and well-written account see Snyder, Timothy: *The Reconstruction of Nations.*

tions but also in a lack of clarity as to who belonged to which ethnicity (or combination of ethnicities). In fact, Belarus was the heartland of what had been the Lithuanian-Polish (or Polish-Lithuanian) Commonwealth and, for a long time, it seemed more logical that Vilnius would become part of Belarus as the natural successor state.[516] Both Marshal Piłsudski and General Zeligowski, whose army occupied Vilnius in 1920 leading to its unification with Poland, considered themselves to be Lithuanian.[517] For instance, after his death in 1936, Piłsudski was buried in Kraków but his heart was buried in Vilnius next to his mother's grave. Even the famous Polish poet, Adam Mickiewicz, considered himself to be Lithuanian. Schoolchildren in independent Lithuania in 1919-1940 learned his masterwork, *Pan Tadeusz,* in a censored format, in which all references to Polish and Poland were cut out.[518] The "father of the nation," Antanas Smetona, had a Polish wife and was very fluent in Polish himself. All in all, this mix of nationalities never was an issue until the twentieth century, when it led not only to complications and people having to choose their "nationality," but also to massive bloodshed and eventually mass murder and ethnic cleansing. The Holocaust was, in that sense, definitely not the only case of extermination and mass killing.[519] Before and after the Holocaust, ethnic groups excelled in killing each other *en masse;* the big difference with the Holocaust being the fact that basically all turned against the Jews – there was nobody who wanted them or was willing to risk his/her own existence by defending them.

According to Vygantas Vareikis, a Klaipėda-based historian, the Holocaust in Lithuania was the result of a combination of five factors. In the first place, the rise of anti-Semitism and various anti-Semitic incidents led to a devaluation of the Jew in the eyes of his Lithuanian neighbors and, thus, a first step had been set to devalue him further to the level that extermination became possible. Secondly, Jews were considered to be almost

516. The initial plan of Stalin was to give the city to Belarus as part of the Belarusian SSR, only later changing it to the plan to give it to Lithuania in exchange for Soviet troops on Lithuanian soil. See *The Reconstruction of Nations*, pp. 80-81.
517. *The Reconstruction of Nations*, p. 69
518. *The Reconstruction of Nations*, p. 78
519. In his book *The Reconstruction of Nations*, Timothy Snyder gives a number of figures that show how effective these killing operations were: in Polish Volhynia (now Volyn district in Ukraine), 98% of the Poles were either killed or expelled, in Galicia a 92% reduction of Poles was achieved by force. In the parts of Galicia that remained part of Poland after the Second World War, 95% of the Ukrainians were either killed or removed. In both regions, 97% of the Jews were murdered, in Volhynia this figure even reached 98.5%, higher than in Lithuania. See *The Reconstruction of Nations*, p. 203

synonymous with Communists and, thus, the Soviet occupation and annexation of 1940, which led to much bloodshed, repression and eventually mass deportations, was mainly blamed on the Jewish population. Also, the fact that the Germans advanced so quickly prevented Jews from fleeing to the Soviet Union. Fourthly, the power vacuum between the quickly retreating Soviet army and the advancing German troops resulted in a situation in which "criminal elements craving for revenge for crimes committed by Soviet repressive structures and wishing to take possession over the property of defenseless citizens of Lithuania" made use of the situation.[520] And fifthly, Vareikis argues, Lithuania had only a limited amount of vast forests, and thus it was harder for Jews to hide. "In Western Belarus, however, abundant forests and good relations between the Byelorussian rural population and their Jewish neighbors enabled a greater number of Jews to escape and join the formations of Soviet partisans."[521]

Part of the argumentation of Vareikis is peculiar, to say the least. On top of that, it is quite contradictory. The fact that the German army advanced so quickly that only few Lithuanian Jews managed to escape is no explanation *why* Jews were killed *en masse* with active participation of Lithuanians; it merely explains why there were still so many Jews in Lithuania that fell victim to the killing machine. In fact, the Soviets only allowed those Lithuanian Jews who could prove they were members of the Communist Party to enter the country. The others were turned back and either killed on their way back home or banned from entering their own homes, as in Kaunas, and, thus, were easy victims of pogroms.

Also, Vareikis argues, on one hand, that the Germans advanced so quickly yet, on the other hand, talks about a 'power vacuum' between the retreating Soviet and advancing German troops. This power vacuum lasted, however, less than a week and, in that period, the first mass killings had already taken place. However, they continued unabatedly after the arrival of the Germans and, by the end of the year, some 137,000 Lithuanian Jews had been massacred. This was not the result of a power vacuum, but the result of a pre-determined plan to exterminate Lithuanian Jewry making use of local collaborators and existing anti-Semitic sentiments. In many cases, the Germans stood by, and *allowed* the murders to take place. Like in Poland, they were often bystanders, while local collaborators did the dirty job. Photos of the mass murder at Lietūkis Garage show Lithuanians doing the killing, while Germans make photographs. The image is no dif-

520. Truska, Liudas, and Vareikis, Vygantas: *The Preconditions for the Holocaust; Anti-Semitism in Lithuania*, p. 120

521. Truska, Liudas, and Vareikis, Vygantas: *The Preconditions for the Holocaust; Anti-Semitism in Lithuania*, p. 120

ferent than that in Jedwabne, where the local population killed their 1,600 person Jewish community while the Germans watched and recorded.

And finally, the idea that Jews had less chance to escape in Lithuania because of the absence of sufficient forestry cannot be taken seriously. Lithuania is a country covered with forests, and rightfully considers its vast forests as one of its national prides – it certainly has much more forest land than The Netherlands, where some 25,000 Jews survived the war by going into hiding.

Equally colored is his reporting on the growing anti-Semitism in Lithuania between the two World Wars, and in particular in the 1930s. Although he lists many cases of anti-Semitic expressions and excesses during this period, which very convincingly show that a climate was created in which violent outbursts against the Jewish population became possible, maybe even inevitable, he maintains a sense of indignation that the Jews preferred a Soviet occupation over a German one. He expresses sympathy for the fact that they hoped that a Soviet occupation would defend them against Hitler, yet he then adds that "there were also insults directed towards Lithuanians, desecration of the state emblem and other insignia, exaggerated allegations against the state of Lithuania and Smetona's regime for the policy of anti-Semitism, etc."[522] A bit further he adds: "Repetition of similar instances led Lithuanians to assume that the Jews had betrayed Lithuania…" yet he offers no further explanation and a listing of these "similar instances." This is a pity because as a result, this claim remains hanging in the air, without proper factual support. Instead, he adds that it was "naive to believe in the Messianic propaganda on equal rights by the Soviet Union." While, looking backwards, this was naïve, especially considering the fact that it later turned out that the Jews suffered proportionally more under Soviet occupation than their Lithuanian fellow countryman, a fact that is confirmed by Vareikis' co-author Liudas Truska.[523] However, for the Jews the choice was basically one between dark and light, because although it was not yet clear how merciless the German policies would turn out to be, it was very clear that life under German rule was not going to be a holiday outing.

Rightly, however, Vareikis points to the "historical and geopolitical situation that could have hardly been less favorable when compared to any-

522. Truska, Liudas, and Vareikis, Vygantas: *The Preconditions for the Holocaust; Anti-Semitism in Lithuania*, p. 170
523. Truska, Liudas, and Vareikis, Vygantas: *The Preconditions for the Holocaust; Anti-Semitism in Lithuania*, p. 176

where else in Europe."[524] In my view, this is where the main explanation of the ferocity of the Holocaust in Lithuania needs to be found.

Vareikis' co-author, Liudas Truska, mentions in his own analysis, several reasons for the Holocaust in Lithuania that have been mentioned by other scholars and observers. First of all, the hopes and fears of Lithuanians and Jews could hardly be more opposite: the Jews feared a German occupation and preferred Soviet rule because it meant survival, while the Lithuanians hoped for a German "liberation" because it might mean a reinstatement of their independence. In a way, the hopes of both populations were crushed. The Jews soon fell victim to Soviet terror, while the Lithuanians soon found out that the Germans had no intention of accepting Lithuania as an independent state and, when the Provisional Government realized that, it more or less disbanded itself (although it was a German decision of August 13 that actually dismissed the government).[525] Still, there is some modification to this crude division, because there were many Jews who did not welcome Soviet occupation. Many sources point out that especially older Jews were not as much in favor as the young and many Jews in Vilnius already knew what to expect from the Soviets. At the same time, there were still quite a few Lithuanian Communists and would have been more followers, as we have seen, if there had been no Jews at Communist rallies and in Communist gatherings to "spoil" it for Lithuanians.

In his analysis, Truska shows in detail how much the Sovietization of Lithuania was initially supported by public figures and even politicians and, as a result of this public support, the general population was at a loss and did not realize that their country was swallowed up by a giant totalitarian neighbor.[526] For instance, in Šiauliai, the Soviet army was not only welcomed by a handful of Jews but also by Colonel Butkevičius, the commander of the Eighth Infantry Regiment, and other officers; Lithuanians even provided the Soviets with fuel because their tanks were empty.[527]

Secondly, the two communities lived side-by-side, totally ignorant of each other's ways of life and beliefs, hopes and convictions. This, of course, is a recipe for disaster and in times of great tension and change this evokes uncontrollable distrust. It undoubtedly ignited or strengthened anti-Semitic sentiments and, in the end, made it much easier to commit mass murder

524. Truska, Liudas, and Vareikis, Vygantas: *The Preconditions for the Holocaust; Anti-Semitism in Lithuania*, p. 120
525. See Brandišauskas, Valentinas, in *Holocaust in Litauen*, p. 51
526. Truska, Liudas, and Vareikis, Vygantas: *The Preconditions for the Holocaust; Anti-Semitism in Lithuania*, p. 205-207
527. Truska, Liudas, and Vareikis, Vygantas: *The Preconditions for the Holocaust; Anti-Semitism in Lithuania*, p. 206

as Lithuanians had already dehumanized Jews, thereby eliminating an important barrier against such extreme acts of violence.

As we saw earlier, this dehumanization is one of the most important factors in preparing society or individuals for mass murder. It is a gradual process, leading from moral disengagement to dehumanization itself. "Moral disengagement is not simply a matter of moral indifference or invisibility," writes James Waller. "Rather, it is an active, but gradual, process of detachment by which some individuals or groups are placed outside the boundary within which moral values, rules, and considerations of fairness apply."[528] And thus, when placed outside the group, it becomes much easier to reduce them to mere "objects," derived of a human quality. Victims are reduced to mere "goods," "logs" or "deliveries," taking away their human face as a result of which killing becomes something mechanical. This was expressly confirmed by Treblinka chief Franz Stangl who, during the interviews with Gitta Sereny, explained how the victims were dehumanized in the most brutal manner before they were killed. This was done not because of sadism but only, as Stangl puts it, "to condition those who actually had to carry out the policies. To make it possible for them to do what they did."[529]

Thirdly, Fascism and National Socialism were widely supported throughout Europe and anti-Semitism was at least an inseparable element in National Socialism's political agenda. Lithuania was, in that sense, no different than other countries and maybe even more liberal. No Lithuanian government adopted anti-Semitic decrees but many rights and specific freedoms for Jews were revoked after 1924. For example, restrictions were imposed on Jewish presence in universities and Jews were no longer hired as civil servants, but these were incomparable to anti-Jewish legislation enacted in some of the other European countries, such as Romania, Poland and Hungary.

Fourthly, the image of Jews being automatically pro-Communist and, thus, supporters of Soviet occupation played a very important role. Whether it was founded on facts or on beliefs is, in this respect, hardly of any importance: Jews were involved in the new repressive Soviet government that ended Lithuanian independence and, thus, they were considered traitors who deserved punishment. In times of crisis or war, sophistication disappears and what is left are crude images that sometimes bear little resemblance to reality. Clearly, this was the case when it came to Jewish support for the Soviet regime. That Jews suffered proportionally more

528. Waller, James: *Becoming Evil*, p. 202
529. Sereny, Gitta: *Into That Darkness*, p. 101

was of interest to no one and would not have altered the picture; by that time, opinions had already been formed and only a miracle would have altered them.

And fifthly, crude old-fashioned anti-Semitism existed in Lithuania for centuries and, even though it did not take on the racially-oriented forms that so characterized national-socialist anti-Semitism in Germany, it did consider Jews to be "defective," if not inferior, and definitely held many strong stereotypes that one could also see in Nazi propaganda: lewd, sly, dangerous to non-Jewish women and girls, lazy, parasitic, profiteering, etc.

Truska adds a sixth factor which, in his view, is perhaps the most important one of all: the fact that Lithuania went through a deep moral crisis in the late 1930s and early 1940s due to the fact that it suffered five humiliations within a very short period of time (the acceptance of the Polish ultimatum in 1938 and forced resumption of diplomatic relations with that country; the loss of Klaipėda region in spring 1939; the refusal of Smetona to take Vilnius in 1939 when Poland was attacked by Nazi-Germany and, a bit later, the Soviet Union; the acceptance of Soviet troops on its soil in 1939 and, fifthly, the acceptance of Moscow's ultimatum and loss of independence in June 1940). In my view, he touches here upon a very important factor that goes much deeper than just these five humiliations.

As I mentioned earlier, in the decade that I have been living in Lithuania, I have found Lithuanians to be a proud people, who – consciously or unconsciously – have a strong feeling of self-victimization and continuously see themselves as victims of history. Lithuanian historian, Liudas Truska, calls this a "heroic-masochistic historical conscience," in which the entire history of the country is presented as an endless series of battles and suffering. After several centuries of fulfilling the role of victim, it is very hard for the nation to accept that it also has a role as a perpetrator.[530] Historian Vygantas Vareikis points out that Lithuanians have a tendency to both feelings of superiority (referring to the great empire they once had during the Lithuanian-Polish union) and feelings of inferiority. In my view, the first is only a cover-up for the second. In other words: Lithuanians have a structural feeling of inferiority, which dominates even politics today. The events of the early 1940s strengthened that feeling of inferiority enormously, not only because it never recovered independence but fell from Soviet hands into Nazi hands and back into Soviet hands, but also because its war history was tarnished by the fact that apart from being victim, it was now also perpetrator.

530. Truska, Liudas, in *Holocaust in Litauen*, p. 263

In 1941, the shame of having lost Lithuania so easily to the Soviets was taken out on the Jewish population and, in "punishing" the scapegoat, the country became an accomplice in a crime that resulted in emotions surpassing the previous shame. The issue was then frozen for fifty years, due to the fact that Soviet rule did not allow public discussion of what happened with the Jews. And so when the country reemerged in 1990-1991, it found an untreated trauma on its plate, a trauma that blocked the closure of a painful chapter and the start of a clean slate. Denial was the result.

Chapter 8 – From Black and White to Shades of Grey

> *The conclusion that every person can become a traitor is, however, not sufficient. More determining for the logics of this notion is much more that under certain conditions, any person can become a traitor. For instance, the total populations of Norway, Holland, France, Greece and Yugoslavia consisted (always in the technical-judicial meaning of the word) of traitors during the German occupation; independent of the fact of whom he considered to be his government, there was always another in whose eyes he committed treason.*
>
> Magnus Enzensberger[531]

> *The time has come that something needs to be done. But he who has the courage to do it, needs to do it knowing full well that he will go into German history as a traitor. But if he doesn't do it, he will be a traitor of his own conscience.*[532]
>
> Von Stauffenberg, July 1944[533]

As discussed earlier in this book, historiography of a period very much mirrors the level in which a society is able to come to terms with it's past and assess it in a less subjective manner.

In The Netherlands, the end of the war was followed by a period in which discussions about the war, in general, and also who was on which side and who was good or bad, were virtually non-existent. The general public had enough of the war and its after-effects, and all efforts were focused on rebuilding the country. Many members of the resistance were disappointed, as all their efforts seemed to have been in vain and no real change in the societal structure emerged. Those who had been in charge of the coun-

531. As quoted in Hofman, J.: *De Collaborateur*, p. 15
532. Quoted in Hofman, J.: *De Collaborateur*, p. 16
533. Von Stauffenberg, a few days before his assassination attempt on Adolf Hitler on July 20, 1941. Quoted in Hofman, J.: *De Collaborateur*, p. 16. Claus Graf von Stauffenberg was a German army officer and Catholic aristocrat who was one of the leading members of the failed July 20 plot of 1944 to assassinate Adolf Hitler and remove the Nazi Party from power. He was one of the central figures of the German Resistance movement within the Wehrmacht. For his involvement in the movement, he was shot shortly after the failed attempt

try remained, by and large, in charge after the war and the same "pillar" structure that dominated public life in the country continued to dominate. The few remaining Jews were ostracized from society and told to be grateful that they were still around and should not stir up any trouble. In 1950 in Amsterdam, a first monument was established in the former Jewish district, which rather cynically thanked the Amsterdam population for the help it had provided to its Jewish compatriots. As Dutch historian Hans Blom rightfully noted, such a monument would have been impossible a few years later – the whole issue of the Holocaust was, by then, already pushed to the background.[534]

It came back in the 1960s, when a certain international relaxation and the return of an acceptable level of comfort in people's lives opened the door to reflection. The issue of the deportation of Jews suddenly became central in publications and in the first television programs on the subject. However, by now a black and white picture was formed, in which the Dutch population - with a few despicable exceptions – had bravely resisted German oppression and the image was carefully created that the Dutch had bravely tried to save the Jews from their extermination. It is the time that people like Abraham Asscher and David Cohen of the *Joodsche Raad* again became subjected to intense criticism and the Dutch public was offered the soothing feeling that it had been one of the staunchest defenders of freedom and democracy. Even now, foreigners are often astonished when they hear that the image is maybe a bit less ideal and that, in fact, the Dutch very much went with the flow and cared mostly about their own skins.

During the late 1970s and the early 1980s, the prevailing debate among historians focusing on the Second World War and its consequences was the shift from a black-and-white picture to one of shades of grey. Renowned historians such as Lou de Jong, director of the State Institute of War Documentation (RIOD) and author of *The Kingdom of the Netherlands during World War II*, a book series of 26 volumes and over 15,000 pages,[535] and

534. Blom, J.C.H.: *In de ban van Goed en Fout*, p. 127

535. Louis ("Lou") de Jong (1914 -2005 in Amsterdam) was a Dutch journalist and historian specializing in the history of the Netherlands in World War II and the Dutch resistance. On January 11, 2011, a Dutch program in "*Het Uur van de Wolf*" revealed that Lou de Jong, who so meticulously documented the Second World War, possessed the last letters and photos from his twin brother Sally, who perished with his wife during the Holocaust, leaving two young boys behind. He never showed these memorabilia to them, and always denied he had anything to satisfy their thirst for information about their parents. The materials were found only after Lou de Jong's death and by sheer coincidence. What made him hide the truth about his son will always remain a guess, yet

Prof. Presser, author of the standard work *Ondergang. De Vervolging en Verdelging van het Nederlandse Jodendom 1940-1945* (Collapse; The persecution and extermination of Dutch Jewry 1940-1945),[536] were proponents of the black-and-white picture, in which all Germans were invariably bad and Dutch society resisted occupation collectively, apart from a small minority of despicable citizens who collaborated with the occupational regime and were, for that reason, justifiably ostracized from society after the liberation. Hans Blom, who succeeded Lou de Jong as Director of the RIOD (later renamed into NIOD), tackled that image and argued that it was a simplification of reality, which was much more diverse and balanced.[537] In his inaugural lecture when appointed Professor at the University of Amsterdam in 1983, titled *Gripped by right and wrong? ("In de Ban van Goed en Kwaad*?") he distanced himself from the right-wrong paradigm of his predecessor Lou de Jong. Several scandals in Dutch society, in which alleged heroes were unmasked as collaborators further stimulated the debate.[538] In particular, the Weinreb case divided Dutch society deeply. Friedrich Weinreb (1910-1988), a Hasidic Jewish storyteller, writer and economist, came originally from a traditional Eastern European Hasidic Judaic family from Vienna. During World War II, Weinreb played a controversial role. He ran a fictional "emigration agency" and created a nonexistent German General, with whom he - in his own words - corresponded. Jews who paid in order to be registered with him were told that by doing so, they could postpone their deportation. Curiously, the German occupiers at least partially participated in the Weinreb initiative: the Amsterdam *Judenrat* temporarily exempted the people on his list from deportation. Even after the failure of this system, when it appeared that

it showed that even a documentarian as Lou de Jong was not free from hiding and distorting history.

536. Jacob (Jacques) Presser (Amsterdam, 1899-1970) was a Dutch historian, writer and poet best known for his book *Ondergang; De Vervolging en Verdelging van het Nederlandse Jodendom 1940-1945* on the history of the persecution of Dutch Jews during the Second World War.

537. Hans Blom (1943), a Dutch historian, was director of the RIOD and professor of Dutch history at the University of Amsterdam. He is renowned because of the Srebrenica report that he and several colleagues wrote in 2002 and which led to the collapse of the Dutch government. In keeping with his lecture, in this report Blom spoke little or no value judgments. This earned him severe criticism from colleagues, publicists, lawyers and politicians. In 2007, Blom retired from the NIOD (former RIOD).

538. The debate is still continuing and not only among historians. In 2009, a public debate focused on the erection of a monument for a German soldier in the town of Riel who, during the last days of the war, saved two Dutch children during a bombardment. The question as to whether a monument for a member of occupation forces was morally justified resulted in sometimes angry and emotional exchanges.

several persons on the list were arrested anyway, he continued, and he later justified this by saying that he offered victims of the Holocaust at least some form of hope.

Weinreb managed to save himself from the Germans in early 1944 by going into hiding. The Special Court of Cassation sentenced Weinreb in 1948 to six years imprisonment. In December of that year, he was pardoned, thanks to the 50-year jubilee of Queen Wilhelmina. Jacques Presser wrote in his book, *De Ondergang,* some laudatory passages about him, and Weinreb, published, with editorial support of two well-known Dutch writers, an autobiography in which he tried to create a positive picture of his activities during the war. The book resulted in a lot of controversy and led to the Weinreb affair. Weinreb's editors sought his rehabilitation, but their efforts took the opposite direction. Several issues in his book proved to be false. In response to this uproar, the then Minister of Justice in 1970 asked the RIOD directed by Dr. Lou de Jong to write a report on this matter. After six years of research, the Institute published a report, which left very little intact of Weinreb's alleged acts of resistance. Numerous witnesses concluded that during the Second World War, Weinreb had, in fact, been guilty of treason and collaboration.

Since the 1980s, many books and studies have appeared in The Netherlands that helped to sophisticate the general picture of the German occupation. Some books were of a more general nature, debating issues of "good and bad" or "right and wrong," others focused on Dutch collaboration with the Nazis, the role of the *Judenrat*, the position of the NSB and the treatment of collaborators after the war. Subsequently also there was focus on many individual stories, such as the Jewish informer, Ans van Dijk, who betrayed dozens of Jews, including several family members and her own partner.[539] In other West-European countries, the perception changed as well and heroes turned out to be either ordinary men or even collaborators. In France, for instance, several collaborators were tried from the 1980s onwards, which resulted in very emotional debates in the country. In 1993, former Vichy official René Bousquet was assassinated while he awaited prosecution in Paris following a 1991 inculpation for crimes against humanity; he had been prosecuted but partially acquitted and immediately amnestied in 1949. A year later, former Vichy official Paul Touvier (1915-1996) was convicted of crimes against humanity. Maurice Papon, a former Budget Minister under President Valéry Giscard d'Estaing and Prime Minister Raymond Barre from 1978 to 1981, had been a civil servant in

539. Groen, Koos: *Als Slachtoffers Daders Worden*. Ambo, Baarn, 1994. Several of the most important books were used as sources for the study of Dutch behavior during the Second World War.

Bordeaux in charge of the "Jewish Questions" during the war. He was convicted after a very long trial (1981-1998) for crimes against humanity. He was released three years later due to ill health and died in 2007. French President Francois Mitterrand, who had been a civil servant in the Vichy regime before joining the resistance, came under attack in 1992 when it was revealed that he had arranged for the laying of a wreath of flowers on the grave of Pétain each Armistice Day since 1987. Three years later, in July1995, President Jacques Chirac recognized the responsibility of the French State for seconding the "criminal folly of the occupying country," particularly the help of the French police in the implementation of the *Endlösung.*[540]

In Germany it took an equally long time for the issue of the Holocaust and the direct and indirect involvement of many thousands of ordinary Germans to become an issue of discussion. A fierce debate erupted when the role of the Wehrmacht was criticized and an exhibition showed the extent to which they had been involved in the mass murder of Jews and other civilians.[541] Thomas Kühne sees three reasons why discussions became more open only in the course of the 1990s. First of all, the generation that consciously lived through the war had retired and was gradually dying out, so the way was open for a more honest and open discussion of what really happened, without attempts to cover up for one's own compliance or collaboration. Secondly, the issue became much more a public one because of films such as "*Schindler's List,*" which, at the same time, showed that people did have a choice and that it was possible to refuse to participate. And thirdly, in the 1990s a new genocidal war raged on "civilized" European soil and, like other Europeans Germans, saw in practice in former Yugoslavia what it meant when individuals and groups enjoyed committing heinous crimes and killing large groups of people only because of their race. The result was a public debate that continues to this very day and which laid bare the simple fact that even under Nazi dictatorship, Germans had a choice. "Numerous Germans joined in anti-Jewish ostracism, approved terror against them, and applauded their deportations and extermination during the war. These Germans constituted a minority, though a large minority. A much smaller minority performed symbolic gestures on behalf of the Jews; but they did so only occasionally, and seldom in public. Most Germans were ambivalent and their actions ambiguous. (...) They looked

540. Historiographical debates are still, today, passionate, with conflicting views on the nature and legitimacy of Vichy's collaborationism with Nazi Germany in the implementation of the Holocaust.

541. For information on this debate see, among others: Förster, Jürgen: *Complicity or Entanglement in: Berenbaum*, Michael: *The Holocaust and History*, pp. 266-283

the other way when Jews were publicly humiliated, or they started blankly as the deportations began."[542]

Lithuania

During Soviet times, the Lithuanian Diaspora tried (and still tries) to ignore the issue of the Holocaust as much as possible. Many of the 56,000 refugees that left the country in 1944 in the wake of the reinstitution of Soviet rule had been directly or indirectly involved in Nazi-German rule in their country and they were often received as heroes and freedom fighters in the various communities abroad. The wish to expose what really happened was totally absent and books published by Lithuanian émigré historians therefore either completely ignore the issue (such as Albertas Gerutis in his standard work *Lithuania 700 years*) or resort to extensive apologetic exposés in which usually Jews are blamed for what had happened and those who had collaborated with the Nazis were presented as Germans or Poles posing as Lithuanians in Lithuanian uniforms.[543]

In Lithuania itself, the debates were basically non-existent, as the country was frozen under Soviet rule and a very one-sided and propagandistic picture emerged. When the Soviet troops returned to Vilnius in July 1944, they found a city in ruins and virtually none of the Jewish inhabitants left. Many of the 7-8,000 Lithuanian Jews who survived the war outside their country did not return. For instance, of the 1,000 Lithuanian Jews who were liberated in Dachau, only 100 came back to Lithuania, the rest preferred to stay in the West.[544]

Initially the remnants of the Jewish communities tried to reestablish a normal daily life, reopening the remaining synagogues, establishing a Jewish museum, setting up monuments in memory of those who had perished and revamping Jewish cultural life. In 1945, a monument was erected in Paneriai, with a plaque in Hebrew and Russian, dedicated to the Jews who perished there. However, soon the Soviet authorities vented the same criticism as during the 1940-1941 occupation of Lithuania; the Jews were nationalists and, thus, a threat to the Soviet concept of multi-nationality and the socialist brotherhood of men and, by 1948, many of the expressions of Jewish culture and traditions were banned, particularly following

542. Kühne, Thomas: *Belonging and Genocide*, pp. 170-171
543. An extensive analysis of Lithuanian émigré historiography on this subject can be found in the chapter Truska, Liudas: *Litauische Historiographie über den Holocaust in Litauen*, in *Holocaust in Litauen*, pp. 262-276
544. Arūnas Bubnys in Nikžentaitis, Alvydas: *The Vanished World of Lithuanian Jews*, p. 218

the murder of the famous Yiddish actor and producer Solomon Mikhoels. Monuments to the murdered Jews were "de-nationalized" and more general terms as "innocent Soviet victims of the Hitlerites" were put in place. In Paneriai, the monument was blown to pieces with dynamite and replaced by a Soviet one, in Soviet style and without any reference to Jews: "to the victims of Fascist terror."[545] Specific mention to the extermination of Jewry was banned. In Vilnius the remains of the Great Synagogue in the Old Town, which still stood like "a massive white building with vestiges of columns and arches"[546] was razed and replaced by an ugly Soviet style kindergarten. Also the City Synagogue, which survived the war intact, was demolished by the Soviets.[547] At the same time, however, Lithuanians who helped Jews survive were afraid to admit it openly, in particular in the provinces. This was not because they feared Soviet reprisals, but because their lives were under threat by the Forest Brothers, who fought Soviet rule and, at the same time, had former murderers of Jews among their ranks.[548] As a result, much of what happened, even positive actions, was covered by a blanket of silence.

The murder of Solomon Mikhoels in Minsk signaled the beginning of an anti-Soviet campaign during the last years of Stalin.[549] A year after his death, a wave of arrests took place among Yiddish cultural figures, all across the Soviet Union and, in 1952, twenty-five of them were tried in Moscow and sentenced to death. Many others were sentenced to long terms of imprisonment in the Gulag. In January 1953, the Soviet newspaper *Pravda* announced the Doctor's Plot, which is generally seen as the culmination point that should have led to Stalin's solution to the "Jewish problem," possibly directed at deporting the Jewish population to Central Asia and Birobidzhan.[550] The death of Iosif Stalin on March 5, 1953, precluded that terrible fate.[551]

545. A 1962 poster advertised Paneriai as "*The Industrial Heart of Vilnius*". See *Jerusalem of Lithuania*, p. 534
546. Venclova, Tomas: *Vilnius; a Personal History*, p. 20
547. *Jerusalem of Lithuania*, p. 530
548. Gitelman, Zvi: *Bitter Legacy*, p. 188
549. See Rubenstein, Joshua: *Stalin's Secret Pogrom*, pp. 1-4
550. See Rubenstein, Joshua: *Stalin's Secret Pogrom*, pp. 62. Also see Klier, John: *The Holocaust and the Soviet Union*, in Stone, Dan: *Historiography of the Holocaust*, pp. 276-295. Stalin's anti-Semitism was already noticeable in 1939 when, during the signing of the Molotov-Ribbentrop Pact, he told German Foreign Minister Joachim von Ribbentrop that "as soon as [there are] adequate cadres of gentiles, he [will] remove all Jews from leading positions." See Rubenstein, p. 34
551. See Gitelman, Zvi: *A Century of Ambivalence*, pp. 150-154.

However, although during the thaw of Khrushchev some of the lost terrain was recovered, the issue of what exactly happened with the Jews during the Nazi occupation in Lithuania remained on the sidelines. In the book about the murder of virtually all Jews in Jurbarkas in the summer of 1941, protocols of interrogations of witnesses and minutes of court sessions are quoted, in which Soviet authorities clearly ask the witnesses not to dwell on what happened with the Jews but, rather, expand on the anti-Soviet nature of the actions of the persons under investigation.[552] Yet at the same time, the Khrushchev Thaw gave the Jewish communities some new vigor. New amateur musical and dance groups were formed, small groups started to learn Hebrew and singers like Nekhama Lifshits became immensely popular and had Yiddish songs in their repertoire. Mass graves of Jews killed in the Holocaust were marked, monuments erected and memorial gatherings were held. By the end of the 1960s, the first beginnings of the mass emigration to Israel and the United States became visible. In the 1970s, they would take on massive numbers but, with the tens of thousands of Jews emigrating, those who were interested in pushing the Holocaust issue also disappeared and, thus, it was shelved, on hold for later times. Those revelations came in 1990 when Lithuania declared its independence as the first Soviet republic to take this step.

552. See Puišytė, Rūta: *Holocaust in Jurbarkas*. BA Thesis, Faculty of History, Vilnius University, 1997

Conclusion

Human cruelty surpasses human imagination.
Abel Herzberg[553]

The Holocaust was not just a Jewish tragedy but the total destruction of our fellow citizens and thus it was a Lithuanian tragedy. Knowledge and understanding of the Holocaust are necessary to overcome nationalist and anti-democratic ideologies, expand society, foster tolerance and understand 'other' cultures.
Arūnas Bubnys[554]

In general terms, one could say that man needs heroes. Mankind has the tendency of distorting history, of "improving" it by deleting some parts and exaggerating some others. It is often not even a deliberate form of whitewashing the past, but more adapting the past to one's current needs. People don't like to admit that it is all a matter of shades of grey, that heroism is only for the few and that even heroes can be impossible characters at the same time. We like success stories, both on an individual as well as on a national level. This is a natural reaction, particularly when coping with bad experiences of the past; yet when these distortions become deliberate and part of an attempt to whitewash the past, they become dangerous. A society built on myths and falsifications, even if built on half-truths, is like a house built on quicksand. Sooner or later, the weak foundations will make it topple and collapse.

Internationally, from the 1970s and 1980s onwards, the issue of the Holocaust has had a fundamental impact on historiography. Until then, singling out the fate of the Jewish victims of Nazism was sporadic and, in broad terms, the Jewish victims were blended into the general population that had suffered at the hand of the oppressor. This was not only the case in the Soviet Union, as mentioned earlier, where all victims, irrespective of their nationality, became innocent or Soviet "victims of Hitlerites,"as part of the desire to create a Soviet uniformity, a Soviet mankind. Also this was a general tendency in Western European countries where many Jewish survivors kept silent, fearing exposure, afraid that their testimonies would not be believed anyway. "Jews and others were instrumentally and psychologically assimilated into the general category of 'victims,' even though they had

553. Quoted in Citroen, Michal: *U Wordt door Niemand Verwacht*, p. 23
554. Nikžentaitis, Alvydas: *The Vanished World of Lithuanian Jews*, p. 219

suffered an undeniable fate, distinct from their compatriots, and therefore could not or only uneasily participate in narratives about the common and tragic fate of the nation."[555] According to some, Jews purposely refused to be portrayed as victims unlike other victims of the Nazis.[556]

Several factors changed the situation rather dramatically and led to an avalanche of interest in the issue. As noted earlier in this book, the German historian Thomas Kühne saw three reasons for this sudden interest in Germany: the emergence of a new "untainted" generation and the retirement of the generation that consciously lived through the Second World War; the popularization of the Holocaust through American-style television programs and films; and the sudden and shocking return of genocidal war on European soil in 1992-1995. Carolyn Dean, looking at it from a more international (yet mostly American and French) perspective, places this sudden increase in interest at an earlier time, caused by the Eichmann trial in Jerusalem in 1961 and the 1967 Arab-Israeli War, which greatly strengthened Jewish pride and thus the wish to link this victory of the Jewish state with earlier suffering. Until then, Carolyn Dean writes, "the near annihilation of European Jews, whose earlier efforts to recount their experiences met mostly if not exclusively... with minimal interest."[557]

With the fundamental changing of focus, history soon became primarily an emphasis on the history of victims rather than of victors, in which the position of the real heroes was taken by those who had suffered. As a result, other groups also claimed their positions as victim, being either African-Americans or the Muslim population from North Africa in France that suffered at the hands of the French colonial government: all claimed to have their "Holocaust," thereby degenerating the term as such. Even the second generation, the children of Holocaust survivors, added to the confusion when they claimed their own position as victims. As Eva Hoffman writes in her book *After such Knowledge*, they too felt "a strange envy towards our survivor parents. Authenticity of experience, in our period, if often conflated with catastrophe, with those traumatic histories with which we are so eager to identify"[558] and, thus, these "children of the Holocaust" tended to feel secondary.

555. Dean, Carolyn: *Aversion and Erasure*, p. 14. In France, this assimilation was forced upon the nation by President Charles de Gaulle's imposition of a coherent and blended narrative of common patriotic suffering of the French. Only after 1995 did the French government recognize the specifics of the suffering of the Jews.
556. For instance Eric Conan and Henri Rousso in *Vichy; and Ever-Present Past.* University of New England Press, 1998, p. 202
557. Dean, Carolyn: *Aversion and Erasure*, p. 16
558. Hoffman, Eva: *After such Knowledge*, p. 175

Yet the heightened interest in the Holocaust and the fate of the Jews not only resulted in empathy but also in aggression. Political scientist Hannah Arendt already foresaw this problem back in 1946, when she wrote to her friend Karl Jaspers that "we Jews are burdened by millions of innocents, by reason of which every Jew alive today can see himself as innocence personified... We are simply not equipped to deal with a guilt that is beyond crime and an innocence that is beyond goodness and virtue."[559] Thus Arendt was clearly aware that if the Jews clung to the image of being the "super victims" of the Second World War, a distorted picture might emerge causing the exploitation of human tragedy and, in the end, the victimization of others. Arendt's premonition proved to be correct and, in reality, more and more people felt that the sudden "moral superiority" of the victims put pressure on them and made their reminiscences and positioning "sacred" and undisputable. Some critics claimed that Jews were experiencing victimization as a surrogate identity, some going as far as saying that Jews had forsaken their history and culture and replaced it with Holocaust trauma as a substitute for collective identity.[560] Thus, in a way, Jews were again blamed for what happened, not so much because of facilitating their own annihilation but for making their non-Jewish compatriots feel guilty about their compliance and collaboration.

In Lithuania, the discussion of the Holocaust started only at the very end of the Soviet regime and, until then, both Soviet and émigré Lithuanian historiography completely ignored what actually happened. The country was entirely - and quite understandably - focused on the effects of Soviet rule, a political regime that truly caused immeasurable suffering.[561] Already long before the country regained independence, Soviet oppression and the liquidation of the country's intelligentsia and bourgeoisie was referred to as genocide.[562] Yet suddenly Lithuanians were confronted with a less pleasant part of their history, one in which they were not as much victims but actual perpetrators. For them, just emerging from a totalitarian past, it was too early for a balanced view on the past. They were the "ultimate victims," rather than the Jews who had been killed, and to make it worse, the whole world pointed to the fact that the Holocaust in Lithuania happened with active participation of some of the Lithuanians, and silent acceptance, if not approval, of virtually all others. The whole debate around the notion "genocide" can be seen in this light, with, for instance, the Museum of Genocide in Vilnius continuing to mention only the Holo-

559. Kohler, Lotte et.al.: *Hannah Arendt-Karl Jaspers*, p. 54
560. See Dean, Carolyn: *Aversion and Erasure*, p. 2
561. As noted earlier, Lithuanians suffered incomparably more under the Soviet regime than under Nazi occupation.
562. See, for instance Pajaujis-Javis, Joseph: *Soviet Genocide in Lithuania*. Manyland Books, New York, 1980

caust in passing and concentrating fully on the suffering of ethnic Lithuanians under totalitarian rule. An amendment to the Lithuanian Criminal Code of June 29, 2010, even forbids the denial of the fact that the deportation and liquidation of Lithuanians by the Soviets was genocide.[563]

Part of the enormous frustration of the Lithuanians over the ever-returning theme of the Holocaust in their country is, in my view, not so much directed at the fact that they are "again" accused of active collaboration with the Nazis and participation in the mass murders, but much more to the fact that it is the Jews who are seen as the victims, whereas the Lithuanians themselves would, in fact, like to claim exclusively the victim role. It seems too early for them to accept the fact that "oppression is not a historical but a human tragedy in which we are all potentially heroes

563. The law reads: "Whosoever approves genocide or other crimes against humanity as defined by legal acts of the Republic of Lithuania or the European Union or by accepted decisions of the courts of the Republic of Lithuania or international courts, whosoever denies or grossly underestimates, if this is done in a threatening, hostile or insulting manner or if it causes disturbance to the public order, as well as anyone who publicly approves of aggression carried out by the USSR or Nazi Germany against the Republic of Lithuania, the crime of genocide or other crimes against humanity or war crimes committed by the USSR or Nazi Germany against Lithuanian residents or on Lithuanian territory, or grave or very grave crimes of aggression committed or abetted by people against the Republic of Lithuania in 1990-1991 or crimes committed against residents of the Republic of Lithuania, or deny or grossly underestimate these crimes, if done in a threatening, hostile or insulting manner or if this disturbs the public order; is punishable by limitation of freedom, arrest or loss of freedom for up to two years." In my view, it is highly debatable whether Soviet terror in Lithuania can be considered "genocide." Of course, it depends on the interpretation of the internationally accepted definition of what genocide is: article 2 of the 1948 United Nations Convention on the Prevention and Punishment of the Crime of Genocide (CP-PCG) defines genocide as "any of the following acts committed with intent to destroy, in whole or in part, a national, ethnical, racial or religious group, as such: killing members of the group; causing serious bodily or mental harm to members of the group; deliberately inflicting on the group conditions of life, calculated to bring about its physical destruction in whole or in part; imposing measures intended to prevent births within the group; [and] forcibly transferring children of the group to another group." I prefer the short and clear definition that Donald Bloxham gives: "Genocide is the physical destruction of a large portion of a group in a limited or unlimited territory with the intention of destroying that group's collective existence." (quoted in Jones, Adam: *Genocide*, p. 20). Keeping this in mind, one has to conclude that the Soviets did not intend to destroy the "collective existence" of Lithuanians and, thus, we cannot speak of genocide.

and victims and all potentially wounded and capable of wounding."[564] In other words, one can be easily victim and perpetrator at the same time, and having one role does not automatically disavow the other.

When looking at the debate on the Holocaust in Lithuania, one cannot escape the impression that the country continues to remain in a state of denial, one of repressed aggression, in which blaming the Jews continues to dominate the debate. On one hand, the historically proven incorrect image of the Jews having brought Soviet rule upon the nation continues to be repeated and, on the other hand, Jews are time and again blamed for "monopolizing" the image of victim that the Lithuanians themselves like to claim for themselves. And it is not that people do not know. Of course, many details are known only to those who study the issue carefully and those who did are usually shocked by what they discover. The scope of the killings, the brutality of the perpetrators, the cruelty and the indifference of the majority of the people who preferred to look the other way, these stories shock every time you read them. Yet the majority of people in Lithuania know, in broad terms, what happened and they know to what extent the Lithuanian nation was involved. However, they prefer not to know, they prefer to believe in the primitive explanations or continue to blame the Jews themselves for what happened to them. And all this is intermingled with fantasies of an anti-Lithuanian conspiracy, of Jewish political power that continues to haunt the Lithuanian nation. As Carolyn Dean writes: "Oddly, fantasies of Jewish power now derive not from Jews' putative cunning and ability to adapt to and thrive parasitically in any environment, but from their recent survival of the Nazi effort to banish them from earth."[565] Thus a general muteness has descended on the country, only broken by sudden outbursts of national indignation when "again" the Lithuanians are accused of active participation. Immediately the country actually repeats the mistake it made back in 1941: it finds an easy scapegoat and washes its hands of any guilt.

Twenty years have passed since the country regained its independence. A new generation has grown up, adults who were born in a free country, yet of parents who were Soviet citizens and grew up in a Soviet environment. The effects of totalitarian thought and behavior are still an integral part of their being, although already much less. Lithuanians today are freer to ask, to wonder, to put events in the right perspective and realize that not all of Lithuanian history will bring them pride. However, in order to be able to assess the past in a balanced and thorough way, they need to be provided with all of the available information. Here we have the paradoxical situa-

564. Dean, Carolyn: *Aversion and Erasure*, p. 25
565. Dean, Carolyn: *Aversion and Erasure*, p. 19

tion; some prefer to continue to cover up and mold the truth to what they think are Lithuania's national needs and, by doing so, they hinder future generations of the country understanding what really happened and learning lessons from it.

What I tried to do in this book is to lay out the facts, to expose what happened during those fateful days. Yet I also tried to put it in an international context, both in terms of the socio-political realities of those days and in comparison to the attitude of people in other countries who faced the same dilemmas and were also forced to choose between compliance, collaboration or resistance. Throughout Europe, collaboration with evil was massive and, even in the present day, new facts adding additional facets to the complex story are uncovered. The Second World War as well as conflicts following that global disaster, show that mankind is able to do the impossible – to be loving people and mass murderers at the same time. The Lithuanians who stood by and those who participated were no different than the Dutch or the French or the Danes. Undoubtedly, if Hitler had conquered Britain, the same would have happened there.[566] In that sense, Lithuanians can be comforted by the fact that they behaved not worse than others, but also not better.

Yet accepting this fact does not take away the moral responsibility of a country, its citizens and its authorities to reveal the true story in all its complexities and to pass it on to future generations in the hope that they will learn from it and maybe find the moral courage to not repeat this history in the future. Unfortunately, fifty years of Communism froze the debate and many witnesses died, emigrated, or gave up on telling what they knew. This is a huge loss, certainly, and many clarifying facts have now faded into oblivion together with those who remembered them. Yet this is no justification for giving up the search for information still available. Fifty years of communism should not be an easy excuse for covering up the story once and for all.

566. The only part of Britain that was occupied by German forces was the Channel Islands. The administration there turned over the small Jewish community to the Nazis. See Bloxham, Donald: *The Final Solution*, p. 1. On the Channel Island of Alderney, where the Germans quickly established four concentration camps, under the eyes of the British population, which were sub-camps of the larger camp Neuengamme near Hamburg: Lager Norderney, Lager Borkum, Lager Sylt and Lager Helgoland. The camps started operating in January 1942 and had a total inmate population of about 6,000. The prisoners in Lager Sylt and Lager Norderney were slave laborers forced to build military fortifications and installations throughout Alderney. Sylt camp held Jewish enforced laborers. Over 700 of the inmates lost their lives before the camps were closed and the remaining inmates transferred to Germany in 1944.

Bibliography

Abramowicz, Hirsz: *Profiles of a Lost World.* Wayne State University Press/YIVO, 1999

Alpert, Nachum: *The Destruction of Slonim Jewry.* Holocaust Library, New York, 1989

Anušauskas, Arvydas: *Terror and Crimes against Humanity; the First Soviet Occupation.* The International Commission for the Evaluation of the Crimes of the Nazi and Soviet Occupation Regimes in Lithuania. Margi raštai, Vilnius, 2006

Arad, Yitzak: *The Holocaust in the Soviet Union.* University of America Press, 2009

Arendt, Hanna: *The Origins of Totalitarianism,* 1951

Atamukas, Solomonas: *The Hard Long Road toward the Truth.* Lituanus, Volume 47, No. 4, Winter 2001 Bak, Samuel: *Painted in Words.* Indiana University Press, 2001

Bakonis, Eduard (ed.): *Jewish Life in Lithuania.* The Vilna Gaon State Museum, Vilnius, 2001

Bart, Michael and Corona, Laurel: *Until our Last Breath; a Holocaust Story of Love and Partisan Resistance.* St. Martins Press, 2008

Bartrop, Paul R. and Jacobs, Steven Leonard: *Fifty Key Thinkers on the Holocaust and Genocide.* Routledge, London, 2011

Bartusevičius, Vincas, Tauber, Joachim and Wette, Wolfram: *Holocaust in Litauen.* Böhlau Verlag, Köln, 2003

Berenbaum, Michael and Peck, Abraham: *The Holocaust and History; the Known, the Unknown, the Disputed and the Reexamined.* Indiana University Press, 1998

Bergen, Doris: *War and Genocide; A Concise History of the Holocaust.* Rowman & Littlefield, New York, 2009

Blom, J.C.H.: *In de Ban van Goed en Fout.* Boom, Leiden, 2007

Bloxham, David: *The Final Solution; a Genocide.* Oxford University Press, 2009

Bloznelis, Mindaugas: *Lietuvių Frontas.* Į Laisve, Kaunas, 2008

Bomba, Jacek: *Overcoming Impossible.* In: Archives of Psychiatry and Psychotherapy, 2010; 1: pp. 61-64

Bosmajian, Haig: *The Language of Oppression.* University Press of America, 1983

Browning, Christopher: *Ordinary Men.* Penguin Books, London, 1998

Browning, Christopher R.: *Fateful Months. Essays on the Emergence of the Final Solution.* Holmes & Meyer, New York, 1985

Bubnys, Arūnas: *Lithuanian Police Battalions and the Holocaust (1941-1943)*

Bubnys, Arūnas: *The Holocaust in the Lithuanian Province 1941*

Carmichael, Cathie: *Genocide before the Holocaust.* Yale University Press, New Haven and London, 2009

Cesarani, David: *The Final Solution; Origins and Implementation.* Routledge, London, 1996

Citroen, Michal: *U wordt door Niemand Verwacht; Nederlandse Joden na Kampen en Onderduik.* Het Spectrum, 1999

Cohen, Israel: *Vilna.* The Jewish Publication Society, Philadelphia-Jerusalem, 1943

Dawidowicz, Lucy S.: *From that Place and Time; A Memoir, 1938-1947.* Rutgers University Press, 2008

Dean, Carolyn: *Aversion and Erasure; the Fate of the Victim after the Holocaust.* Cornell University Press, 2010

Dieckmann, Christoph, and Sužiedėlis, Saulius: *The Persecution and Mass Murder of Lithuanian Jews during Summer and Fall of 1941.* The International Commission for the Evaluation of the Crimes of the Nazi and Soviet Occupation Regimes in Lithuania. Margi raštai, Vilnius, 2004

Dieckmann, Christoph: Alytus 1941-1944; *Massenmorde in einer Kleinstadt.* http://www.lfpr.lt/uploads/File/2001-8/Dieckmann.pdf

Donat, Alexander: *The Holocaust Kingdom.* Secker & Warburg, New York, 1965

Donskis, Leonidas: *The End of Ideology and Utopia?,* New York, 2000

Donskis, Leonidas: *Troubled Identity and the Modern World,* New York, 2009

Donskis, Leonidas (ed.): *A Litmus Test Case of Modernity.* Peter Lang, Bern, 2010

Earl, Hilary: *The Nuremberg SS-Einsatzgruppen Trial 1945-1958.* Cambridge University Press, Cambridge, 2009

Faitelson, Alex: *The Truth and Nothing but the Truth; Jewish Resistance in Lithuania.* Gefen, Jerusalem/New York, 2006

Figes, Orlando: *The Whisperers: Private Life in Stalin's Russia,* London, 2008

Fritze, Lothar: *Täter mit guttem Gewissen.* Böhlau Verlag, Köln, 1998

Gerrits, André: *The Myth of Jewish Communism.* Peter Lang, Brussels, 2009

Gerutis, Albertas: *Lithuania 700 Years.* Manyland Books, New York, 1969

Gieseke, Jens: *Der Mielke Konzern,* München, 2001

Ginaitė-Rubisonienė, S.: *Atminimo knyga.* Vilnius, 1999

Gitelman, Zvi: *A Century of Ambivalence,* Indiana University Press, Bloomington, IN, 2002

Gitelman, Zvi (ed.) *Bitter Legacy; Confronting the Holocaust in the USSR.* Indiana University Press, 1997

Goldhagen, Daniel Jonah: *Hitler's Willing Executioners.* Vintage Books, 1996

Gordon, Harry: *The Shadow of Death; the Holocaust in Lithuania*, University of Kentucky Press, 1992

Greenbaum, Masha: *The Jews of Lithuania.* Gefen Publishing House, Jerusalem, 1995

Gross, Jan T.: *Neighbors.* Penguin, London, 2001

Gourevitch, Philip: *We Wish to Inform you that Tomorrow we will be Killed with our Families.* Picador, 1999

Hidden History of the Kovno Ghetto. United States Holocaust Memorial Museum, Washington D.C., 1997

Hiden, John and Housden, Martyn: *Neighbours or Enemies? Germans, the Baltics and Beyond.* Rodopi, Amsterdam/New York, 2008

Hilberg, Raul (et.al.): *The Warsaw Diary of Adam Czerniakow.* Elephant paperbacks, 1999

Hilberg, Raul: *The Destruction of European Jews, Revised and Definite Edition.* Holmes and Meier, New York, 1985

Hilberg, Raul: *Perpetrators, Victims, Bystanders.* Harper Collins, New York, 1992

Hilbrink, Dr. C.: *In het Belang van het Nederlandse Volk.* SDU, Den Haag, 1995

Hoess, Rudolf: *Commandant of Auschwitz.* Phoenix Press, London, 2000
Höhne, Heinz: *The Order of the Death's Head; The Story of Hitler's SS.* Pan Books, London, 1969

Hoffman, Eva: *After Such Knowledge; Memory, History and the Legacy of the Holocaust.* Public Affairs, New York, 2004

Hofman, J.: *De Collaborateur. Een Sociaal-Psychologisch Onderzoek naar Misdadig Gedrag in dienst van de Duitse Bezetter.* Boom, Meppel,Amsterdam, 1981

Jones, Adam: *Genocide; a Comprehensive Introduction.* Routledge, London, 2011

Katsh, Abraham: *Scroll of Agony; the Warsaw Diary of Chaim A. Kaplan*. Collier Books, 1973

Katz, Dovid: *Lithuanian Jewish Culture*. Baltos Lankos, 2010

Kerz-Rühling, Ingrid, and Plänkers, Thomas, *Verräter oder Verführte*, Berlin, 2004

Klee, Ernst: *The Good Old Days; The Holocaust as Seen by its Perpetrators and Bystanders*. The Free Press, 1991

Kochan, Lionel (ed.): *The Jews in Soviet Russia since 1917*. Oxford University Press, Oxford, 1978

Kohler, Lotte and Saner, Hans (ed.): *Hannah Arendt-Karl Jaspers; Correspondence 1926-1969*. Harcourt Brace Jovanovich, New York, 1992

Kruk, Herman: *The Last Days of the Jerusalem of Lithuania*, Yale University Press, 2002

Kühne, Thomas: *Belonging and Genocide; Hitler's Community, 1918-1945*. Yale University Press, 2010

Kuodytė, Dalia and Stankevičius: *Whoever Saves One Life; The Efforts to Save Jews in Lithuania between 1941 and 1944*. Garnelis, Vilnius, 2002

Kwiet, Konrad: *Hitler's Willing Executioners and Ordinary Germans; Some Comments on Goldhagen's Ideas. http://web.ceu.hu/jewishstudies/pdf/01_kwiet.pdf*

Lammers, C.J.: *Vreemde Overheersing; Bezetten en Bezetting in Sociologisch Perspectief*. Bert Bakker, Amsterdam, 2005

Liekis, Šarūnas: *1939 – The Year that Changed Everything in Lithuania's History*. Rodopi, Amsterdam/New York, 2010

Lifton, Robert Jay: *The Nazi Doctors*. Basic Books, 2000

Littman, Sol: *Rauca of Kaunas; War Criminal on Trial*. Key Porter Books, Toronto, 1993

Lukša, Juozas: *Forest Brothers*. Central European University Press, 2009

Maslauskienė, Nijolė and Petravičiūtė, Inga: *Occupants and Collaborators; the First Soviet Occupation*. The International Commission for the Evaluation of the Crimes of the Nazi and Soviet Occupation Regimes in Lithuania. Margi raštai, Vilnius, 2007

Mattas, David, and Charendoff, Susan: *Justice Delayed; Nazi War Criminals in Canada*. Summerhill Press, Toronto, 1987

Miller, Barbara: *Narratives of Guilt and Compliance in Unified Germany*. Routledge, London/New York, 1999

Misiunas, Romuald and Taagepeera, Rein: *The Baltic States – Years of Dependence*. Hurst, London, 1983

Nikžentaitis, A., Schreiner S. and Staliūnas, D. (ed.): *The Vanished World of Lithuanian Jews*. Rodopi, Amsterdam/New York, 2004

Petersen, Roger D.: *Resistance and Rebellion; Lessons from Eastern Europe*. Cambridge University Press, 2001

Presser, Dr. Jacques: *Ondergang; De Vervolging en Verdelging van het Nederlandse Jodendom*. Staatsuitgeverij, Den Haag, 1965

Puišytė, Rūta: *Holocaust in Jurbarkas*. BA Thesis, Faculty of History, Vilnius University, 1997

Rabinovici, Schoschana: *Thanks to my Mother*. Puffin Books, 1998

Ran, Leyzer: *Jerusalem of Lithuania*. The Laureate Press, New York, 1974

Remeikis, Thomas: *Opposition to Soviet Rule in Lithuania 1945-1980*. Institute of Luthuanian Studies Press, 1980

Rislakki, Jukka: *The Case for Latvia; Disinformation Campaigns against a Small Nation*. Rodopi, Amsterdam/New York, 2008

Röhr, Werner: *Die fasistische Okkupationspolitik in Polen (1939-1945)*. Deutscher Verlag der Wissenschaften, Berlin 1989

Rubenstein, Joshua and Altman, Ilya: *The Unknown Black Book; the Holocaust in the German-Occupied Soviet Territories*. Indiana University Press, 2008

Rubenstein, Joshua and Naumov, Vladimir: *Stalin's Secret Pogrom; the Postwar Inquisition of the Jewish Anti-Fascist Committee.* Yale University Press, 2001

Sakowicz, Kazimierz: *Ponary Diary 1941-1943; a Bystander's Account of Mass Murder.* Yale University Press, 2005

Schoenburg, Nancy and Schoenburg, Stuart: *Lithuanian Jewish Communities.* Jason Aronson, New Jersey, 1996

Sereny, Gitta: *Into that Darkness.* New York, 1983

Shneer, David: *Through Soviet Jewish Eyes; Photography, War, and the Holocaust.* Rutgers University Press, 2011

Shneidman, N.N.: *The Three Tragic Heroes of the Vilnius Ghetto.* Mosaic Press, 2002

Shneidman, N.N.: *Jerusalem of Lithuania; The Rise and Fall of Jewish Vilnius.* Mosaic Press, 1998

Slezkine, Yuri: *The Jewish Century.* Princeton University Press, 2004

Smith, Helmut Walser (ed.): *The Holocaust and other Genocides.* Vanderbilt University Press, 2002

Snyder, Timothy: *The Reconstruction of Nations.* Yale University Press, 2003

Stone, Dan (ed.): *The Historiography of the Holocaust.* Palgrave McMillan, 2005

Sutskever, Abraham: *Iz Vilenskogo Getto; Vospominaniya.* MIK, Moscow-Ekaterinburg, 2008

Sutton, Karen: *The Massacre of the Jews in Lithuania.* Gefen, Jerusalem/New York, 2008

Sužiedėlis, Saulius: *The Burden of 1941.* In: Lituanus, Volume 47, No. 4 - Winter 2001

Szur, Grigori: *De Joden van Wilno.* Jan Mets, Amsterdam, 1997

Todorov, Tzvetan: *Facing the Extreme; Moral Life in the Concentration Camps.* Metropolitan Books, New York, 1996

Todorov, Tzvetan: *Hope and Memory*. Princeton, 2003

Tory, Avraham: *Surviving the Holocaust; the Kovno Ghetto Diary*. Harvard University Press, 1990

Truska, Liudas and Vareikis, Vygantas: *The Preconditions for the Holocaust; Anti-Semitism in Lithuania*. The International Commission for the Evaluation of the Crimes of the Nazi and Soviet Occupation Regimes in Lithuania. Margi Raštai, Vilnius, 2004

Van Kaam, Ben: *Opstand der Gezagsgetrouwen*. Zomer & Keunings, Wageningen, 1966

Van der Heijden, Chris: *Grijs Verleden; Nederland en de Tweede Wereldoorlog*. Contact, 2003

Van Zijl, Annejet: *Bernhard; een verborgen geschiedenis*. Querido, 2010

Van Voren, Robert: *Op Zoek naar Robert van Voren*. Kok, Kampen, 1986

Van Voren, Robert: *Lost History: Memories of Pre-War Podbrodz-Pabradė in Lithuania*. In Donskis, L. (ed.), A Litmus Test Case of Modernity; Baltic volume of the Eastern Europe Studies series by Peter Lang, 2009

Van Voren, Robert: *Cold War in Psychiatry*. Rodopi, Amsterdam/New York, 2010

Venclova, Tomas: *Vilnius; a Personal History*. The Sheep Meadow Press, New York, 2009

Volkan, Vamik: *Bloodlines*. Farrar, Straus and Giroux, New York, 1997

Weeks, Theodore R.: *From "Russian" to "Polish"; Vilna-Wilno 1900-1925*. National Council for Eurasian and East European Research, Washington D.C., 2004

With a Needle in the Heart; Memoirs of Former Prisoners of Ghettos and Concentration Camps. Garnelis, Vilnius, 2003

Yakovlev, Aleksei: *The Tragedy of Lithuania: 1941-1944; New Documents on Crimes of Lithuanian Collaborators during the Second World War*. 2004

Žydų darbo stovykla HKP - The H.K.P. Jewish Labor Camp. Valstybinis Vilniaus Gaono Žydų Muziejus, Vilnius, 2002

Index of Names

About the Author

Robert van Voren (1959) is a Sovietologist by education. A graduate of Amsterdam University, he obtained his PhD at the Vytautas Magnus University in Kaunas (Lithuania) where he currently teaches political science. He is also Director of the Center for Cold War Studies at the Ilia State University in Tbilisi, Georgia, where he also teaches.

Starting in 1977, he became active in the Soviet human rights movement. For many years, he traveled to the USSR as a courier. In 1980, he co-founded the International Association on Political Use of Psychiatry and became its General Secretary in 1986. He is still Chief Executive of its successor organization, the Global Initiative on Psychiatry.

Van Voren has written extensively on Soviet issues, the Second World War, and issues related to mental health and human rights. A dozen of his books have been published. Rodopi previously published *On Dissidents and Madness* (2009) and *Cold War in Psychiatry* (2010). He has been living in Lithuania over the past ten years and also holds Lithuanian citizenship.

Lightning Source UK Ltd.
Milton Keynes UK
UKOW051337120112

185250UK00001B/481/P

9 789042 033719